LANDMARK COLLECTOR'S LIBRARY

E. W. Twining: Model Maker Artist & Engineer

Stan Buck

E. W. Twining: Model Maker Artist & Engineer

Stan Buck

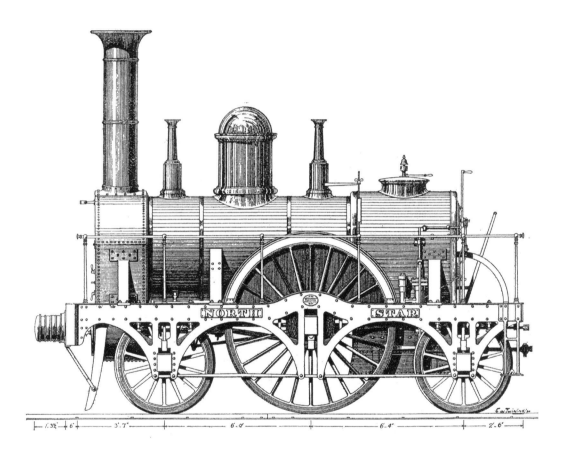

Landmark Publishing

Published by

Ashbourne Hall, Cokayne Ave
Ashbourne, Derbyshire DE6 1EJ England
Tel: (01335) 347349 Fax: (01335) 347303
e-mail: landmark@clara.net
web site: www.landmarkpublishing.co.uk

1st edition

ISBN 1 84306 143 0

Printed by Cromwell Press

Design & reproduction by Simon Hartshorne

Cover captions:

Front cover: Twining Models Ltd, Engineering Models brochure
Back cover: A selection of the work of Ernest Twining and his company

Contents

Introduction

Ernest Twining? Who was he? A few years ago I might have asked the same question. Actually, I had already met some of his work on several occasions over the years, but had not realised it.

The first occasion was around the end of WWII, when my older brother (whose idea of entertaining me was a walk to Guide Bridge station, outside Manchester, or across neighbouring fields to the LNER ex Great Central mainline to Sheffield) picked up some old copies of *Locomotive Magazine*. One had Twining's article on his narrow gauge ideas, although I did not think much of them at the time; Belle Vue's *Little Giants* and pictures I had seen of Romney Hythe and Dymchurch locos were then much more to my taste.

A few years later my brother and I were subscribing to *Model Engineer* and I saw Twining's *Crampton* series. Without thought of the author's name I was fascinated both by the quality of the drawings and by the elegant locomotives they represented.

By 1976 I was already taking a serious interest in miniature and narrow gauge railways when the Fairbourne Railway's 2-4-2 *Siân* paid her first visit to the Ravenglass and Eskdale Railway. Smitten like many others by this most attractive engine, I was horrified at her transmogrification into *Sydney*; and subsequently only too pleased to be able to help in restoring her original appearance.

As part of the group who now own *Siân*, I started researching her history and became aware of the link between these three, and of the wide range of other interests of Ernest Twining and of Twining Models Ltd. Uncovering more and more items linked to Twining in libraries, museums, churches and on railways around the UK is where the idea for this book germinated.

Born in 1875 Ernest Twining was very typical of his period, a reserved and private man but displaying two very Victorian characteristics. He was honest, considerate and courteous to everyone he dealt with yet also a man of many parts, successfully tackling a wide range of work and interests. Although not to the exclusion of many others, three subjects in particular appealed to him: art, flight and railways, and all three were pursued in one form or another from his early teens to the end of his life.

An independent and self-sufficient individual, Twining seems always to have been his own man, to have "ploughed his own furrow", and was self-employed or running his own company for most of his working life. This self-sufficiency spilled over into his technical activities and he was always prepared to work things out for himself; whether the aerodynamics of model aircraft, the design of locomotive valve-gears or the chemistry of stained glass. He was also prepared to undertake painstaking historical research, for example into the design of early locomotives or the rigging of wooden warships.

Whilst a very practical man, both in his designs and his own handiwork, he always showed creative initiative, technical foresight and great interest in new developments. This is well exemplified by his early interest in helicopters, by the incorporation of roller bearings in his last 15in gauge loco design (contemporary with their application to BR standard designs) and the inclusion of a super heater into his 1915 3 $^1/2$in gauge pacific for *Model Engineer*.

Both a gentleman and a gentle man, he typically maintained cordial relations over more than 40 years with three very fiery characters: miniature railway pioneer Henry Greenly, entrepreneur W. J. Bassett-Lowke and editor of *Practical Mechanics* F. J. Camm. His friendship with Trevor Guest also lasted from the late 1930s until his death in 1956. His work has perhaps been overlooked or neglected in part because much of it was done for, or in association with, Greenly or Bassett-Lowke. Neither man was noted for "hiding his light under a bushel" and Twining's gentle nature perhaps allowed these and others a greater share of the credit for some projects than they deserved.

Ernest Twining was born in Bristol, into an essentially working class family, but by the time he was in his teens sufficient funds were available so that he could be apprenticed as an electrical engineer and soon afterwards start at art college too. Some of his teenage years must have been spent at Bristol Temple Meads station because he describes both discussions with engine drivers and his affection for the broad gauge singles. He also started experimenting with model aircraft at this time.

With his apprenticeship completed, but whilst still at art college, he married Mary Davies, a widow with four children. The eldest, and only boy, was Cuthbert, with whom he seems to have got on well; apprenticed to Henry Greenly, Cuthbert subsequently became Twining's partner in the Twining Aeroplane Co. so clearly their interests must have coincided. The lack of customers for either model or man-carrying build-your-own aircraft forced Twining into sub-contract work for both Greenly and Bassett-Lowke, leading eventually to the establishment of Twining Models Ltd.

Finally leaving his company in 1940, to work as a draughtsman for the Bristol Aeroplane Company, Twining returned to his home town. It seems likely Mary would have known she was terminally ill for some time and they may have planned accordingly. Twining subsequently remarried, and after his wartime service remained in Bristol, reviving his railway, writing and artistic interests.

Ernest Twining worked in many fields over more than 60 years, the most significant being art, flight, model railways, static models, stained glass and larger locomotive models. He was also a prolific writer, producing several books and contributing to *Model Engineer, Practical Mechanics*, aeronautical publications and serious railway journals such as the *Locomotive Railway Carriage and Wagon Review*. Subjects ranged from wooden ships to helicopters, from microscopes to telescopes, garden railways to historic locomotives; a truly diverse range with significant research and useful facts and ideas in every article.

His skills as artist and in engineering drawing led to a variety of work for his friend Alfred Rosling Bennett, to advertising material especially for Bassett-Lowke and for his own company, and ultimately to a book on the subject. He seems to have painted for pleasure throughout his life – for example as a member of the Northampton Town and County Art Society. His second wife Edna clearly knew him best as an artist and his death certificate describes him as "artist, retired".

Interest in flight he claimed arose from reading Jules Verne in his youth, evolving through model aircraft design (including aerodynamic studies) to man-carrying designs for his Twining Aeroplane Co. He was almost certainly a member of the Northampton Aero Club at Sywell, before his spell with Bristol – and was writing about helicopters and their potential not long before his death.

Similarly railway interest progressed from the full size engines and trains seen in his youth, through model railways and rolling stock, to miniature steam designs, then right up to the 15in gauge designs of his last years. All these were backed by up comprehensive drawing and writing on many aspects of steam locomotive design and history.

His interest in stained glass is fairly attributed to his maternal grandfather. After designing and making his own panels, Twining Models Ltd was also led into this field – examples of their work are in several local churches. His book *The Art and Craft of Stained Glass* was also written at this time, and was for many years a standard work on the practical aspects of the subject. He also returned to this field of work after WWII with the Bristol firm of Bells.

Finally there is the range of Twining Models' better known activities, notably the architectural models which kick-started the company and the glass case railway models still in museums around the

UK. They also made a major contribution to the Queen's Dolls House Project as well as making telescopes; astronomy and photography were yet more of his many interests!

Twining has long been neglected and his work seriously overlooked – typical reactions to his name even amongst model engineers being "he made model buildings for Bassett-Lowke didn't he?" or " he made paper aeroplanes before WWI." He certainly did both of those things; but a whole lot more besides, much of it still significant in relevant fields of work or hobbies.

This volume and variety of material would probably have made a straightforward chronological account of his activities far too complex, with constantly changing subjects. Consequently a summary of his family and career to put things in perspective is followed by consideration of each of the major areas of his work, more or less in the order in which each became a significant source of income.

The justification for this book is really the view that this man who worked so successfully (if not always profitably) in so many fields, was significant in several of them; model aircraft, stained glass, miniature/narrow gauge locomotives, technical historical research, and deserves to be better known. His many surviving drawings, paintings, writings and models make it easy to illustrate his work, but recognition of its importance and significance is also long overdue.

Acknowledgements

This book would not have been possible without the help of numerous individuals and organisations who provided information, notes and pictures, and often the opportunity to take further photographs. Equally important were the people whose clues and ideas led to these sources, often by fairly tortuous routes. Notable were Finlay Skinner for the loan of his salvaged Twining Models Limited photograph albums, Gerry Nichols for his researches in Bristol, Martin Harrison for advice on stained glass and the staff of Northampton Central Museum for repeated access to their reserve collection.

Particular thanks are due to Tony Woolrich and Michael Gilkes, without whose help, encouragement and persuasion, the idea I had been nursing for some years would probably never have matured into this story of Ernest Twining and his work.

A very special mention is due to several people without whose help the work would have been far less complete. Firstly to Michael Gilkes again, for access to his vast library of technical and hobby magazines and his willingness to search them on my behalf, and for his numerous suggestions and ideas. Secondly to the late Bryan Clifton and his family; and finally to Ernest Twining's family: grand-daughter Mrs Anne Blake and niece Mrs Diana Cornwell. Their own recollections of Ernest Twining, and their collections of his drawings, writings, photographs and paintings provided unique background to many of his projects and much valuable family information.

This book is published with the approval of Ernest Twining's family and their consent to the use of any relevant drawings or pictures. I hope they feel that I have done justice to the man and his work.

Finally without my wife's patience over the last two years none of this could have been completed; how she managed to put up with my detachment from normal life throughout this time is far from clear!

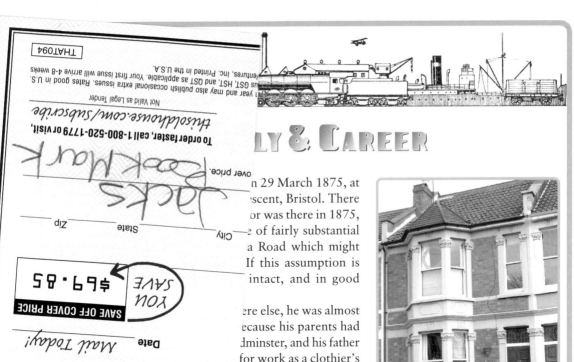

...LY & CAREER

...n 29 March 1875, at
...scent, Bristol. There
...or was there in 1875,
...e of fairly substantial
...a Road which might
...If this assumption is
...intact, and in good

...ere else, he was almost
...ecause his parents had
...dminster, and his father
...for work as a clothier's
...inly came of farming
...aac) being a farmer at
...gardener in Gloucester.
...married his cousin Ann
Twining, each being the last survivor of their respective branches of the family. There is no evidence of any significant wealth, but this consolidation of such resources as there may have been is perhaps what made possible Ernest's apprenticeship and art training, as well as his father's eventual setting up of his own business.

Ernest Twining's mother, Rosina Maria, was the daughter of William Jones of Bristol. His many years as a glass painter are mentioned later and it was to him that Ernest Twining attributed his artistic abilities and consequently dedicated his book on stained glass. William Gilbert Jones, Rosina's brother and Ernest's uncle, was also to become a glass painter, a trade at which he spent all his working life. This seems to have been the long-lived side of the family too – Ernest's mother lived into her 97th year, dying only in 1946, whilst her younger daughter Mildred, born in 1878, died exactly 100 years later.

By 1881 the family had moved a short distance, to 19 Wood Street, a house they would occupy for the next 15 years or so. This is a much smaller property, which they presumably rented for themselves – Ernest's two sisters had arrived by this time, Florence in 1877 and Mildred in 1878. The house still exists, but the frontage has been considerably altered and modernised. Wood Street is near to the St Mark's Church of England school, which catered for both infants and separate boys and girls junior classes. Ernest Twining spent at least some of his school years here, perhaps significantly close to Stapleton Road railway station. Again the school building still exists, although it has now become a mosque, whilst the adjacent church has been deconsecrated and is used as a meeting centre for social activities.

Ernest Twining subsequently received private tuition from Dr John Abel PSS MRCP at Wiltshire

Above: Mina Road, Bristol, which may have been Twining's birthplace. photo – author

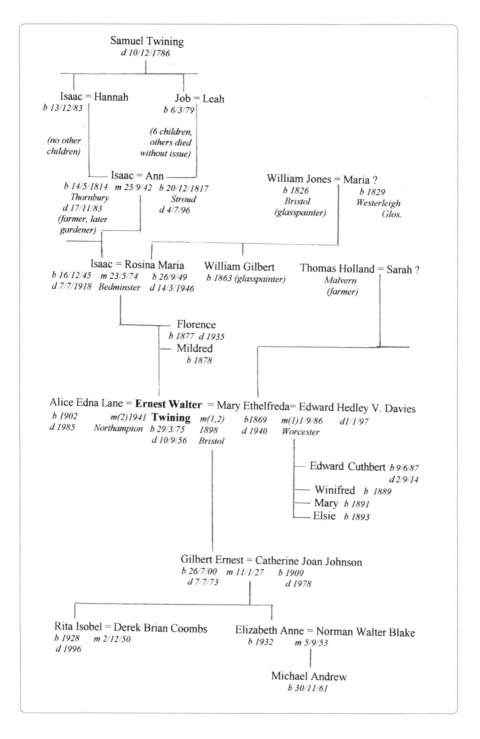

Samuel Twining
d 10/12/1786

Isaac = Hannah
b 13/12/83

Job = Leah
b 6/3/79

(no other children)

(6 children, others died without issue)

Isaac = Ann
b 14/5/1814   m 25/9/42   b 20/12/1817
Thornbury   Stroud
d 17/11/83   d 4/7/96
(farmer, later gardener)

William Jones = Maria ?
b 1826   b 1829
Bristol   Westerleigh
(glasspainter)   Glos.

Isaac = Rosina Maria
b 16/12/45   m 23/5/74   b 26/9/49
d 7/7/1918   Bedminster   d 14/3/1946

William Gilbert
b 1863 (glasspainter)

Thomas Holland = Sarah ?
*Malvern
(farmer)*

Florence
b 1877 d 1935
Mildred
b 1878

Alice Edna Lane = **Ernest Walter**
b 1902   m(2)1941 **Twining**
d 1985   Northampton   b 29/3/75
d 10/9/56

= Mary Ethelfreda= Edward Hedley V. Davies
m(1,2)   b1869   m(1)1/9/86   d1/1/97
1898   d 1940   Worcester
Bristol

Edward Cuthbert *b 9/6/87*
d 2/9/14
Winifred *b 1889*
Mary *b 1891*
Elsie *b 1893*

Gilbert Ernest = Catherine Joan Johnson
b 26/7/00   m 11/1/27   b 1909
d 7/7/73   d 1978

Rita Isobel = Derek Brian Coombs
b 1928   m 2/12/50
d 1996

Elizabeth Anne = Norman Walter Blake
b 1932   m 5/9/53

Michael Andrew
b 30/11/61

This page: Family tree of Ernest Twining. Opposite top: Ernest Twining's father Isaac. photo – Twining family. Opposite bottom: Ernest Twining's mother Rosina Maria, née Jones. photo - Twining family

Villa, now 303 Stapleton Road, and this part-time education may well be how he found time for his early experience in the stained glass industry. His account of waiting for successive episodes of Jules Verne's *Clipper of the Clouds* mentions reading these with a prefect at his school, so perhaps this was the establishment. This would have been in 1887, when he was 12 or 13, and led to his first aeronautical experiments a year or two later.

At some point in his teens, presumably before starting his engineering apprenticeship around 1891, he also gained significant experience in the practical aspects of stained glass work. This was no doubt with his maternal grandfather and uncle, both then employed by Bells ecclesiastical glaziers in College Green, Bristol. How this experience was undertaken there is absolutely no indication, but it was sufficiently comprehensive to have considerable later significance.

In about 1891 Twining started an apprenticeship as an electrical engineer with the Western Counties and South Wales Telephone Company. The firm's premises were in Queen Victoria Buildings, High Street, Bristol at this time, property occupied by the United Telephone Company prior to 1886. The WC&SW Coy was set up as a subsidiary of United and like the many other local subsidiaries was absorbed into the National Telephone Company from 1892 as the industry consolidated; the change had no effect on Twining's career.

Photographs of the area during this period show a positive cats' cradle of aerial telephone cables. In fact Twining joined the industry at a time of considerable expansion (Bristol subscribers increased 5-fold between 1891 and 1901) and then reorganisation, both technical and financial. After completing his apprenticeship (say 1896) he rapidly became involved in the major task of putting many of these cables underground, eventually becoming assistant engineer for underground works. This work was prompted by changing technology, as the original single wire and earth return gave way to the 2-wire system. Bristol actually buried 17 miles of cable, representing over 4000 miles of circuits, in 1900 alone.

An interesting photograph showing Twining supervising a cable-laying operation has survived, presumably from the late 1890s. It is not perhaps a coincidence that it shows work almost outside the Bristol Academy of Fine Art which he was still attending, and only a few yards from his then, or shortly to be, home in Westbourne Place.

As was to be his custom throughout his life Twining was by now clearly becoming involved in many different activities at the same time. Aeronautical experiments had temporarily lapsed but he developed what were to be lifelong interests in photography, astronomy and locomotives, designing a 1in to 1ft scale model in 1895. A more significant activity at this period however was a long association with the Bristol Academy for the Promotion of Fine Arts, now the Royal West of England Academy. This overlapped with most of his apprenticeship and continued for some time afterwards, because although student records are not available for this period his work certainly appears in their exhibition catalogues for 1893, 1895 and 1899.

Ernest Twining was also married at this time, on 19 July 1898, to Mary Davies, a widow with four young children. It is a family understanding that Mary's first husband, Edward Hedley Davies was employed, directly or as a contractor, by the same telephone company as Ernest Twining. Certainly Davies is described as an electrical engineer on the certificate of his marriage to Mary and as a telephone company manager on his death certificate.

Mary, born 1869, was the youngest daughter of Thomas Holland, a farmer from near Malvern, and had married Edward Davies in Worcester in 1886. The records of their family show the life of a contract engineer, then and now. Their four children were born respectively in Cardiff (Cuthbert 1887), Christchurch (Winifred 1889), Westbury (Mary 1891) and Bristol (Elsie 1893), whilst Edward Davies died of pneumonia in Cheltenham, aged only 39, on 11 January 1897.

In the following year Mary and her family were living at Westbourne Place, Clifton, Bristol; in fact it seems likely they had remained in Bristol although Edward was working in Cheltenham. Mary was with him when he died however and it was she who registered his death. Meanwhile the Twining family, sometime in 1897 or 1898, had moved to Daisy Road, Easton. Isaac Twining now had his own wholesale clothiers (tailors) business, perhaps courtesy of a small inheritance from grandmother Ann (who died in 1896), and the family could afford a larger house in a better area. Ernest Twining moved in with Mary and her family on their marriage in 1898.

Mary and Ernest's only child, Gilbert Ernest, was born at Westbourne Place on 20 July 1900, and the whole family was still there at the 1901 census. Subsequently Ernest Twining obtained a position

Top: Queen Victoria Buildings, Bristol in the 1890s. The complex framework on the roof is for telephone cables before these were buried.
photo – collection Gerry Nichols

Left: Ernest Twining supervising a cable-laying operation near the Bristol Fine Art Academy in the late 1890s.
photo – Twining family

with the Glasgow Corporation Telephone Company as District Superintendent for Underground Operations – obviously exploiting the specific skills and experience he had gained with the Bristol company.

Whether Mary and family went to Scotland too is uncertain, but perhaps unlikely with all four of the Davies children at school and Gilbert barely a year old. Ernest certainly visited Bristol in 1902, photographing ships in the Avon Gorge on more than one occasion. In 1903 he was living at an address in Glasgow given just as Queen's Crescent, although the nearest Queen's Crescent to the city centre today is at Bellshill, well out in the suburbs; perhaps there were others 100 years ago.

Apart from his engineering work the period in Glasgow probably brought him into contact with the work of Charles Rennie Mackintosh and the "Glasgow School". Certainly something persuaded Twining he could make a living from his artistic abilities and training.

The other significance of the years in Glasgow was that he met Alfred Rosling Bennett, who was to provide him with useful initial work for his own studio. Rosling Bennett is probably best known these days for his writings on railway subjects, particularly his *Chronicles of Boulton's Siding* but, like Twining he was an electrical engineer in the telephone industry. After more than 20 years of experience with telephone and telegraph companies around the world he had set up practice as a consulting engineer in 1893, acting as consultant to several municipal companies, including that in Glasgow between 1900 and 1904. Glasgow Corporation sold their telephone system to the Post Office in around 1904, and Rosling Bennett's contract may then have come to an end, or he may have anticipated the change in organisation and decided to leave.

The date may be particularly relevant because it was in that year that Twining also left Glasgow, and the telephone industry, to move to London and set up his own art studio in Lavender Hill. Here his first job was assisting Rosling Bennett with his *Proposal for London Improvements*. This was basically a scheme to build a new bridge over the Thames, with a new city hall incorporated in the bridge. Twining's job was to produce the majority of the water colours used to illustrate the proposal document, although it is clear from his notes that he also assisted with many of the calculations. The document was completed in 1904, although one of Twining's accompanying paintings actually appeared in the 1906 RA Exhibition. Twining had by then completed his second task for Rosling Bennett, preparing the very detailed and highly researched locomotive illustrations for *Historic Locomotives and Moving Accidents by Steam and Rail*.

He had soon started other work too, articles for the *Model Engineer* and for *Woodworker and Art Metalworker* as well as designs for furniture and household items. The move back south had a further advantage in that stepson Cuthbert was able to start an apprenticeship with Henry Greenly, staying during the week with the Greenly family at Watford at least until April 1908. How the contact with Greenly was made is unclear, but Rosling Bennett was a member of the Institution of Locomotive Engineers and may well have known Greenly. Twining's *Model Engineer* articles did not start until 1905 so the contact must have been with Henry Greenly first, before Twining met Percival Marshall who published the magazine.

The Twinings moved to Hanwell in 1907, setting up Aldwick (or Alnwick?) Studio in Milton Terrace. He also set up a 1 inch scale garden railway there too, perhaps to operate the loco he had designed in 1895. (There had been an earlier gauge 1 line which appeared in his *Model Engineer* articles). Sometime about this period the link with Greenly and Percival Marshall also led to W. J. Bassett-Lowke, although perhaps not until his aeronautical activities had restarted.

Prompted by successful manned flights in Europe, Ernest Twining started taking an interest in aviation again, with a series of experiments which were subsequently written up in *Model Engineer* and in *Aero* magazine. When Cuthbert completed his apprenticeship in 1908 the two formed a partnership as the "Twining Aeroplane Company". Initially this was intended to make and supply model aircraft and model aircraft kits, but they then branched out into full sized aircraft. For this work a nearby property, 29b Grosvenor Road, was leased as a workshop. The house frontage here remains, with access beneath at street level to where the workshop may have been, but of this there is no trace. The company exhibited at both *Model Engineer* and Olympia *Aero* exhibitions for some years, with Mary conscripted to man the stand on at least one occasion.

Unfortunately the move to full size aircraft was not successful and the Twining Aeroplane Company was short-lived. By the end of 1912 Cuthbert Davies had set up a motor cycle repair business, whilst Twining himself had moved to Northampton to help Bassett-Lowke with specialised models, initially architectural work and dioramas. This work expanded rapidly and by 1914 extra help was recruited in the form of E.H. (Harry) Clifton, who although straight from school soon proved a competent and versatile model maker. For several years Ernest Twining lived at Harborough Road, Kingsthorpe, although when Mary and Gilbert also moved to Northampton is uncertain.

When WWI broke out, Cuthbert immediately volunteered, and with his motor cycle skills became a dispatch rider. Unfortunately he was killed in action in France almost at once, on 2 September 1914. At this early stage in hostilities military cemeteries had not been established, so Cuthbert, Private MS/1685, 27th Company Army Service Corps, is buried in Ermenon Communal Cemetery, Oise.

In early 1915, the *Model Engineer* printed two miniature locomotive design series by Ernest Twining, the last things he was to have published for several years. This was initially because he was heavily involved with Bassett-Lowke's war effort. Although never actually a Bassett-Lowke employee he played a major role at this time, supervising, amongst other things, their production of precision gauges for the armaments industry and the range of ship recognition models they made for the Admiralty. After the war he was soon heavily involved in other modelling projects and the setting up of Twining Models Limited. Gilbert was also involved in the company from an early stage, some items were even labelled "E.W. Twining, Son and Co", but none can be precisely dated. How Gilbert's

Top: Twining with his 1in scale freelance 4-4-0 in about 1907. Stepson Cuthbert Davies on the left, son Gilbert Ernest on the right. photo – Twining family.
Left: Twining with his *Model Engineer* Challenge Cup winning aircraft in June 1911. *photo - Model Engineer*

service career, presumably only in the closing stages of the war, fits in with the formation of the company is also unclear.

An interesting sideline at this point, worth including because it provides both another picture of Ernest Twining and another insight into his character, is his ownership of a White Steam Car, of model "OO", which he ran for several years. It was originally the property of N.R. Franklin, Bassett-Lowke's Finance Director, and must have been imported in 1910 or 1911, just before the company changed over to internal combustion engines. Many years later Twining wrote of overhauling the car's engine (a 2 cylinder compound fed by 600 psi steam) after 10 years of use; unfortunately it is not clear if all these 10 years were spent in Franklin's hands or whether ownership had been transferred earlier. Janet Bassett-Lowke, in her biography of her uncle W.J. refers to the vehicle but claims it ended up at the Beaulieu Museum. Unfortunately they have no White cars at all and in any case Twining wrote that he eventually scrapped the car and sold the engine and steam generator for use in a launch.

In around 1920 Twining Models Limited was formed, with Bassett-Lowke's encouragement, to be an independent but largely subordinate company, which would handle most of their architectural and glass case model commissions, but for whose modelling work Bassett-Lowke Ltd would be sole concessionaires. The Twinings moved to Abington Crescent, Northampton around this time and Ernest Twining started writing for *Model Engineer* again, with a series on his own models followed by one on early model warships.

By 1922 Twining Models had expanded from their original studio at Bassett-Lowke's facilities into workshops in Dychurch Lane. They also now branched out into telescope production, making use of Twining's interests in astronomy and optical equipment for a product line outside the Bassett-Lowke agreement. The 1922 telescope catalogue does not however seem to have been repeated or updated, perhaps there was no need to update their range, or because the company soon became very busy with work for organizations anxious to have models of their products or facilities for the forthcoming British

Top: Mary Twining manning the Twining Aeroplane Company stand at the October 1909 Model Engineer exhibition. Photo – Twining family.
Left: Gilbert Twining in uniform in the closing months of WWI. photo – Twining family.

Empire Exhibition at Wembley. Twining Models' work for this eventually encompassed a variety of railway, road and military vehicles, a huge diorama of Durban (SA) and its harbour, factory models for several companies, and a significant contribution to Queen Mary's Dolls House, which was also exhibited.

Twining had also been writing his *Pageant of English Naval History*, a beautifully illustrated and carefully researched booklet, available separately or as accompaniment to a Bassett-Lowke set of ship models, which he also designed. Some at least of these, along with a large range of smaller models they marketed at the time, exploited the methods developed during WWI for the mass production of small water-line ship models for recognition purposes.

The 1920s continued to be a busy period for Twining Models, which moved to still larger premises in Pike Lane, whilst both Gilbert Twining and Harry Clifton became directors. The Twinings moved again, this time to Duncan House, St George's Avenue. Here they stayed at least until Gilbert's marriage, on 11th January 1927, to Catharine Joan Johnson. Grand-daughters arrived in 1928 (Rita Isobel) and 1932 (Elizabeth Anne). A family photograph from 1928 shows four Twining generations, from Ernest's mother Rosina Maria down to baby Rita Isobel.

In the late 1920s Twining Models branched out into a new area, again one outside the Bassett-Lowke agreement on "sole concessionaires for models". This built on yet another of Ernest Twining's

Above: Ernest Twining with his White Steam Car, Model OO, registration NH 1898.
photo – Twining family

interests, this time the making of stained glass windows, techniques learnt from his maternal grandfather and uncle. In fact the latter, William Gilbert Jones, was at the time still working for Bells of Bristol.

Gathering together all the practical bases of this craft, in order to put it into commercial practice, prompted Twining to produce a substantial book *The Art and Craft of Stained Glass* in 1928; a book which was to prove a significant source of practical information for workers in the field for over 50 years. This book was followed a few years later by *Art in Advertising*, written jointly with Dorothy Holditch. Ernest Twining had long produced publicity material for his own companies, for Bassett-Lowke and for other local organizations, and his ideas on the subject clearly appealed to his publisher. A further collaboration with Dorothy Holditch was *Heraldry*, a substantial article in a multi-volume work on home and commercial decorating.

Socially, Twining was now involved with the Northampton Town and County Art Society throughout this period, took a keen interest in the Northamptonshire Aero Club (actual membership cannot be confirmed) and encouraged the formation of the Northampton Model Aero Club, of which he was first president.

By the mid 1930s, Twining Models, like other companies, was laying off staff, perhaps partly because the agreement with Bassett-Lowke had been rescinded and they were making some of their own models, but largely because few organisations had spare funds for such "extras", unless models formed

Above: Twining family group taken in 1928, showing four generations: Ernest in the back row, Gilbert sitting on the floor; and in the middle row Mary, Ernest's mother Rosina, and Gilbert's wife with baby Rita. photo – Twining family

essential components of orders, for example valve gear models to go with export locomotive contracts.

Ernest Twining himself started writing magazine articles again on a regular basis after his second book – although a third, on model railways, may already have been in the pipeline. Initially articles were on aircraft and model aircraft for *Hobbies* magazine, but then on model aircraft, model railways and miniature steam locomotives for *Practical Mechanics*. Most significant in the long term was his 1934 article for a "professional" railway journal, *Locomotive* magazine (strictly *The Locomotive, Railway Carriage and Wagon Review*) advocating the use of "designed for the job" steam locomotives for public passenger hauling railways, rather than the pseudo scale steam locos and steam outline diesels then in use. This idea was to have particular importance many years later, but unfortunately not until the last years of his life and afterwards.

The period also saw two further house moves, although still in Northampton, first to The Crescent, Phippsville in 1934 and three years later to Kettering Road. (It is not clear who was the restless partner, Mary or Ernest, or Marie and Ern as they were known to family and friends. Perhaps Mary had developed a taste for frequent moves in her early married life with Edward Davies.)

In the late 1930s Twining Models' fortunes revived, with a very large South African diorama, a model for the Euston Centenary Exhibition, and their first (and only) large steam locomotive, a 10 1/4in gauge 4-6-0 for Trevor Guest.

However Mary's health was deteriorating, and soon after the outbreak of WWII both Ernest and Gilbert Twining sold their interests in Twining Models to Harry Clifton, who then traded as Twining Models (EH Clifton) Ltd, eventually moving again, to Nelson Street, until they ceased trading in 1967. Gilbert became a development engineer on war work, with another of Bassett-Lowke's associate companies, Winteringhams. Mary and Ernest moved back to Bristol, to Fishponds Road. Ernest Twining started work for the Bristol Aeroplane Company but on 26 October 1940 Mary died of cancer, whilst they were on holiday at Blickley, Gloucestershire.

The following year Ernest Twining married again, Edna Lane, who he had already known for many years; she had been a librarian in Northampton and probably helped with the research for his books, and she was also a contemporary of Dorothy Holditch. They shortly moved to a flat in Iddesleigh Gardens, Redland, Bristol, where Twining was to spend the rest of his life. He remained at Bristol's throughout WWII (chapter four speculates on what he might have done there) leaving at the end of hostilities.

After the war Ernest Twining's stained glass skills were immediately in demand. Many churches and their windows had of course been damaged and were in need of repair or replacement. His contacts with Bells, perhaps as a result of family members working there previously, soon found scope for his abilities, assisting with Bells' projects but allowed also to carry out his own commissions in their workshops: the four memorial windows in Wolverton Catholic Church date from this period (Wolverton

Above: Ernest Twining with two of his staff, working on the 10 1/4in gauge 4-6-0 for Trevor Guest. Twining Models' workshop in 1938/9. Photo – Twining family.

is now effectively a suburb of Milton Keynes). The report of the dedication of these windows confirms that by this date he had himself become a Catholic. He had shown an increasing interest in religion, especially religious paintings, throughout the 1930s, and perhaps especially after the nature of Mary's illness became apparent. His subsequent marriage to a lady who was herself a Roman Catholic now completed his conversion.

Throughout the war he had obviously continued to think about locomotive designs, although not publishing anything, but in 1949 a further article in *Locomotive* magazine covered a narrow gauge design with a number of novel Twining features, chief amongst which was his own design of valve gear, subsequently used on his final 15in gauge design. Trevor Guest had meanwhile regauged his Dudley Zoo Railway from 10 1/4in to 15in and was starting two 15in gauge locomotives to Twining's design. These two were nominally of scale or fullsize outline, but were followed after a few years by *Katie*, a 2-4-2 of narrow gauge proportions; "designed for the job" as Twining had so long advocated. After almost 20 years an engine incorporating his ideas had at last appeared, ultimately marking a major change in the design policy for public miniature railways.

The post war period continued to be a busy time, although the only family developments of note were the marriages of both granddaughters and Gilbert's move from engineering into the licensed trade, keeping a series of public houses in the Northampton/Daventry area for the rest of his life.

Ernest Twining meanwhile was engaged with numerous articles for *Practical Mechanics* on railways, aviation and model boat designs for example, and a major series for *Model Engineer* on the Crampton Locomotives of Great Britain. He was also still painting, for himself and his

Top: Marriage of Ernest Twining and Edna Lane, in 1941. photo - Twining family
Right: Iddesleigh Gardens, showing the first floor flat which was the Twining's home from 1941 to 1956. photo – author

family, for local exhibitions, and privately commissioned railway works.

His "magnum opus" in the railway field, 2-4-2 *Katie* noted above, carries 1954 worksplates, but probably was not completed and in service until 1956; evidence is far from clear. No doubt he was kept up to date on progress by Trevor Guest because he would have expected no less, but it is however rather sad if, as seems likely, he died without seeing his engine operating.

He actually died on 10 September 1956, and was buried in a family grave with his parents and elder sister Florence, at Greenbank Cemetery in the same Bristol district as he had been born. His widow Edna subsequently returned to Northampton to live with an unmarried brother. She died in 1985, leaving a substantial collection of papers, drawings and photographs to her niece. Other material, which had been retained by Gilbert, eventually passed to Ernest Twining's younger granddaughter. These two sources have proved invaluable in piecing together and illuminating the story. After Twining Models (EH Clifton) Ltd closed down almost all their records were destroyed, apart from some of their "official" photograph albums which were the source of many of the pictures of models used here.

Above: Gilbert Twining outside his last public house, the *New Inn*, Buckby Wharf.
photo - Twining family
Below: The Twining family grave, Ernest with his parents and elder sister, in Greenbank Cemetery, Bristol. photo – Gerry Nichols

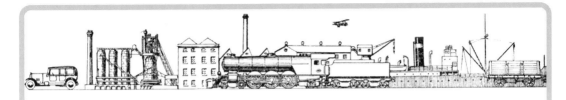

Railways & Model Railways

RAILWAYS IN HIS EARLY YEARS

Ernest Twining's interest in railways seems to have started at an early age. This is not perhaps surprising in view of the number of railways near his childhood home – like most Victorian cities or larger towns, Bristol had an elaborate network. When he was born, in 1875, there were three principal lines in north-east Bristol, all passing within a mile of his home. To the east was the Midland (formerly Bristol and Gloucester) to Mangotsfield Junction, Gloucester and Birmingham; to the west, and probably closest was the Great Western (Bristol and South Wales Union Railway) through Stapleton Road to Filton and New Passage for the South Wales ferries; whilst the triangle was completed by the Midland line linking their main line to the Joint MR/GWR Clifton Extension railway. The latter joined with the Bristol Port Railway and formed the railway outlet from the dock being built at Avonmouth, which opened in 1877, sending goods traffic through Stapleton Road station and across the "13 Arches", the Frome valley viaduct on the Midland connection.

The Severn Tunnel was also being planned, with work actually starting in 1877. Problems with this project, for example repeated threats from the "Great Spring", must have been common knowledge amongst the Twining family's neighbours by the time Ernest was old enough to understand. Wood Street was after all barely 10 miles from the tunnel's English portal. The Severn Tunnel finally opened in September 1886, with passenger trains from 1 December 1886, and London to South Wales expresses were diverted from their previous Gloucester route in July 1887. To cope with the extra traffic the line through Stapleton Road Station was quadrupled in

Great Western Railway broad gauge single *Hirondelle*, one of Twining's favourites.
photo – Stephenson Locomotive Society

1891; although he left this school several years earlier some of Ernest Twining's education had been at St Mark's school, only 100yds from this station.

Twining's busy but unexciting freight and suburban passenger branch had now become a main line, part of two major through routes. It was now used by trains from London to South Wales (until the Badminton cut-off opened, after Twining had left Bristol) and also by trains from Bristol and the West Country via Hereford to the Midlands and North West of England. Standard gauge GWR express engines would now be common sights and it is not surprising they form many of his favourite designs.

The nearby Midland was not entirely neglected however, and he once described the Johnson singles as the most beautiful engines ever built. He probably saw them from an early stage in their careers in fact because according to E. L. Ahrons many of the batch built in 1892 were immediately based at Bristol and Birmingham to speed up important expresses and match the GWR's now much more serious competition on this route. (1)

Great Western broad gauge activity ceased in this part of the city in the late 1870s (the Bristol and South Wales Union had already been re-gauged in 1873 for example) before young Ernest could really have been aware of trains, but he later described his particular affection for the Gooch broad gauge singles. Many of these lasted until the end of the 7ft gauge in 1892, just after Twining started his apprenticeship, so some of his early teens was spent on Temple Meads station or other vantage point! *Hirondelle* of 1848 ("renewed" in kind in 1873) seems to have been a particular favourite, although according to Ahrons it was a London-based engine throughout its life. Twining later built a 1in to 1ft scale model of *Hirondelle* which is discussed later.

Another favourite type was the standard gauge 2-2-2 of the 157-166 class. These were Dean rebuilds of Gooch locos, which Ahrons claims spent most of their time on Birmingham trains but clearly they occasionally reached Bristol too. Twining later painted this type, featured it in several articles and started a 1 $^{1}/_{2}$in to 1ft scale model; only a few basic parts remain unfortunately.

He also described talking to the driver of one of the later and much better known Dean singles (3031 class 4-2-2) when these were first introduced as standard gauge 2-2-2. The driver complained bitterly about their unstable riding compared to the broad gauge engines he was used to. These locos appeared on the standard gauge from January 1892 (a few were turned out as broad gauge convertibles from April 1891), but after the derailment of No 3021 *Wigmore Castle* in Box Tunnel on 16/7/93 all were rapidly rebuilt as 4-2-2 by the end of 1894. One of Twining's visits to Temple Meads was presumably in 1892 or early '93.

Twining's railway interests continued for the rest of his life, interspersed with his non-railway activities, and with his railway historical research, railway modelling and miniature locomotive design often overlapping. Each subject area is perhaps best dealt with separately and semi-chronologically.

RAILWAY RESEARCH

Twining's first historical study to appear in print was his collaboration with Alfred Rosling Bennett in *Historic Locomotives and Moving Accidents by Steam and Rail*. Twining probably met him in Glasgow, where they both worked for the Corporation Telephone Department. Both returned south to London in 1904 and he then illustrated several items for Rosling Bennett. (2)

In this case his part in the work was ten watercolours, not of railway accidents but of the types of locomotives Rosling Bennett discussed in the text. The designs involved ranged from a Bristol and Exeter broad gauge 4-2-4T to a Caledonian Railway Connor 8ft single, by way of South Eastern Railway Cramptons. Each of these paintings must have needed considerable study into the locomotive designs and livery details, and they now represent important historical records. The whereabouts of six of the originals is unknown, but four, two London Brighton & South Coast Railway and two South Eastern Railway, each about 12in by 15in, are in the permanent collection of the National

GWR standard gauge 2-2-2 No 158, another of Twining's favourite
prototypes. collection – Reg Davis

Railway Museum. [Fig.c1 - colour section at back of book]

Twining's railway links with Rosling Bennett continued the following year in an article for *The Railway Magazine* on a number of continental Crampton locomotives. Whilst far from a complete survey of continental Cramptons this article covered those of the Paris-Lyon-Mediterranée railway in France and of the Baden State and Hesse-Ludwig railways of Germany. Twining again researched and supplied the illustrations, in this case side elevation drawings. (3)

For the first time his characteristic line shading appeared, a technique of which he with F.C. Hambleton might have been regarded as the last exponents except that John Milner has recently revived it, appropriately enough for a drawing of the Fairbourne Railway's 15in gauge Pacific *Ernest W Twining*.(4)

Twenty years later Rosling Bennett produced his *Chronicles of Boulton's Siding*, the story of a Victorian entrepreneur who overhauled and hired out secondhand (often very secondhand) locomotives to civil engineering contractors and to impecunious mainline railways. This is illustrated with numerous drawings of small steam locos, of designs from almost the dawn of mainline railways to mid-Victorian. Whilst there is no evidence of Twining's involvement in this book it would certainly have been a project dear to his heart if he and Rosling Bennett were still in contact.

Research that Twining definitely did undertake, however, concerned the

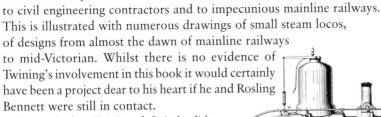

Right: Twining's drawing of Baden Railway's *Crampton Eagle* for Rosling Bennett's 1907 article for *Railway Magazine.*

23

Newcastle and Carlisle Railway's locomotive *Comet*. Built by R.& W. Hawthorn in 1835 *Comet* took part in the NCR's opening later that year. In 1920, Hawthorn Leslie (successors to R.& W. Hawthorn) asked Twining Models to make a $^3/_4$in to 1ft model of this, their first ever locomotive design. In fact three copies were made, all of which still exist, two in store for the proposed Tyneside Museum of Science and Industry and the third in the National Railway Museum.

Fortunately some drawings of the locomotive had survived, although they gave no clue as to the livery, which was assumed to be the fairly universal dark green of early locomotives, with polished wood boiler lagging and a fair amount of polished brass. A much more significant problem was that the surviving drawings were only a side elevation and a plan from beneath, and the latter showed four eccentrics.

Prior to this two eccentrics only had been used, one per cylinder, loose on the axle but engaged with stops at 90 degrees to the cranks. To reverse his engine the driver had to depress a treadle to disconnect the eccentrics from their valve spindles, then work the valves by hand levers until the locomotive moved off. Then he could re-engage the eccentric rods with the valve spindles. But if this engine had four eccentrics how did they operate? Hawthorn's own valve-gear was not patented until 1840, and the eccentric rod extensions did not seem to be gabs, which in any case were probably not in use by 1835. Twining comments "Although no historical work gave complete particulars of the pre gab gear . . . one old book at least gave a drawing of an eccentric rod which fitted the case." This matched the plan view in every respect " and there can be no question that the gear shown, peculiar as it may appear, was that fitted to the original *Comet*.

Comet's four eccentric gear dispensed with the treadle, although not entirely with the hand gear, which would be needed if the locomotive came to rest in forward gear and only then did the driver find he had to reverse. If he put the engine into back gear before stopping the hand mechanism would not be needed. Nevertheless *Comet* introduced four eccentrics and proper reversing gear. Soon afterwards however gab gear came on the scene, leading rapidly to Stephenson's link motion, which made all early valve-gears obsolete. (5) [Fig. c2]

In 1934 Twining produced for *Practical Mechanics* a series Modelling Historic Locomotives. Each part consisted of 2–3 pages of historical background and technical description and up to three of his characteristic drawings. It is his view "that it is a great pity that the reproduction of historic engines is so much neglected. It is a deplorable fact that of dozens of famous . . . classes of

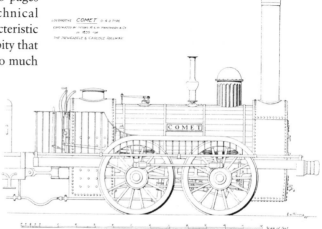

Top: One of Twining Models' *Comet* models. photo – Skinner Collection
Right: Newcastle and Carlisle Railway's *Comet*, built by Hawthorn's, redrawn by Ernest Twining for a 1921 article in *Locomotive* magazine.

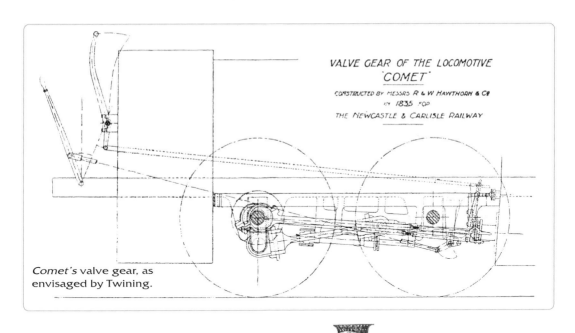

VALVE GEAR OF THE LOCOMOTIVE
'COMET'
CONSTRUCTED BY MESSRS R & W HAWTHORN & Cº
IN 1835 FOR
THE NEWCASTLE & CARLISLE RAILWAY

Comet's valve gear, as
envisaged by Twining.

Right & below: Lancashire Witch and *North Star*
for Twining's *Practical Mechanics* series

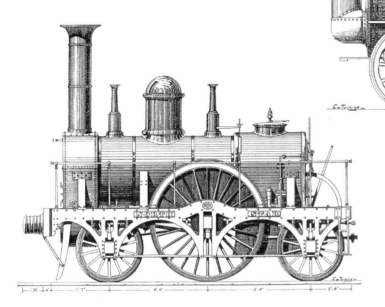

locomotives . . . not a single model exists. I write these articles with the object of urging model makers . . . to devote their attention . . . to making good the omissions of the past by providing future generations with tangible records." His belief is that "Models of old engines are better not made to steam, because such ability to work involves modification. . . and correct appearance is unavoidably spoiled." (6)

His series covers the period from 1803 to 1934, in approximately 8-year steps, and so includes over 20 of his drawings. Starting from the Trevithick beginnings, and explaining in detail the design of his 1805 Gateshead loco, Twining proceeds by way of Stephenson's evolving designs to Robert Stephenson's *North Star*. This provided a link to *Great Western* history and practice, which he elects to follow because " it would be confusing to dodge about from one railway to another, and because it was on the broad gauge that . . . the most outstanding advances were made in size, speed and power." The choice had nothing to do with his personal preference of course.

His particular favourites, the broad gauge singles appear in no less than four forms. Starting from Stephenson's 1837 *North Star*, most successful of the original Great Western engines, the series proceeds to Gooch's 1846 *Great Western*. Originally also a 2-2-2 this was rebuilt as the first of the celebrated 4-2-2 broad gauge singles. By 1851 *Lord of the Isles* represented the final design, which survived to the end of the 7ft gauge in 1892, although many were re-boilered or renewed in 1876-80. The very last variation illustrated was *Tornado* of 1888, now with a cab, vacuum brakes and continuous inside and outside frames.

The articles also included one of his other favourites, the standard gauge Gooch/Dean 2-2-2 of the 157-166 class; before turning to the Dean 3031 class singles, then *City of Truro* and concluding with *The Great Bear* and *King George V*. As a sop to the rest of Britain's railways he includes a Midland Railway Johnson 4-2-2 as a sort of postscript, calling it ". . a magnificent engineering achievement . . . designed as a complete unit".

Altogether the series comprises an excellent set of drawings and background material for early locomotive progress and then how GWR express types developed. It is however not truly representative of Great Western practice in general, much less Britain as a whole, but many of the drawings are minor works of art and represent a considerable body of work. Most are actually dated 1934, showing the short timescale in which they were all produced.

In 1938 a further series appeared, this time written by W.J. Bassett-Lowke and illustrated by Twining (although he may well have "ghosted" the text also), 'Milestones in the Progress of the British Steam Locomotive'. This contains much less technical or historical background, and the drawings are simplified side elevations, with no shading and essential detail only. Nevertheless there are 29 drawings in the 6 parts, so his pencil must have been busy. The drawings are said to represent *Bassett-Lowke's* own favourites and so are less partisan than Twining's own series, inevitably most of the early engines are the same and most of the broad gauge designs but such locos as *London & North Western Railway's Charles Dickens* and the *North Eastern's* first express 4-6-0 appear. The series concludes with the LNER's *Silver Link* and *LMS Coronation* before adding a section that is not British at all: Chapelon's 240A class 4-8-0 in France, Deutsch Reichsbahn's 05 class 4-6-4, and Southern Pacific's GS2 class 4-8-4, all fairly recently introduced. (7)

Even apart from *Comet* Twining's railway research was not restricted to writing and drawing, because he and/or his company made several other models of early locomotives, notably the Killingworth model for the Science Museum (which is believed not to be that now on show at York) and a sectioned model of *Rocket* as built. Following his own favourite themes there were also two Great Western models; broad gauge *Hirondelle* and a 2-2-2 of the 157-166 class.

The former was actually started by Twining himself in 1906/7, after *Lord of the Isles* was broken up, as a replica of that engine. He later changed the model to a different loco so he could incorporate his preferred sandwich framed tender. He ". . adopted the name of one of the other engines *Hirondelle* because of its euphonious nature". In 1927 the model was loaned to the Science Museum for 5 years,

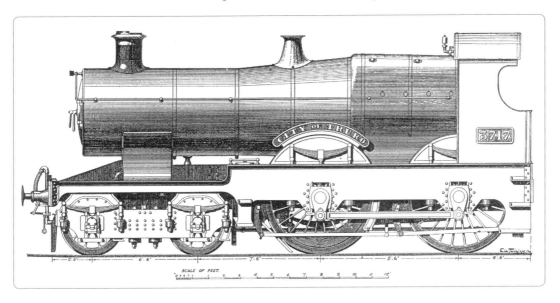

GWR *City of Truro* also drawn for the *Practical Mechanics* articles.

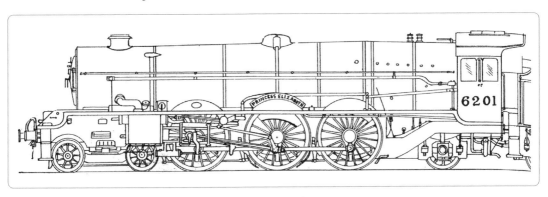

Twining's drawing of LMS No 6201 for the series written for *Practical Mechanics* by W.J.Bassett-Lowke. A much simpler style than the more traditional illustrations for his a own earlier series.

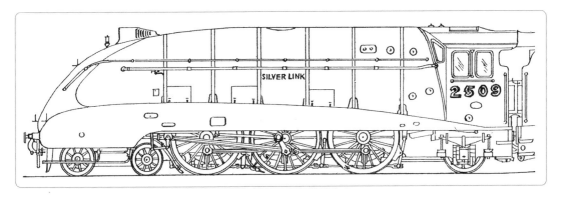

LNER 2501 also for W.J.Bassett-Lowke's *Practical Mechanics* articles.

until reclaimed by Twining Models. He tried to sell it to the museum, who declined it because they already had a broad gauge model. Years later, after WWII, the Museum tried to renew the loan, only to discover the model had passed to Bassett-Lowke Ltd and then in turn to the Scottish National Museum in Edinburgh, where it still is. Twining comments this is a long way from the broad gauge system the engine represents and wishes he still had the model to remind him of it ". . for I am old enough to have known and remember all those beautiful Gooch singles". The model is however still in Edinburgh, in the Museum's reserve collection, and can be viewed by arrangement.

The last correspondence on this engine also reveals the existence of a part built 1 $^{1}/_{2}$in to 1ft model of the 157-166 class standard gauge 2-2-2. Designed by Daniel Gooch, built at Swindon in 1878/9 and later rebuilt by William Dean, these seem to have been favourites of many railway enthusiasts of the time. Ahrons describes them as ". . celebrated and amongst the most handsome express engines ever built". It is not surprising that they keep turning up in Twining's work.

This particular model, perhaps started in the 1930s was presumably laid aside when Twining's wife became ill and he subsequently left Northampton, leaving it in store at Twining Models. From his 1952 description all major components except the boiler were then in existence, although wheels and cylinders were un-machined. What happened to this model over the years is uncertain, but some items are still believed to exist.

The *Hirondelle* model meanwhile was used to illustrate a further series for *Practical Mechanics*. This was itself of course a highly detailed "glass case" model but in January 1937 Twining started a series aimed at model engineers making a working model of a broad gauge GWR single wheeler. The series as a whole is most appropriately dealt with later, under small steam locos, but the first two parts were almost entirely devoted to information about the class, and so merit inclusion at this point. It might be argued that the information Twining sets out does not really constitute research as it is readily available; and so it is nowadays, e.g. in the GWR series compiled by the Railway Correspondence and Travel Society. Twining however was writing in 1937, when such material was much less accessible, especially from an organisation like the GWR which could be very secretive.

Twining concentrates on *Lord of the Isles* in her final condition; but aims to provide modellers (and incidentally historians) with information on all the other engines. He points out that not only were there significant differences between the batches as these were built, rebuilt or renewed at different dates, but also each individual engine changed in appearance over the years as modifications were made. *Lord of the Isles*, for example, ended her days with a Dean chimney and flanged driving wheels, but never received engine brakes, injector or cab.

Twining's view is that the class prototype, the original *Great Western* of 1846, was not really a member of the class proper, because her boiler, wheelbase and other features were always non-standard. The remainder form three distinct groups, with significant differences in outside frame shape for those built in 1847, between 1848 and 1855, and finally those built or "renewed" after 1878. The class also carried six different chimney designs over the years, due to Gooch himself, to Joseph Armstrong, and eventually to Dean. All sorts of other items varied over the years; e.g. size,

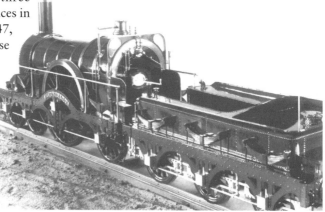

Ernest Twining's own model of GWR *Hirondelle*, now in the National Museum of Scotland, Edinburgh.
photo - Twining family

number and location of sand boxes, addition of weatherboard or later cab, addition of hand then vacuum brakes, changing shape and height of leading wheel splashers, fitting of proper spring buffers instead of leather stuffed with horsehair. The range of changes is vast and Twining obviously delved into the archives in some detail; he thanks C.B.Collett, GWR Chief Mechanical Engineer, for information on chimney designs for example. Clearly for someone as anxious as he to achieve accuracy in a model this level of information is essential, and as in other cases he provides a wealth of material on this well known and historically important class of locomotives.

Twining Models produced a further item of historical significance around this time. This was a model of the original Euston Station, as it opened in July 1838, for the LMS Euston Centenary Exhibition in 1938. The National Railway Museum have such a model but have no information except that it was passed to them from the British Railways Board in 1970. In fact this is much inferior to the Twining article as described at the time, much smaller in scale, with no real attempt to represent the track and no locomotive in sight.

At least at the time the Twining model was being made some drawings and information on the original structure would still have existed, and as with Hawthorn's *Comet* their significance would have been appreciated. The number of organizational changes our railways and other major companies have gone through in more recent years means that is often no longer the case. The National Railway Museum is not the only organization using volunteers to sort out archives of drawings, photographs and company records which have been deposited inadequately catalogued.

In terms of railway research, Ernest Twining's "magnum opus" is undoubtedly the series of articles for *Model Engineer* on British Crampton locomotives. Thomas Crampton was assistant to Daniel Gooch at Swindon during construction of the early 7ft gauge singles (*Firefly* class 2-2-2) but saw the possibilities of designing standard gauge locomotives which might be as fast and powerful as their broad gauge contemporaries. To combine the features of large single driving wheels and low centre of gravity, both then thought essential for speed and stability, his patents of 1842 (when he was only 26) were for an outside cylinder stern wheeler, the design with which his name is always associated.

Twining seems always to have been interested in the stern wheel Cramptons (but not the later jack-shaft drive types which he dismisses as aberrations) and like some Great Western classes they appear repeatedly in his painting, drawing and writing. In this case he apparently offered a series of articles to the *Model Engineer*, collecting together his information on British Cramptons and illustrating this with his own drawings. Many of the drawings are in fact dated 1950-2, although the articles appeared between 12/3/53 and 25/3/54. (8)

The editor commented on the quality of the drawings. "Readers will surely agree with us that the drawings . . are magnificent, in spite of his age (he was then in his late 70s) Mr Twining has not lost that touch which has always made his drawings such a delight to study". However he was still only paid £6 per episode, £66 in total. Twining covered all 25 British rear driver Cramptons in this series; 20 built new and 5 on the South Eastern Railway rebuilt from conventional locos, with side and end elevations, plus extra detail drawings where appropriate.

The first engines were a batch of six built by Tulk and Ley, of Lowca Foundry, Whitehaven, to Thomas Crampton's own design, perhaps even as a speculative venture. The six went to three different railways and the London and North Western Railway then ordered an enlarged version from the same builders, this became their *London*. Drawing this particular engine caused Twining problems, due to finding different dimensions in different sources. This was especially true of the boiler, which like some other Cramptons was not circular but oval in cross section. It was also pressed to 100psi, a very high figure for 1847, and one reason for the Crampton's success on some railways, particularly in France.

Twining is very critical of the layout of the Stephenson's valve-gear on these seven locos, and goes into considerable detail to explain how this was improved upon in the next Crampton to be built. This was the LNWR's *Courier* built at Crewe in the following year. Presumably due to the influence of

Twining's beautiful side elevation of London and North Western Railway's Crampton *Liverpool.*

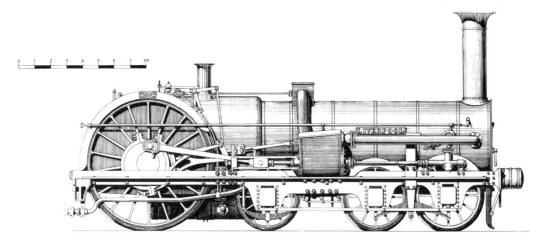

Crampton himself in the construction of this engine Gooch valve-gear was used, for the first and only time on a Crewe-built engine. This greatly simplified valve-gear arrangement and design of *Courier* compared with its predecessors.

The next three episodes were all devoted to LNWR's *Liverpool,* largest and best known of British Cramptons, built by Bury Curtis and Kennedy in 1848. There must be a story behind the LNWR buying three Cramptons in two years, all of different designs and from different builders, but Twining does not explore it unfortunately. He notes however that he would anticipate *Liverpool* being most popular amongst model makers, and having comprehensive information on the prototype he ". . proposes to give a full description of the engine and to prepare drawings showing, in addition to external elevations, cross sections, a longitudinal section giving details of the boiler, plan views and drawings of the tender." This totals 10 drawings, of which the side elevation and longitudinal section are magnificent pieces of work.

As with *London* Twining found it necessary to reconcile conflicting sources of information, and particularly sort out common misconceptions about the engine; e.g. the chimney was almost certainly parallel not tapered and the wooden boiler lagging was covered. Nor was the engine painted red as in a popular oil painting by C. Hamilton Ellis; the McConnell red livery of the LNWR Southern Division was not introduced until two years after *Liverpool* was scrapped.

He may well have uncovered the reason behind the engine's reputation for spreading track. Apparently her third pair of carrying wheels (she was a 6-2-0) were flangeless, and whilst this was common knowledge, what Twining noted was that these were only the same width as the tread portion of the other wheels, whereas later practice would have made them at least as wide as the other wheels including their flanges. His contention, which seems very

Right: Crampton No 112 of the Eastern Counties Railway.
Model Engineer.
Opposite top: Crampton loco No 81 of the South Eastern Railway.
Model Engineer.

reasonable, is that these wheels could have dropped at least partially within a rail sufficiently to apply considerable side force to what was at that time very poorly and lightly constructed track, far from that of the "Premier Line" it was to become. (This incidentally is why No 92220 *Evening Star* is no longer allowed on the mainline, check rails are now allowed to be higher than running rails and could derail her wide flangeless wheels).

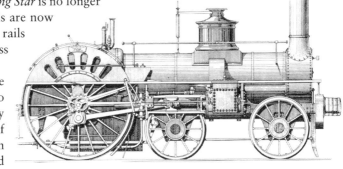

His other major investigation in the Crampton series concerned the two Midland Railway examples, built by Kitsons in1848. The existence of drawings for parts of these engines in the Science Museum both helped and hindered his study, because the complete side elevation showed part of a different type of valve-gear than that shown in the accompanying drawings of the full valve-gear and reversing mechanism!

The elevation is undated, but Twining argues that it is the later of the two drawings, because the valve-gear shown in detail is that of Isaac Dobbs, already long obsolete in 1848. He suggests this might have originally been proposed, because of space limitations, only to be replaced by a better design as construction proceeded. His initial conclusion, based on the partial gear shown on the full side elevation, was that Gooch valve-gear had again been incorporated, but an attempt to lay this out still showed insufficient space. He suggests therefore that a modified Stephenson valve-gear may have been used, with the eccentric rod led backwards instead of forwards and then via a rocking shaft. He provides a detailed drawing of this "hypothetical" arrangement, putting ". . this forward as a probable solution of this little problem, which to the locomotive historian is extremely interesting" and a matter of major importance to any model engineer attempting to model one of these engines.

This particular study is typical of his work on this fascinating and historically invaluable archive. Some writers have criticised parts of the work, but no one else has attempted to pull all the British Crampton threads together. Forty years on W. Sharman (a modeller of early and unusual steam locos) re-used many of the drawings and other Twining material in his book *The Crampton Locomotive*, commenting ". . the very fine drawings (of *Liverpool* especially) . . . really do her justice and from the modellers' stand point are superb". He was convinced these were the most accurate of the many drawings and prints of this particular engine. The whole series is certainly a most interesting piece of work and some of the drawings deserve considerable study and admiration. (9)

MODEL RAILWAYS

Ernest Twining's very first published articles were on model railways, starting in the *Model Engineer* in August 1905, and he continued to write on various aspects of the subject for almost 50 years, off and on. In 1905 of course the term "model railways" did not mean quite the same as it does today, and initially he was writing for garden railways of gauge 1(1 ^{3}/4in) upwards. This first series was entitled "Picturesqueness" in model railways, really describing what would now be termed scenic features. In fact this started a theme common to most of his writings on the subject; that of improving the appearance, whether by scenic features, more realistic locos, stock and buildings, 2-rail electrification, or better model trees, all aimed at making layouts more scenic and more realistic.

In his very first article he bemoans the fact that (at that time) few "model railway engineers" considered the need for landscape or scenic effects, many being satisfied with "a bare track upon which they can run their locomotives". Where tunnels, bridges and the like were incorporated into model railways he was concerned that they were generally of unsuitable proportions. His artistic sense as well as his engineering training was clearly offended by tunnels which were too high, or too narrow, or by bridges out of scale for the trains they carried.

To this end he used the series to design and describe a series of bridges and tunnel mouths, some freelance and others based on actual GWR and LNWR prototypes. Detailed instructions were given for simple but robust construction methods and the articles were illustrated by his usual elegant drawings, by his own watercolours and also by photographs. These were also presumably his own, including some of the prototype structures and examples of the models on his own garden railway.

The designs were all for $^3/4$in to 1ft scale (as noted above, "model" railways were built to larger scales in those days), although his own line was half that size, 1 $^3/4$in gauge or $^3/8$in to 1ft scale. One photograph on his own railway showed a model GWR loco emerging from a typically Brunellian Gothic tunnel onto Brunel longitudinal sleepered track. This is of note because a similar view, from a slightly different angle, appeared in the introduction of Bassett-Lowke's model railway catalogues for a number of editions a few years later.

In spite of these articles, and his own garden line, his model railway interests were not restricted to larger sizes. Steam outline electric locos were beginning to be marketed in "O" gauge (1 $^1/4$in, 7mm or $^1/4$in to 1ft scale) but it would not be until after WWII that commercial models appeared in still smaller sizes, initially as HO (i.e. half O gauge) from Bassett-Lowke and Stewart Reidpath. However as early as 1906 Twining used his electrical engineering skills to produce an 1/8in to 1ft scale model of a 4-4-2.

This used the boiler as field winding for the motor with the armature filling the wide firebox, the only way it then seemed possible to get the necessary components into the available space of what was effectively the first electric HO loco model. He subsequently (*Practical Mechanics* June 1935) described a 4-6-2 version, with either permanent or electro-magnet, having (in his words) "copywrited the locomotive as an electric motor".

In view of later developments this was really an evolutionary dead end but its significance, like many of Twining's projects, was to show what really was possible. One of the biggest handicaps to technical progress in any field is that something which has not yet been achieved is felt by some to be impossible. Conversely once a breakthrough is made, however crudely, improved designs and methods follow. Twining never seems to have suffered from the idea that something could not be done, and consequently pioneered many fields over the years.

After the early *Model Engineer* articles, Twining's interests, or at least his published work, turned away from model railways for several years. In the 1930s however he produced articles for *Hobbies Weekly* and for *Practical Mechanics*. These started with "Model Railways and how to make them," which evolved into "Realistic Model Locomotives and how to make them"; details of how to make best use of commercial electric motors in model locomotives; details of model railway control and signalling systems, and finally a long series on "Adapting (i.e. improving) the Twin-Train Table Railway," later more usually called the Trix-Twin system.

All this culminated in his 1937 publication *Indoor Model Railways*, devoted exclusively to HO/OO systems. Like W.A.Mozart however Ernest Twining was not in the habit of wasting good ideas and the book reuses much earlier material; e.g. the tunnels and bridges from 1905-8 reappear in the smaller scale, as do some ideas to improve the realism of the Twin-Train system. There is however much useful basic information in the book and some of it is still relevant 60 years later.

Twining was very unhappy about the emergence of the British OO scale, using 4mm/1ft rolling stock on 16.5mm gauge track. The early commercial models, e.g. those of Bassett-Lowke and Stewart Reidpath post WWII had been to a scale of 3.5mm to 1ft (i.e. HO or half O). This has a very accurate scale/gauge ratio with track only 0.02mm too narrow – and the rest of the world's modellers of

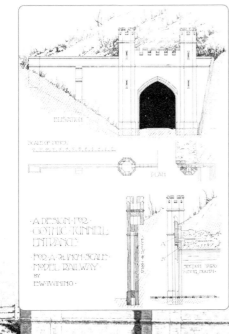

Left: A drawing from Twining's 1905/6 series for *Model Engineer* on Picturesqueness in model railways. *Model Engineer*.
Middle: A watercolour from the 1908 series on engineering features. *Model Engineer*.
Bottom: Twining's $1/8$in to 1ft model 4-4-2 of 1906, one of the first electric model locomotives in roughly HO gauge.

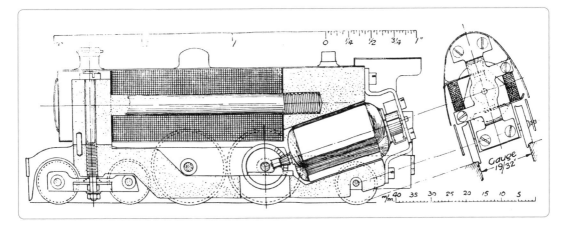

standard gauge railways have adhered to this. Unfortunately some British producers, perhaps for ease of manufacture, increased the scale of their engines and rolling stock to 4mm/1ft but still on 16.5mm gauge. As he points out this discrepancy makes true finescale modelling impossible, and he would no doubt have been pleased by the later emergence of first 18mm and then exact 18.83mm gauge track for fine scale 4mm/1ft modelling.

The other "political" issue of the book is his advocacy of two rail electrical systems. These were already being used in the USA as the book was written, and Twining Models were about to use them in at least two architectural/landscape dioramas. With his unspoken objective being to improve the general realism of all model railways this was a natural route to follow. He notes that many of his colleagues in the trade are opposed on the grounds of cost, due to the need to insulate frames and/or wheels, however "if the quantities called for are large enough nothing in this way is impossible". It took almost 20 years for British commercial models to make the change but as so often he was right in the end.

Enlarging on this subject, the book covers control and wiring arrangements for 2-rail systems in some detail, together with relevant features of complex trackwork and locomotive design including how to convert a locomotive from 3-rail to 2-rail. The earlier *Practical Mechanics* articles had covered only the then common 3-rail system, but clearly the book him gave an opportunity for propaganda for this much needed improvement.

Another theme picked up from the earlier articles is that of adapting or improving the realism of the Trix-Twin Railway system, then being strongly promoted by Bassett-Lowke Ltd. For those unfamiliar with this, it used fully insulated 3-rail track, with a common centre return rail but separate feeds to the outer rails. Two suitably insulated locomotives could thus be operated simultaneously but separately on the same layout. Early Twin-Train track and locos were very crude by today's standards, although the original 0-4-0T and 0-4-0 tender locomotives were supplemented by 4-6-2s in the late 1930s, and by other types after WWII.

From the winter of 1935/6 the Trix-Twin or Twin-Train table railway was initially sold as just that – intended for assembly on the dining room table for use, then packed way again afterwards. Twining's articles and chapters in the book are concerned to exploit its possibilities for permanent layouts, at the same time adapting the locomotives to more British outlines and providing stations, tunnels, bridges and other lineside equipment; familiar themes. Suggested locos include (necessarily) freelance 2-4-0 tank and tender engines, with cabs and boiler mountings to match any of the "Big Four" railways. Other ideas included extending the loco into a 2-6-0 tender engine of GWR appearance, although this would need curves of larger radius than TTR's standard 14". (10)

Twining also helped to develop a Southern Railway emu motor coach, using the standard motor and control system, and for Bassett-Lowke redesigned the Many-Ways station system, based on the Trix system. This was a modular design, "made either in parts of hard wood, die-cast metal or steel stampings and arranged in definite and precisely dimensioned units which will build up into various formations without tools or attachments"; in other words capable of assembly in many different ways, so as to give a range of stations from suburban or country halt to city terminus. All were based on the simple concrete structures of the 1930s, many of which still survive on London Transport and the erstwhile Southern Region of British Railways. "The combination of pleasing lines with proportionate masses is essential in the study of architecture. Only an artist is capable of combining these and the . . designers have excelled themselves in this respect".

Another section of the book recalls his earlier "Realistic Model Locomotives and how to make them," showing how the limited designs of electric motors then available could be incorporated into a wide range of prototypes. As candidates he provides no less than 24 locomotive side elevations carefully drawn to HO scale and with main features shown but not excessive detail. These range from mid-Victorian to LMS *Princess Elizabeth*, and inevitably include his old favourites from the GWR

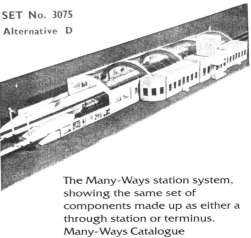

SET No. 3075
Alternative D

SET No. 3075
Alternative H

The Many-Ways station system, showing the same set of components made up as either a through station or terminus. Many-Ways Catalogue

Left: The Trix-Twin or Twin-Train system as it was originally intended to be used, with the author aged about 5. Author's collection

Below: Twining's adaptation of the Trix-Twin power unit for a pseudo-Southern Railway electric motor car. *Practical Mechanics*

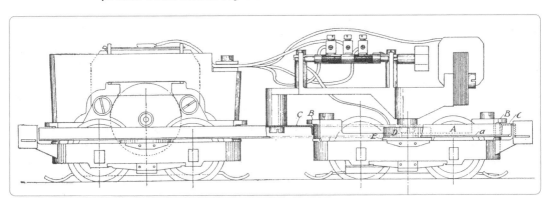

such as the Dean 157-166 class 2-2-2 and Dean 4-4-0 No 8 *Gooch*.

Indoor Model Railways also contains much useful information on the design and construction of scenery. By the time it was published Twining himself had not only had many years of railway modelling but he and his company had also constructed many model factories and landscape models, several on a huge scale and others incorporating working model railways.

Whilst his bridge and tunnel designs are merely scaled down from those of the much earlier *Model Engineer* articles the station schemes are much more modern, reflecting similar styles to those of the Many Ways series. On actual layouts he describes how to design the railway system, then the timber structure to support it and finally his suggestions for "realistic natural modelling". For this he proposes plywood frames, with coal to represent rock faces (painted as necessary), then soil made either from plaster mixed with chopped hair, or with sawdust or just sawdust with glue-and-water size. Actual quantities needed would not be very great because of the plywood supports, to which the "soil" would be keyed by protruding brads or tacks. He is emphatic about the need for trees, as many as possible, and modelled to their prototypes, and finally about the appropriate painting of all surfaces of the model and of the back scene.

His final model railway articles were again for *Practical Mechanics*, in 1951-3. The first was a scheme to operate very small-scale railways by having all the moving parts below the baseboard, really a variation of the system once seen on fairgrounds but with points and junctions. This does not really seem an idea worthy of his imagination, especially as 2mm / 1ft scale OOO gauge (later N) was not far in the future.

Likewise his O gauge garden railway of May to November 1953 covered all aspects of such a system but in very skimpy detail, the spirit fired *Britannia* 4-6-2 to haul the trains was dealt with in a single article for example. Interesting ideas but totally inadequate information for a potential modeller to follow up, except someone already familiar with garden railway design, for whom there would be little new.

Clearly some articles were dashed off in rather a hurry, either to satisfy a friend's request (e.g. F.J.Camm for *Practical Mechanics*) or just for the money! A much earlier aberration was the November /December 1935 article for *Practical Mechanics* on a 4 ^{3}/4in (1in to 1ft) gauge passenger carrying Electric Model Garden Railway, for use by juveniles or those unskilled with steam locos but operating direct from the 220 volt mains supply! The simple locos (4 different 0-6-0 prototypes are shown) were to operate from a large motor in the firebox, supplied from twin conductor rails mounted within the running rails and completely boxed-in apart from a slot in the top of the box for the contact arms, and therefore visually very similar to the conduit system sometimes used for trams. Our present day safety culture would have found this concept interesting to say the least!

Ernest Twining's major contribution to model railways was his passion to achieve as great a realism as currently available equipment allowed, together with advocacy of further improvements (smaller, more powerful motors, 2-rail systems), all aimed ultimately at the same objective. Whether his work or writing significantly affected the course of model railway development is unlikely ever to be known, but he would certainly be pleased at the progress actually achieved, in model realism, in still smaller scales for indoor systems, and things like radio control of outdoor steam powered lines – something even he could perhaps never have imagined.

Small Steam Locomotives

Ernest Twining designed and/or built several small passenger hauling steam locomotives. According to *Model Engineer's* series Who's Who in Model Engineering he first prepared a set of working drawings for a 1in scale engine in 1895, towards the end of his apprenticeship. This is perhaps the rather elegant outside cylinder 4-4-0 shown in the family picture of some 12 years later. Around

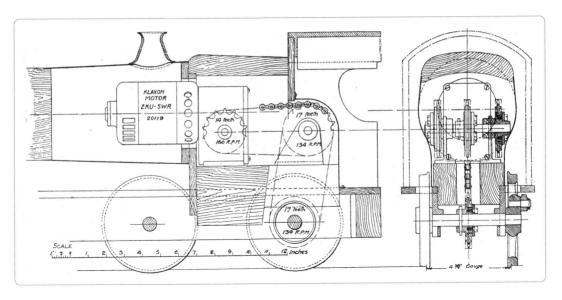

Simple mains voltage 1in scale 4 ^{3}/4in gauge locomotive. *Practical Mechanics*

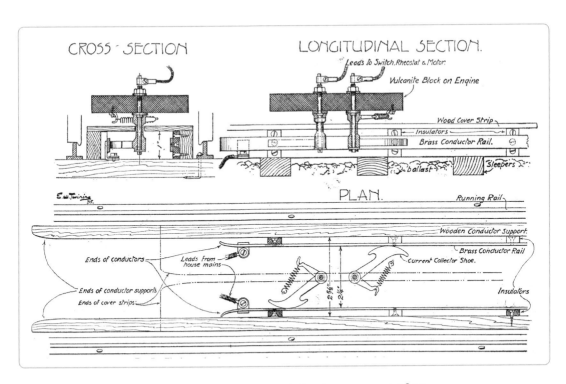

Conduit style conductor rails for the proposed 4 ^{3}/4in
gauge mains voltage system. *Practical Mechanics*

1914/15 he also built a 7 ^{1}/4in gauge Midland Railway 0-4-4T loco, No 1830. This was typically highly detailed, but clearly has an overscale boiler with chimney and dome cut down to match, this was common practice then of course. Built apparently for a particular customer, the engine still exists, and is now with a collector in Warwickshire. (12) *[Fig. c3]*

Later several of his designs were published in *Model Engineer* and in *Practical Mechanics* and it is these which are of the greatest interest. Although appearing over a period of more than 20 years the designs all included some of Ernest Twining's original ideas and several common themes. The early models for example all used the then universal riveted and soft soldered boiler principle, and although he silver-soldered specific parts of some designs, he never accepted LBSC's fully brazed boiler ideas. The models were often rather lightly constructed by later standards, for example ^{1}/16in frames for the 2 ^{1}/2in gauge *Castle*, and a typical Twining touch was that several incorporated unusual valve-gear. All were either freelance or GWR prototypes.

As usual his reasons for choosing to model Great Western engines were not exactly unbiased – in the introductory paragraph of the first series he says ". . on a stormy day . . . go first to the station of the company whose engines are black and note the mud splashings from buffer to buffer and from rail level to the top of the chimney. Then cross to Paddington, where the brasswork glistens and the green paint is polished clean, whilst even the wheels have nothing but a film of oil on their spokes." Hardly a fair comparison of an engine just arrived from (say) Birmingham with one about to start its day's work.

The first model was a ^{3}/4 inch scale Model GWR Express Locomotive and was based on one of his favourites, the Dean 4-4-0 No 8 *Gooch*, starting in *Model Engineer* from 11 March 1915, on p198. These locos were a class of four (Nos 7,8,14&16) originally built as broad gauge convertible 2-4-0s in 1888, although some contained parts e.g. driving wheel centres, from earlier engines. Withdrawn with the end of the 7ft gauge they reappeared as standard gauge 4-4-0s in 1894, and with 7ft wheels closely resembled the famous Dean 4-2-2s. Between 1901 and 1911 they were rebuilt with Churchward domeless tapered boilers. No 8 was last to be dealt with and was turned out with a superheater.

Twining's model is in this later rebuilt form, but deviates from the prototype. The rebuilds had widened cabs so the rear splashers were now largely hidden, but he felt it ". . a pity to spoil the symmetry of the two splashers . . by this adherence to accuracy". His own model, and his drawings, therefore retain the original appearance by making the cab narrower and splashers wider than the full

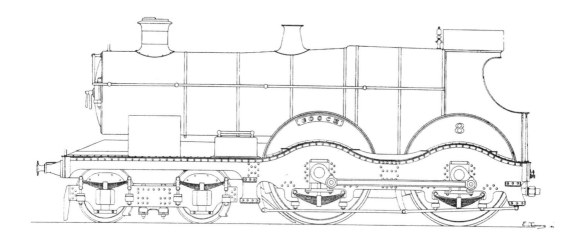

Design for 3 ^{1}/2in gauge GWR 4-4-0 No 8 *Gooch*.

size engine. The model had a Smithies boiler, intended for spirit or paraffin oil firing, both common practice at the time. A Twining variation however was to use Joy instead of the correct Stephenson valve-gear. Whether he felt this easier to make or to fit into the available space is unclear; he does not make clear his reasoning in this case. However he always had a fascination with valve-gear, which was to culminate in a design of his own, used on his last 15in gauge loco.

The 4-4-0 makes a most elegant model, in fact he comments elsewhere that the prototypes were probably more beautiful than their better known 4-2-2 sisters, whether in the typical Twining side elevation drawing or in the photograph of his own example. He notes in part one that he is building the engine himself, surely an encouragement to anyone else proposing to do so. Although the series was brief, in nothing like the detail that "LBSC" (L Lawrence) was later to make standard practice, it was still a significant improvement on previous "how to do it" articles, with a detailed parts list, side and end elevations and detailed drawings of several components.

It seems possible that this design was not actually commissioned by *Model Engineer* but that Twining was already building it for himself and was asked by Percival Marshall to write it up for the magazine. Henry Greenly was at this time contracted to supply model locomotive and similar articles for *Model Engineer* but he and Marshall were not on good terms at this point due to him falling behind with this commitment, perhaps due to pressure of work for Narrow Gauge Railways Ltd. Ten years or so later Bassett-Lowke added the engine to their range, selling completed models for £160, complete sets of parts and material for £14.10.0, or sets of castings alone for £4.17.6. These were described as being made from Mr Twining's own patterns, which "we confidently recommend to the amateur loco builder as the best yet produced for this class of work".

Possibly because of Greenly's other commitments, Twining had not long before been asked by Bassett-Lowke (presumably with Greenly's approval) to undertake the design of a 15in gauge 4-6-2 derived from Greenly's *Little Giant* 4-4-2 series. This project now provided the inspiration for the next 3 1/2in gauge design, 'A Maximum Loading Gauge 3/4in scale Locomotive'. (13)

This is probably the most interesting of his small locomotive designs and completely different from its predecessor, incorporating several innovations but still quite practical. His original intention apparently had been to design a quarter size copy of the Bassett-Lowke class 60 *Pacific*, but realising there was scope for improvement he introduced a series of changes. The dome was abolished as being too small to be of value, and a proper radial trailing truck provided. Essentially cosmetic changes are the deeply-domed smokebox door, outside framed bogie, and short, round-roofed cab. These give the engine a very French appearance and several people have commented on the design's resemblance to the Nord (Northern Railway of France) pair of 4-6-4 locomotives, designed by du Bousquet and built in 1910. These were at the time amongst the largest passenger engines in Europe, larger in all respects than *Great Bear*, but

Twining's own model of No 8 *Gooch*. Only the cab fittings reveal it is a working model.
photo – Skinner Collection

not as heavy as the Belgium Railway's Flamme Pacifics. Their visual influence on Twining's ideas is perhaps not surprising.

Whilst describing the engine as of "maximum loading gauge", which in full size would have dwarfed GWR's *Great Bear* (the largest loco in Britain then and for some years to come) he admits that claims of locos having reached the limit of Britain's (somewhat limited) loading gauge have been made many times before, only to be overtaken by later progress. So it would have been with this engine, because whilst its boiler might have been higher pitched than that of a Stanier Duchess, its maximum diameter is much the same, and significantly smaller than that for the Stanier 4-6-4 proposal of 1938/42.

This time the loco is designed to burn coal, with a proper grate (but no ashpan – these were many years in the future for small steam locos) and an injector for boiler feed water. A more significant feature is the inclusion of a proper flue-tube superheater for the first time in a model, when indeed they were far from universal in fullsize UK practice. His final innovation is, inevitably, an unusual valve-gear, a revival of that designed by Daniel Gooch and used on many broad gauge engines. He notes it has the same number of parts as Stephenson's gear but has the merit ". . that the lead of the valve is of the same amount in all positions of the reversing lever (whereas) in Stephenson's gear wear of the die block is considerable and in time productive of much lost motion, even in a model".

Apart from the appropriate drawings the article is illustrated by a photograph of the 15in gauge prototype retouched by Twining ("faked" in his words) to provide a view of the model, or if one ignores the cab fittings and the track, a realistic impression of what a fullsize version might look like. As with the GWR 4-4-0 Bassett-Lowke again subsequently sold items for this engine. In this case however they just offered sets of drawings at £1.12.0 or castings at £12. Prices for small items and finished fittings were available on request.

Although we can have no idea how many such models were actually made, at least one still survives, albeit not in working order. This example was built, in 1933, by Mr J. Todd, an Englishman living in Holland. When he died the model passed to Nienord, a municipal park in Northern Holland, with railway tracks from 3 1/2in to 20cm. The locomotive was then completed by Rob van Dort and steamed occasionally. Trouble was experienced with the boiler, built to the usual early model system of riveting with soft solder caulking (Twining did however stress the need for brazing of the superheater components). Although this has been repaired the engine still awaits reassembly. An interesting touch is that like Twining's "faked" picture the engine is named *Pacific* and numbered for its year of construction.

As in the model railway field there was now a long gap in Twining's small steam loco activities – at least in any published work, and some 18 years passed before the next design. This was a 1/2in scale GWR *Castle* for *Practical Mechanics* magazine. The series started in October 1933 (p31) and if built to the drawings and finished as recommended would have

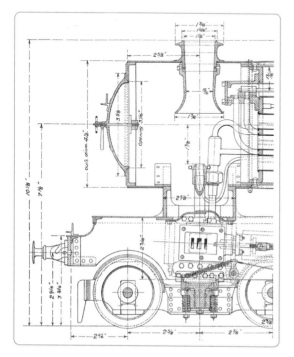

Left: Twining's 3 1/2in gauge 4-6-2 for *Model Engineer*, part section showing superheater. *Model Engineer*

produced an attractive and realistic model locomotive. It was however very lightly built and one wonders how robust it would have been in practice. This is particularly true of the frames, which although braced by cross members or other components at five locations were still only made of ^{1}/16in steel plate, i.e. about scale thickness. As the fullsize class was far from immune from frame troubles, and as O gauge models, whether steam, electric or clockwork, usually have frames this thick, it seems much too thin for the rigidity required.

The other curiosity of this design is his solution to the complex mechanism of a four cylinder locomotive with inside valve-gear in this scale. The usual method would be to omit the inside cylinders and just have the outside ones, a solution used on sizes right up to 15in gauge. Twining however has an alternative, turning this idea on its head.

In his solution the two outside cylinders are dummies whilst two larger ones are fitted inside, not in their correct location but farther back, above the bogie centre where most space is available and short steam and exhaust pipes can be arranged. This poses another problem however, of how the

connecting rods are to avoid the leading driving axle. This in turn is resolved by making a two piece connecting rod which is assembled with a large elliptical opening embracing the leading axle.

The other answer to simplifying the machinery is to avoid Walschaert valve-gear in favour of a system ". . to take the motion for the valve of one cylinder from the piston rod or crosshead of the other cylinder and let this motion operate an expansion link as employed in Walschaerts gear". The idea is not original, variations on the theme have been used on several full size designs, notably the Midland Railway's 4-4-0s of the 999 class and Churchward's very first 4 cylinder 4-6-0 *North Star*. In full size applications however a further link would join each crosshead to its own valve spindle to provide lead for the valve. Twining felt this unnecessary in 2 ^{1}/2in gauge and for simplicity it was omitted.

Top: Twining's photograph of Captain J.E.P.Howey's *John Anthony* retouched to represent his 3 ^{1}/2in gauge design for *Model Engineer. Model Engineer*

Middle: Dutch made example of Twining's 3 ^{1}/2in gauge *Pacific* design at Nienord.
photo – Rob van Dort

The rest of the engine including the boiler is much more conventional, coal-fired with a proper grate but still no ashpan. The boiler barrel is parallel and the firebox round topped, taper and belpaire firebox top being provided by the lagging, whilst a simple Greenly smokebox superheater is fitted. Twining offers the alternatives of traditional rivet and caulk construction or hard soldering, so he was clearly by now familiar with this development.

Altogether this design seems disappointing, the only one of his small passenger hauling locos where his attempts, presumably to design something less complex to build, included so many fresh ideas in one engine. Was the *Castle* with its complicated inside machinery his choice of prototype or did F.J.Camm of *Practical Mechanics* ask for this? If Twining had just wanted a modern express design his beloved GWR could have supplied the mechanically much simpler *Saint* with large outside cylinders and nothing but the valve-gear inside, although the class was a few years older and would presumably have had a less popular image in the 1930'. It would be interesting to know how many *Castle* models were actually built and how successfully they operated. By the following spring Bassett-Lowke Ltd were selling sets of plans and castings (as they had for the earlier designs) at two guineas (£2.10p) for drawings or eight guineas (£8.40p) for drawings and castings, so no doubt there are, or were, several examples around the British Isles.

Shortly after the *Castle* design, Twining produced for *Practical Mechanics* something much more workmanlike and down-to-earth. This was a 4 3/4in gauge 0-4-2 of narrow gauge outline, the series starting in January 1934 (p 185), continuing in February and March before concluding in January 1935. A follow-up in March 1935 described suitable track.

He explains the prototype had originated as a request from a builder of full size locomotives for a modern 18in – 20in gauge design, simple and cheap to produce and operate, with a high tractive effort and short rigid wheelbase. In fact this scheme was to appear in its entirety, later in 1934, in *Locomotive* magazine (strictly *The Locomotive Railway Carriage and Wagon Review*) and will be considered later. For a heavy duty, hard working passenger hauling loco on a smaller scale much the same arguments as to simplicity and robustness apply so the only thing to decide was the gauge. 4 3/4in offers a more stable platform for passengers, so it was preferred to a smaller gauge. (4 3/4in was then in common use, and still is in the USA, although largely displaced by 5in in this country.)

The machine is a robust and substantial one, with 1 1/4in by 2in cylinders, a well proportioned, short fat boiler and large firebox with plenty of grate and heating surface area. All bearings and

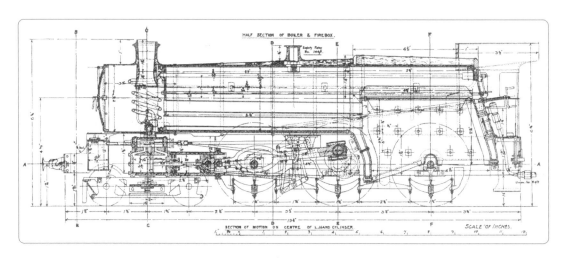

Sectional elevation Twining's 2 1/2in gauge GWR Castle design for
Practical Mechanics, showing unusual valve gear layout.

2 ^{1}/₂in gauge *Windsor Castle* built to Twining's *Practical Mechanics* design.
photo – Skinner Collection

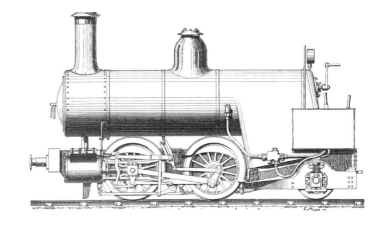

4 ^{3}/₄in gauge narrow gauge outline 0-4-2 based on his 18-22in gauge scheme. *Practical Mechanics*

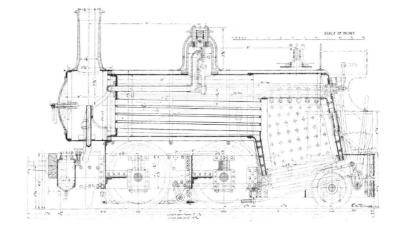

Sectional elevation of the passenger hauling 0-4-2. *Practical Mechanics*

moving parts are solidly designed but again it suffers from thin frames, only $3/32$in thick, although heavily braced and reinforced.

For once straight forward Walschaert valve-gear is used, with a detailed explanation as to how it should be set out; Twining Models were heavily involved in making valve gear models at this period and he seems to have realised the model engineering fraternity could well benefit from the same sort of information. In fact the whole series, whilst still less explanatory than that for an "LBSC" design nevertheless contains much more detail, both in drawing and description, than any of Twining's previous models. This is particularly significant because although larger than previous designs this one is much simpler than the 2 $1/2$in gauge *Castle* or 3 $1/2$in gauge 4-6-2.

The thin frames, which could easily be replaced by thicker material, are perhaps the engine's main weakness, although the boiler design has reverted to rivet and soft solder, Twining claims it is too large to braze but no doubt "LBSC" would beg to differ!

What seems to have been Twining's last significant small steam loco design started in January 1937 (*Practical Mechanics* p229), as noted earlier in the historical railway section. The model was a $3/4$in to 1ft *Lord of the Isles*, the Great Western broad gauge single of 1851. The series actually gave dimensions for $1/2$in and 1in scales, as well as going into considerable detail to cover the numerous variations in the class so any one of them could be modelled.

Apart from the gauge most features of his design were quite conventional; slide valve cylinders and the correct Gooch valve-gear, and a riveted and soft solder caulked boiler, albeit with a silver-soldered inner firebox. Twining again suggests this boiler is too large to be a single brazed unit – he was clearly wary of this technique in spite of its very successful and wide spread application.

Complications in this case arose from basic design features of the original, where apart from the very last few built the inside frames were very short. In effect the outside frames acted as a carriage whilst the inside frames connected cylinders and driving axle together and attached them to the boiler; almost as if a stationary engine had been fixed beneath the boiler, then the whole thing mounted on wheels.

"The main purpose served by the outside sandwich frame was to carry the boiler and machinery, and these outside frames took up none of the working stresses. There were inside frames, which extended only from the back of the cylinders to the front corners of the firebox. In these there were horns and axleboxes, and all the thrusting and pulling of the pistons and the shocks of the reciprocating masses were taken up by these frames". This means the machinery of the engine cannot be built separately from the boiler as is usual, because these inner frames and the parts they carry are attached to the boiler, a further complication being that the cylinders and steam chests are effectively incorporated into the lower part of the smokebox.

Although Twining attempted to simplify the mechanical design, in ways which would not eventually be visible, for example by omitting the fifth driving axle bearing fixed to the bottom of the boiler (there were the usual four in the two sets of frames), assembly was still going to be complex and he carefully outlines this. He proposes installing the cylinders in the smokebox, then attaching the completed boiler to the inside frames. Next assemble the motion parts, driving axle etc., and finally outside frames and wheels.

This should have made a most practical yet very accurate working model – although the $3/4$in scale version would have needed track specially laid to 5 $1/4$in gauge. The $1/2$in and 1in scale versions would have been able to use standard 3 $1/2$in and 7 $1/4$in tracks presumably. The series was interrupted for several months, and was only concluded shortly before the outbreak of war.

LARGER STEAM LOCOMOTIVES

Ernest Twining's first involvement with larger scale locomotives seems to have been in 1912/13. Captain J.E.P.Howey (later of Romney, Hythe and Dymchurch Railway fame) had decided to upgrade his existing 9 ^{1}/2in gauge garden railway at Staughton Manor to 15in gauge. He therefore asked Bassett-Lowke if they could provide a larger engine than the Greenly 4-4-2s they were then building for 15in gauge lines.

Twining was asked to undertake the job of enlarging the biggest of these, the Class 30, into a Pacific, later known as the Class 60. The design was of course Henry Greenly's, and with his reputation for a fiery temperament the work was presumably done with his approval, perhaps even at his suggestion. After all Cuthbert Davis, Twining's stepson, had been Greenly's apprentice, so the two men already knew each other. Greenly himself must have been otherwise engaged, perhaps with the activities of Narrow Gauge Railways Ltd.

Twining had previously designed and built small steam locomotives, but this may have been a somewhat daunting proposition, not just the biggest locomotive he had tackled but the largest 15in gauge engine built in Britain up to that date. Clearly existing parts and designs would be used as far as possible, "I had not altogether a free hand, for reasons of economy", but new boiler and frame designs would be needed.

Using existing patterns still allowed the cylinders to be enlarged from 4in diameter by 6in stroke to 4 ^{1}/4in by 6 ^{3}/4in; but new cylinder covers would be needed and careful consideration of the wheels to confirm the crankpins could be moved ^{3}/8in farther from the centre. He later noted that using the existing cylinder design meant retaining the valve chests above them and using a rocking shaft; extra linkages meant more scope for wear, something he was always anxious to avoid, especially in valve-gear.

The other area he was unhappy about was the use of radial axleboxes for the trailing truck, when a radial truck would have allowed a deeper firebox as well as giving a more flexible wheelbase. Actually, with hindsight the locomotive was far too lightly built; ^{5}/16in frames, small bearing surfaces and small section motion parts, but it was being designed for someone's garden railway, not for the very much harder task in Cumbria to which it eventually migrated.

Twining's general arrangement drawing in *Model Engineer* carries the name *Gigantic* and the number 1913 for its year of construction – a characteristic touch. Capt. Howey named the engine *John Anthony* but she later became the Ravenglass and Eskdale Railway's *Colossus*. WWI stopped Bassett-Lowke from exploiting this design; their 1914 *Miniature Railways and Equipment catalogue* offered the Class 60 Pacific at £500, as opposed to the Class 30 Atlantic at £450 or the smaller Class 20 Atlantic at £320 (or £360 with bogie tender). After the war Bassett-Lowke was no longer building 15in gauge locomotives, so that when the R&ER wanted another one they had to go to a different builder, upsetting Henry Greenly in the process as he regarded Twining's drawings as his own copyright!

This seems to have been Twining's last direct involvement with larger scale loco construction until his work with Trevor Guest in the late 1930s, but as usual pencil and drawing board were far from still. In fact Twining had by 1934 sufficiently clarified his ideas on small public passenger-hauling locomotives that he prepared a lengthy article for *Locomotive* magazine, 'Small Power Locomotives for Narrow Gauge Railways', illustrated by general arrangement drawings for 0-4-2 and 0-6-2 tender engines. Why 1934? Perhaps because by then Bassett-Lowke had lost interest in larger sizes, only building one or two more engines above 7 ^{1}/4in gauge, whilst public passenger-hauling seemed to be going down the steam outline, diesel powered route. Ten such lines had been built or planned, four using Hudswell-Clarke diesel powered replicas, LNER or LMS Pacifics or freelance 4-6-4T; and the others much cruder steam outline locos built by Baguley. In his article, perhaps in reaction to the brief UK popularity of 20 – 22in gauges, e.g. these steam outline powered lines, Twining supported this track gauge as well as advocating engines of narrow gauge rather than scale proportions. Subsequently in 1940 he proposed a 15in gauge version of the 0-4-2, smaller all round, but otherwise identical. (14)

Twining had been maintaining his railway contacts too. He later recorded driving *Colossus* from Ravenglass to Boot; an interesting experience because the loco's trailing truck was found to be derailed at the end of the journey! It is not clear when this occurred but Greenly made numerous visits in the early 1920s before becoming heavily involved with the Romney line, so no doubt Twining accompanied him on one or more of them, bringing back pictures of Muncaster Castle and Muncaster Mill to prove it, as well as making a sketch of one of the Eskdale Railway's locos that was subsequently used for publicity. In locomotive design terms the significance of the trip was that he was very forcibly made aware of some of the deficiencies of "scale" models by a loco with whose design he was intimately acquainted; and when the generally run-down mechanical condition of the R&ER's "scale" locos was obvious.

Colossus lasted longest of all the Ravenglass & Eskdale's scale models, arriving in 1916 but still withdrawn in 1927 after only 12 seasons. Twining pointed out that on this railway "when fully laden this locomotive regularly hauled loads equal to 700 tons full size". An obvious analogy is with the prodigious WWII loads on the East Coast mainline, which had equally disastrous consequences for the "weakest" components of the locos involved i.e. the Gresley conjugated valve gear and middle big ends of the V2's and Pacifics. However Twining had himself been responsible for the detail design of *Colossus*, albeit constrained by Bassett-Lowke and Greenly to use Class 30 components as far as possible to keep down costs. For a line in the grounds of a private house this would have been adequate, but the loads, speeds and gradients of the R&ER clearly showed him the inadequacies of such a design philosophy for the operation of a busy service for the general public.

Early in Ravenglass & Eskdale Railway 15in days Greenly had himself begun to appreciate the shortcomings of "scale" locos, making proposals for much larger machines. The railway however settled for the 1/3rd scale *River Esk*, and the RHDR followed the same pattern. Twining clearly felt a return to the principles of Sir Arthur Heywood, suitably updated, provided a better solution as "the great technical objection to the scale model is the very fact that it is a miniature in all respects of a prototype and that, consequently, it is not specially designed for its job. Journals, bearings, rods, pins and bushes are all too small; wearing surfaces are of insufficient area and often boilers have to be worked too hard. The result is that either the life of the locomotive is too short or it spends a considerable portion of its time undergoing repairs or renewals". Heywood on the other hand had pioneered the idea of 15in gauge railways as a practical transport method, using robust and reliable machinery, only to see them overtaken by the internal combustion road vehicle.

Whilst these factors were largely overcome in the 1/3rd full size engines that Greenly had designed for the R&ER and for the RHDR, Twining was critical also of the need to cramp the height of boiler

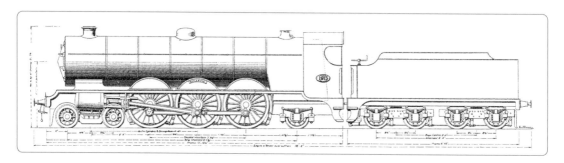

Twining's general arrangement for the Bassett-Lowke Class 60 Pacific which he scaled up from Greenly's Class 30 Atlantic. *Model Engineer*

mountings and the engine generally to a loading gauge which is an imaginary one, and which is exceeded by the coaches forming the train. This is "particularly noticeable in the dome, which, from the point of view of usefulness (i.e. raising the regulator above the water level in the boiler) might just as well be omitted. The chimney, too, would be more efficient if it were increased in height". He argued that it was absurd to use engines whose chimneys are below the level of the passengers' heads and the driver perched on the tender. In both engineering and aesthetic terms it would be better to regard the passengers' heads or the carriage roofs as the loading gauge and build locos to match, thus permitting all the above technical advantages. Nowadays we take this philosophy for granted but just think how outrageous some people must have found it in the 1930s.

Consequently Twining's proposals featured Heywood maximum adhesion ideals as exemplified by his Duffield Bank designs, but modified, with a trailing truck to allow a proper grate and deep firebox, and separate tender to allow adequate fuel and water for longer runs, or at least less frequent replenishment. Details such as running boards, steps and handrails were omitted and splashers were bicycle type – reminiscent of the engines of Edward Bury. A tall chimney provided good draughting, and a tall dome placed the regulator well above the water line, whilst safety valves on top of this meant only one hole was needed in the barrel. The 1940 15in gauge version of the 0-4-2 was smaller all round; but the only significant differences were an articulated tender chassis to cope with sharp curves, and deletion of the cab roof in favour of a Heywood style spectacle plate.

The next step was completely different, not just designing a locomotive but this time actually building one to 10 $^1/_4$in gauge for Trevor Guest and his Dudley Zoo Railway. Trevor Guest was born in 1906, one of the sons of a family building firm, A.H. Guest Ltd of Amblecote near Stourbridge. Originally intent upon a maritime career his plans changed when his father died prematurely so that in 1924 Trevor and his brother had to take over the family business. A great sportsman in his youth, playing both rugby and cricket for Worcestershire, he then moved into motor boat and motor car racing and ultimately competed at Brooklands, Le Mans and Monte Carlo as a works driver for Singer Motors.

In the mid 1930s he and a neighbour, Capt Raymond Saunders, both with an interest in small steam engines, decided to build something larger, and so contacted J.N.Maskelyne to design a freelance 10 $^1/_4$in gauge 4-4-2. G&S Light Engineering was set up to build two such machines, at a workshop at Wollaston, Stourbridge, in a sand quarry belonging to A.H.Guest Ltd. Eventually three buildings were used: the machine shop equipped with machine tools large enough for all work on 15in gauge locos except the boilers, a storage shed for components and finished work, and after the war a concrete

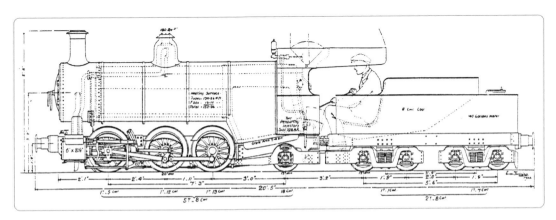

Twining's response to the steam outline 20in gauge engines of the early 1930s, a robust and cheap 18-22in gauge 0-6-2 design. *Locomotive Magazine*

shop in which such things as concrete sleepers were made. About 1976 the quarry was sold and a new workshop built at A.H.Guest's Amblecote works; some Fairbourne Railway items returned here for overhaul, although probably none of the locos by that date.

A conversation with the proprietor of the Crown Hotel in Wychbold provided a site for their first year's running, but Dudley Zoo also opened in 1937 and following an approach by its directors the line moved there in the following year, still operated by G&S. The original 4-4-2 became No 1001 and the second No 1002 (No 1001 is now believed to be in Hampshire, but 1002's whereabouts are unknown). The zoo line's gradients, up to 1 in 50 with severe curvature, were too much for these engines so a pair of 4-6-0 using the same wheel, cylinder and other patterns was schemed out. Guest actually started construction of the 4-6-0s himself but progress was slow due to pressure of other work, so in 1938 Twining Models was asked to build the engines, intended to be *Himley Hall* and *Dudley Hall* according to a local paper. There are several pictures of 4-6-0 No 3 under construction in Twining Models workshop, which is of course to be expected, but there are also pictures of 4-4-2 No 1 under construction too, although the location cannot be identified. The location of the view of it operating however is more obvious! Did Ernest Twining just take the photographs for Trevor Guest, or was he in some way also involved in the 4-4-2's design or construction?

According to the *Northampton Independent* the first 4-6-0 entered service in the summer of 1939, but presumably because of the onset of the war it was the only one completed. It was a good copy of a GWR Saint apart from the outside valve gear, used to ensure operational reliability and for standardisation with the 4-4-2s. Cylinders were enlarged to 3 ^{1}/4in by 5in and Goodhand supplied a 125 psi boiler. This engine still exists, having, like so many Twining designs or products, led a pretty nomadic life. In fact E.S.Tonks, preparing *Light & Miniature Railway Locomotives* (1950) received a letter from Ernest Twining about it. Apparently his wife Edna, visiting Northampton, had picked up a local newspaper item referring to its working on a temporary line at nearby Billing. Twining commented the "poor thing has been trying to find its way home!" He would be pleased to learn its wanderings are now at an end. Rebuilt first for the Hastings Miniature Railway in 1958/9 it then went to Oakhill Manor and eventually was given a new boiler and complete overhaul by Neil Simkins. Now with proper inside valve gear it forms an excellent representation of GWR Saint class No 2943 *Hampton Court*, and operates on the Stapleford Miniature Railway. This is a private railway, but usually has a couple of weekends of public operations every year. (15)

As noted elsewhere Twining left his company at the outbreak of WWII, any railway activities being confined to research and the drawing board. By the end of the war this had borne fruit. In the 15 June 1949 *Locomotive* magazine he produced a scheme for a large 30in gauge 2-6-2T. The interest is not particularly in the design itself, which like the earlier 0-6-2/0-4-2 schemes was perhaps prepared for a loco builder wanting to submit a proposal

Trevor Guest's 10 ^{1}/4in gauge 4-4-2 No1 (later No 1001) under construction. photo – Twining family

The same engine at work on the Dudley Zoo Railway. photo – Twining family

Dudley Zoo Railway 4-6-0 No 3 under construction in Twining Models' workshops in 1938/9. photo - Twining family

to some overseas project. Certainly Twining Models was not going to build or sell models of such large size. Much more significant are some of the features which the design incorporates, perhaps the result of a few years' thinking on railway themes with no chance to do anything about them; several of the ideas turn up again later on the 15in gauge locos.

Firstly couplings are attached to the radial trucks, requiring the truck pivots to be strengthened but reducing side loads on the couplings and on the track; secondly the cylinders have combined automatic and manual relief valves; and there are claimed improvements to both safety valves and the steam brake system. Finally, and most significantly, the engine has Twining's own design of valve-gear.

As noted earlier, Twining's significant interest in valve gear first became apparent in the *Model Engineer* schemes of 1915, where the GWR 4-4-0 model used Joy instead of Stephenson valve gear, and the large 4-6-2 uniquely had Gooch valve gear. His subsequent investigation of Newcastle and Carlisle Railway's *Comet*, when his company was asked to model it, had shown this to have probably been the first locomotive to have had four fixed eccentrics instead of two movable ones as was previously customary; and made clear Twining's deep interest in, and understanding of, steam locomotive valve gears.

His own design was intended particularly for locomotives spending their time shuttling short distances backwards and forwards and has in fact only been used on three 15in gauge engines. His objective in designing this hybrid between Walschaert's and Joy gear was particularly to eliminate the slip of the dieblock in the expansion link, and of the sliding block in the radius rod, an especial problem where much of an engine's work is in back gear. Twining's gear aims to minimise wear by having no sliding parts (except the valve spindle cross head), using ball bearings rolling on hardened faces instead of dieblocks and providing right angle motion for the eccentric rod via a bell crank pivoted off the lower slide bar bracket.

Soon after this however he was involved with miniature railways again when Trevor Guest, still owner/operator of the Dudley Zoo Railway, decided to re-gauge this to 15in. The line re-opened at Whitsun 1947, initially with internal combustion locos, but a steam engine was soon needed. Twining designed an engine based on a Stanier "Black 5"; with 5in by 8in cylinders and 20in driving wheels this was larger than $1/4$ scale but not as big as Greenly's $1/3$rd scale engines. The large cylinders and more robust frames, bearings and motion were an improvement on the earlier designs although

Below: Twining valve gear, as first described in the *Locomotive Magazine* in 1949.

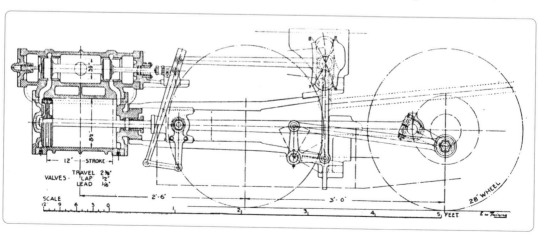

proportions were similar to the Greenly 4-4-2 with their overscale boilers so the 4-6-0 subsequently looked very well alongside Fairbourne Railway's Class 30 *Count Louis*. The locomotive appeared in 1949 (G&S No 9/1949) with the number 5751 which it has carried throughout its life. The significance is unknown, 5751 was not a Black 5 or even a Jubilee (highest No 5742), so whether the number was significant to Guest like the family/friend names he used later, or whether it was some kind of progress number in the Guest workshop remains problematic. The next engine, started to the same design, was 57512 however, suggesting the latter explanation.

The locomotive worked happily enough on the DZR, although its narrow firebox was not really satisfactory, a 15in gauge loco with its firebox between the frames is limited to a grate only some 9in wide at most. It was followed next year by G&S No 10/1950, which had the same front end and coupled wheels but extended into a 4-6-2 with a much bigger boiler and wide firebox. Perhaps Twining's views were starting to prevail, but in any case the 4-6-0's deficiencies provided him with the opportunity to design for Trevor Guest the sort of narrow gauge outline machine he had long advocated.

Whether Twining had by now had second thoughts about the rather basic outlines of the 1934/1940 schemes or whether Trevor Guest requested something more decorative is uncertain, but *Katie*

emerged as a neo-colonial 2-4-2, with the (in this size) purely decorative features of running boards and buffers, which had been omitted in the earlier proposals. In fact a photograph exists of a 7 ^{1}/4in gauge (probably) scheme, which is very like a ^{1}/2 size *Katie*, except for the slide valve cylinders and Walschaert's valve gear of the earlier proposals, so Twining had probably sketched this before designing his own valve gear.

How long *Katie* was in Trevor Guest's workshop is uncertain (*Katie* after Guest's mother, first of the family/friend namings); after all he operated the DZR as well as his own family business and Guest Engineering & Maintenance (previously G&S Light Engineering), so construction would have to be fitted in between other work. Some detail drawings e.g. cylinders, are dated 1951 but these are common with the earlier locos and the date may represent Twining "signing off" an "as built" drawing

Above: Twining valve gear on 15in gauge 2-4-2 *Siân*. photo - author

rather than something specific for the new engine. One of the DZR's i/c locos expired in 1952 however, which would have increased the need for the engine. Whilst *Katie's* works plates are No 14/1954, there is general consensus that she entered service only in 1956, and in any case Trevor Guest did not fit worksplates originally, these being added later, perhaps at Fairbourne, and with possible inaccuracies in both numbers and dates.

The significance of the delivery date however is that although he was fit and active in his later years, and probably saw her under construction, it is unlikely Ernest Twining saw the engine in service, as he died in September 1956. Whether he saw his design operating or not he should have been pleased with it. The narrow gauge "colonial" appearance well matches 15in gauge passenger stock, especially covered, and closely resembles many 2ft to 2ft 6in locos built in Britain for service overseas – Cyprus Railway 4-4-0 for example. All the features Twining had been advocating were incorporated; tall chimney for good draughting, tall dome for well raised regulator, deep firebox with generous grate and ashpan, outside frames and adequate bearing surfaces, front coupling and tender drawbar pivoted on the pony trucks to minimise side loads on couplings, combined manual/automatic cylinder relief valves and Twining's own valve gear. All this was fitted into a neat and elegant little engine, which has since been found very attractive by all who have seen her.

Katie performed more than adequately on the Dudley line but only the next year (assumed 1957) Trevor Guest was approached to sell the engine to a Captain Vivian Hewitt of Anglesey. It is claimed that Guest, not very seriously, named an outrageous price, which was immediately accepted! So *Katie* went into store at the Guest workshops until moved in 1961 to the Captain's Estate. Captain Hewitt is supposed to have wanted her for a proposed Caribbean coconut plantation railway (Bagnalls, who had built the boiler, were even asked if it would steam on coconut husks!). The whole idea conjures

Guest/Twining 2-4-2 *Katie*, in as-built condition on
the Dudley Zoo Railway. photo – G.A.Barlow

up a vision of Lewis Carroll's "Jabberwock with eyes of flame came whiffling through the tulgey wood". Hewitt shortly ordered 4 and 6 wheel bogies for wagons, and then an extended 2-6-2 version of *Katie*. Unfortunately for the Captain, but not for UK 15in gauge enthusiasts, his death prevented the scheme from being carried out and all the items remained in the UK, the loco eventually appearing as steam outline petrol-hydraulic *Tracey-Jo*.

At this point, with the locos owned and ordered by Hewitt on his estate and in Guest's workshop respectively, a further locomotive to the Twining design was ordered, this time by John Wilkins for his Fairbourne Railway in Wales. Originally a horse drawn tramway, this had, like the Ravenglass and Eskdale, been revived as a 15in gauge line by Narrow Gauge Railways Ltd in 1916; i.e. by Bassett-Lowke, Greenly *et al*. Falling on hard times in the 1930s it became moribund during WWII, until purchased and revived by a syndicate led by John Wilkins. By the early 1960s business was good enough for a new steam loco to be considered and the Guest/Twining "scale" locos were meanwhile loaned to the line, the 4-6-0 in 1960/1 and the 4-6-2 from 1961. [Fig. c4]

Guest Engineering & Maintenance were at this time the only people building engines of this size. Discussions between John Wilkins and Trevor Guest agreed to follow the Twining ideals exemplified by *Katie*, suitably modified for Fairbourne conditions. Various delivery dates have been quoted but Ken Leighton gave a graphic eyewitness account of her July 1963 arrival and first run on the FMR in the Bulletin of the Ipswich and District Historical Transport Society. She was named *Siân*, for the daughter of Glanmor Jones, John Wilkin's solicitor.

Compared with *Katie* the locomotive had a steel boiler and firebox, sealed bearings to keep out the blowing sands of the Mawddach Estuary, and wider cab, tender and running boards. This improves the appearance because *Katie* perhaps looks a little too narrow when viewed head on; and gives more cab space and coal capacity. The wider tender tank was deceptive however, containing an inner galvanised tank of the same size as *Katie's*. However economies do seem to have been made in construction, to save either cost or time. The steel firebox may have been one of these, but a smaller example is the tender and engine truck spring hangers, where *Katie* has proper forgings whilst *Siân* just has long bolts. Air brakes were also fitted; supplied from an axle-driven tender compressor, which was the only such application for over 30 years until the Bure Valley Railway took up the idea. Ernest Twining would have been proud of this innovation even if some of the other items did not meet his exacting standards!

These five are all of the 15in gauge engines built directly to Ernest Twining's design, all by Trevor Guest's workshops. If we except the original ordering of the 2-6-2 by Capt. Hewitt, all were built either for the DZR (on which all except *Siân* ran at one time or another) or the FMR, on which all of them operated, 3 simultaneously from 1966 to 1984. However the Dudley Zoo line was sold by Guest in 1968 (but not the locos, which he retained), whilst the Fairbourne Railway was sold in 1984 and re-gauged in 1985. Consequently all of them became homeless and have since led very nomadic lives. Between them they have operated regularly on at least 12 railways and visited two others. The five have also carried 11 different names, although only 6 numbers!

No 5751, the 4-6-0 of 1949, was soon named *Prince Charles* and operated on the DZR until 1960, when it was loaned to the Fairbourne Railway for a year or so. This was the final straw in demonstrating its inadequacies, especially the narrow firebox on a much longer run. It was stored at Trevor Guest's Wollaston workshop for some years, then rebuilt in 1968 with a trailing truck and larger boiler and firebox like the second engine. After Guest sold the Dudley Zoo Railway *Prince Charles* was sold to Sir William McAlpine in 1969. After 5 or 6 years' storage, partly on the RH&DR, the loco moved to Blenheim Palace in early 1975, appropriately renamed *Sir Winston Churchill* but still No 5751. [Fig. c5]

In 1982 it was displaced by a steam outline diesel, then sold to Pat Kelly who operated it on the 15in Cragbank line at Steamtown, Carnforth. By 1984 it had been named *Prince William*. This line ceased regular operations in 1996 and the engine went into storage at the East Lancs Railway, Bury, with occasional outings on mixed 15in/std gauge. In the following year it was loaned to Windmill Farm Railway, Burscough, Lancs, where it operated regularly for several years. In the winter of 2002/3 the locomotive was sold to Helen and Jim Shackle and will operate on their line at the Evesham Country Park in Worcestershire.

The 1950 4-6-2 was to have been *Princess Anne* but the name was never carried, instead it was numbered 57512. After the 4-6-0's unsatisfactory performance at Fairbourne the larger locomotive was loaned instead in around 1961, the FMR soon naming it *Ernest W Twining*. A nice compliment, but he had already been dead five years and the loco surely was not really a type which he would have wished as a memorial, being neither a detailed and accurate model nor a workmanlike but elegant "design for the job". In 1964 the Fairbourne Railway bought the engine and shortly gave it a major overhaul with new boiler, firebox, cab and larger tender, the loco going to Trevor Guest's workshop at the end of the '64 season (29 September) and returning to the railway on 25 September 1966.

The engine was then regularly used until the 1984 sale of the railway when *EWT* remained with the original owners and was stored at Milner Engineering, Chester. Two years later it was briefly exhibited at the Birmingham Railway Museum, Tyseley, before being sold to the "Rainbow Village" at Shuzenji, Japan. Here it is back-up to two Ravenglass built copies of R&ER's *Northern Rock* and two diesels, seeing little service. It has actually been reported that, apart from initial trials on first arriving in Japan, the loco has never been steamed. [Fig. c6]

Katie, the first Twining narrow gauge loco, operated successfully at Dudley for a year or so before its sale to Capt. Hewitt and eventual storage at his estate at Bryn Aber, Cemaes Bay, Anglesey. After failure of the Caribbean scheme and then the Captain's death, John Wilkins was able to buy *Katie* for the princely sum of £1,760. Arriving at Fairbourne for the 1966 season, very opportunely with EWT halfway through rebuilding at Wollaston, *Katie* then settled down with sister *Siân* for many years steady operation before the sale to John Ellerton. She was briefly renamed *Shôn*, but was soon sold to Wigan Metropolitan Borough (1985) for a proposed line in their country park at Haigh Hall; this opened 5 July 1986 (official opening 23 August) and *Katie* arrived from overhaul soon afterwards.

Here she became, in Great Western style, *Haigh Hall*, No 7204; except that GWR Halls were X9XX series, and the 72XX's were 2-8-2T. Like Trevor Guest's 5751 the number was no doubt significant to someone. Overhauled again in the winter of 1989/90 (reputedly at Bala Lake Railway workshop) she was eventually displaced by an Alan Keef steam outline 0-6-2T (No 41/92) in 1994. The now unserviceable *Katie* was loaned to the Cleethorpes Coast Light Railway for their September 1994 Gala. After a winter overhaul she operated there for three seasons but from 1997 languished in need of a new boiler. In early 2001 she was advertised and sold to Austin Moss at Windmill Farm, Burscough, Lancs, where a rebuild to working order is in hand. [Fig. c7]

Of all the locomotives none has had a more complex history than *Tracey-Jo*, the 2-6-2 which Hewitt ordered. This was cancelled, perhaps even before his death, and completed (No 20/64) as a steam outline petrol hydraulic with a 3.5l Daimler engine instead of a boiler. The chassis was however complete with cylinders and Twining valve gear, no doubt an indication of the stage at which the work was cancelled, and from buffer beam to driving wheels was identical to *Katie*. After trials on the DZR it went to Fairbourne (26 September 1964) and was named *Tracey-Jo* for Trevor Guest's grand-daughter (*Rachel*, *Clara*, & *Sylvia* were also i/c engines from the Guest workshop). Although not wholly successful *Tracey-Jo* stayed on the FMR for two years as spare for the absent *Ernest W Twining* before returning to Guest's workshop in late 1966 after the 4-6-2 came back. Sold along with 5751 to Sir William McAlpine in 1969, she was stored until 1974, also partly on the Romney Hythe & Dymchurch Railway, then rebuilt with mechanical transmission, going to join 5751 at Blenheim Palace the following year.

In 1981 she was out of use but by 1984 had joined 5751 at Steamtown, Carnforth. Next year she briefly went to Lightwater Valley, but was sold in 1986 to Brian Taylor for construction of the Kirklees Light Railway on an ex BR-branch (originally L&Y), near Huddersfield. Used for works trains and

Steam outline 2-6-2T *Tracey-Jo*, newly out-shopped by
Trevor Guest's works. collection - J.Challingsworth

early operations, she received a Peugeot diesel engine and further transmission rebuild but was still
not very satisfactory. Finally in 1991 the infant Bure Valley Railway was desperate to establish its own
loco fleet and *Tracey-Jo* went to Norfolk, arriving 9/4/91. The following winter she was rebuilt by
Winson Engineering as a proper steam 2-6-4T, retaining all the Twining chassis features, valve gear,
tall dome and chimney, and returned as *Wroxham Broad*, BVR No 1. She then became a mainstay of
the railway's fleet until arrival of the third of the line's big ZB models (2-6-2T No 8), when No 1 was
sold to a consortium of BVR members. She remains at Aylsham, and in regular use, but not as intensively
as previously. [Fig. c8]

Siân (G&S 18/63) arrived at Fairbourne in July 1963 and immediately settled down to more than
20 years' steady operation (apart from a 7/4/82 level crossing incident!) before the line was bought by
John Ellerton. She was then Americanised with numerous but fortunately cosmetic changes, especially
to cab and tender, and became *Sydney*, No 362 (respectively the name of John Ellerton's father and
the railway's telephone number). After re-gauging of the FMR to 12 $1/4$in in late '85 *Siân/Sydney*
moved (2 December 1985) to Littlecote House (Wiltshire) for a newly built line. Policy here changed
after a few years and she was offered for sale on 30 September 1990. Acquired by the Bure Valley
Railway she arrived at Aylsham as their No 4 on 9 April 1991. Some American excrescence's were
immediately removed, followed by more tidying during the following winter, along with a boiler
overhaul and new inner firebox to permit operation at 180 instead of 120 psi. Ernest Twining would
probably not have approved of this, regarding it as modifying the loco for heavier work than it was
designed for!

She and *Wroxham Broad* were then the only reliable steam locos on the line for the 1992 and '93
seasons before the BVR decided to obtain new motive power. In early 1994 the first of their large
locos arrived from Winson Engineering and *Siân* was sold to a group of Ravenglass and Eskdale

Railway Preservation Society members (the Siân Project Group) who have restored her original appearance with new cab, tender body and dome cover, as well as carrying out further major boiler work. *Siân* was hired to the Cleethorpes Coast Light Railway for 1995/6/7, ran on the Kirklees Light Railway in 1998 and is currently based on the Windmill Farm Railway; the first time she and 5751 have lived together. Over the years she has also visited the RHDR four times and the R&ER on numerous occasions. [Fig. c9 & Fig. c10]

Ernest Twining's experience with 15in gauge railways, together with his own design and construction work, led him to believe that "scale" models of full-size locomotives were unsuitable for public passenger-hauling, because many aspects of their detail design could not be made robust enough for continuous heavy use without ruining their "scale" appearance; which in any case was not necessarily appropriate for over-scale carriages and passengers.

Economic operation of such railways requires their locomotives to be robust and reliable, easy to maintain and convenient to operate. To minimise capital cost they should also be as simple in design as possible, without redundant features provided just for appearance. His artistic sensibilities however ensured that such a machine in the form of *Katie* was attractive to enthusiasts and general public alike on its own merits.

It would be an exaggeration to claim his ideas and designs were alone responsible for the major post-war change which occurred in steam loco design policy for public passenger-hauling 15in gauge railways. He must however be regarded as a pioneer, by over 30 years, in advocating "designs for the job" as several railways and builders consciously or unconsciously followed his lead. One might argue an analogy with the Churchward revolution in early 20th–century British steam locomotive design, where application of most of his design principles was effectively universal - but only after a sufficient proving period.

Once operation on the Dudley Zoo and Fairbourne Railways had confirmed their practical advantages, and the narrow gauge twins had also shown themselves to be as attractive to the passengers as scale models, so overcoming any aesthetic objections, then the future policy for 15in gauge passenger hauling steam was clear. Individuals would still build (or have built for them) scale models of favourite designs for their own private railways but public lines would follow Twining ideas because of their economic and operational advantages.

Since *Katie's* appearance in the 1950s, at least 20 steam engines have been built for 15in gauge public railways in the UK, but only one of them to pseudo-scale proportions, *River Mite* of the Ravenglass & Eskdale. This was a special case however, because construction began from the remains of *River Esk's* experimental steam tender, which was an 0-8-0 chassis of similar proportions to *Esk* herself. This factor, together with the design period coinciding with *Katie* being stored for Captain Hewitt and *Siân* having only just entered service perhaps explains why no alternative to a *River Esk* clone seems to have even been considered.

In the late 1960s, after *Katie* and *Siân*, David Curwen (who had started building locos of narrow gauge proportions but in smaller gauges) co-operated with Severn Lamb to build 15in gauge locos to Twining outline for Longleat and Lappa Valley. Subsequently the R&ER, having in 1973 fitted a new boiler to 0-8-2 *River Irt* (with the chassis of Heywood's *Muriel*), gave her a new cab, boiler mountings and tender of narrow gauge proportions, improving her appearance and steaming abilities as well as increasing coal and water capacity.

Three years later the R&ER's *Northern Rock* appeared, looking very much like *Siân's* big sister. The survivors of the *Northern Rock* design and construction team deny any Twining influence, but the original scheme was prepared by the R&ER's engineer Tom Jones, who died several years ago. Tom was a resident of Eskdale and employee of the railway from 1925 (was he there when Twining visited?) but maintained strong links with his native North Wales and with developments in the narrow gauge field. He certainly saw *Siân* and *Katie* at work at Fairbourne, would have been aware of their performance, and of their Twining features which would fit so well with the R&E's desire for a return to Heywood principles. After all what were Twining designs if not modernised Heywood engines?

It seems clear from the mechanical evidence in the chassis of BVR No 1 that Trevor Guest interpreted Capt. Hewitt's 2-6-2 request as a simple stretching out of the engine; certainly cylinders and chassis components were unchanged. However if the loco was intended for harder work than *Katie* then it seems unlikely that experience with *Colossus* as a "stretched" Class 30 would have allowed Twining to fall into this trap had he still been alive. Certainly in his 1934 proposals the 0-6-2 is larger all round than the 0-4-2, with 50% greater cylinder volume and grate-area; heating surface and tender capacity to match. Had *Katie* been similarly enlarged the resulting 2-6-2 would have been very similar to *Northern Rock*, with identical 20in driving wheels, 6in by 9in cylinders, and a boiler at least as large.

Clearly Twining's ideas proved much more acceptable in the late 20th–century than 30 - 40 years earlier. The merits of being able to do the same work with fewer moving parts but larger bearing surfaces and better boiler/firebox proportions not surprisingly appealed to designers whether they were conscious of the Twining influence or not. Meanwhile the operating advantages of larger fuel/water capacities, easier lubrication/maintenance access and more commodious cabs were not lost on the drivers.

In realising that "scale" models were inadequate for routine heavy work, and in then designing engines which were suitable, Twining led the 15in gauge world back to the tenets of Sir Arthur Heywood and the robust and reliable machines that he had built. Unfortunately Twining's ideas took many years to come to fruition and he then died before he could further effect their implementation – what might he have made of the Hewitt 2-6-2?

The widespread adoption of such locomotives on 15in gauge might have happened anyway – but no one else undertook to break the Greenly/RHDR mould; the RHDR even toyed with further "scale" proposals in the post-war period. Once *Katie* and *Siân* had proven themselves however, both for their technical and operational advantages, and in terms of public acceptability of their narrow gauge outlines, then further such designs could be proposed without fear of their rejection.

1. *Ahrons, EL: Locomotive and train working in the latter part of the nineteenth century – W. Heffer & Sons, 1953*
2. *Twining, EW and Rosling Bennett, A: Historic Locomotives and Moving Accidents by Steam and Rail – Cassell 1906*
3. *Rosling Bennett, A: Crampton locomotives on the Continent – The Railway Magazine April 1907, p303*
4. *Milner, J: Rails through the Sands – Rail Romances*
5. *Locomotive Railway Carriage and Wagon Review, May 14th 1921 p126 et seq*
6. *Practical Mechanics, May 1934 to November 1934, 7 parts*
7. *Practical Mechanics, February 1938 to July 1938, 6 parts*
8. *Model Engineer, 12/3/53 to 25/3/54, 11 parts*
9. *Sharman, W: The Crampton Locomotive – published by the author, 1983*
10. *Practical Mechanics, from March 1936*
11. *"Many-Ways" catalogue, second edition July 1938*
12. *Model Engineer, Who's who in Model Engineering No 44 23/10/37 p610*
13. *Model Engineer, July 1st, 8th and 15th, 1915*
14. *The Narrow Gauge No 102, Autumn 2003, p37*
15. *Northampton Independent 25/8/39*

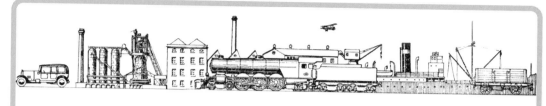

Art & Design

Bristol Academy for the Promotion of the Fine Arts

Ernest Twining painted for most of his life, largely for his own pleasure but often as part of his many projects. The earliest known pictures are dated 1891, probably the year he started his engineering apprenticeship, whilst the last were painted only a year before his death. These were done especially for his two granddaughters, both then recently married. One of these paintings survives but the other succumbed to the South African climate. As well as painting for pleasure he undertook a lengthy course of study, and subsequently made use of this training and experience in many ways throughout his career.

Twining attributed his artistic skills and tastes to his maternal grandfather, who for most of his life was a glass painter with Bells of Bristol, and to whom he dedicated his book on stained glass. William Jones was not the only artistic family member however, and young Ernest must have come under both his influence and that of his son, i.e. Ernest's uncle, William Gilbert Jones. William Gilbert was only 12 years older than Ernest and may well have been more like an older brother than an uncle. Twining's earliest knowledge and experience of stained glass work must also have come from these two, perhaps whilst he was in his later school years.

The earliest paintings that he kept, or thought worth keeping, are careful studies of flowers and butterflies, dating from 1891. Two years later there is a highly detailed botanical study of a passion flower; it is clear he had already spent some time in an engineering drawing office in the interval, because the flower is shown in a precise and detailed form, with each of its components separated out. [Fig. c11, Fig. c12]

By this time (1893) Ernest Twining was also attending the Bristol Academy for the Promotion of the Fine Arts – now the Royal West of England Academy. Academy archives do not have detailed lists of students for the late 19th–century but they do have complete lists of student's work in their annual exhibitions, which includes Ernest Twining in 1893, 1895 and 1899. His first piece in 1893 was entitled 'Homeward'; in 1895 two works were both based on themes from Shakespeare's *Macbeth*; and in 1899 he entered 'The long ripple washing in the reeds' (Tennyson) and 'Moonlight and Mere', the latter priced at £20, not a bad price for a student's work in 1899. (1)

How exactly art studies fitted in with his apprenticeship and then work for the National Telephone Company (as it had now become) is not clear – presumably taking the form of evening classes, although contemporary apprentices have written of having to do engineering studies in their own time. The gap between 1895 and 1899 was probably due to his being otherwise engaged; Edward Davies died in early 1897 and if Twining was already a friend of the family then Mary no doubt welcomed his support. They were eventually married some 18 months later, no doubt further interrupting his studies.

GLASGOW AND LONDON

Ernest Twining spent the years 1901 to 1904 in Glasgow, and whilst the Corporation no doubt kept him occupied Monday to Friday and on Saturday mornings, he would still have found the time to investigate artistic life in the city and especially any new developments. It is always possible of course that his choice of work in Glasgow was influenced by this factor, and not just a desire to further his career in the telephone industry.

By the time he arrived in Glasgow, 'The Four' had already outgrown the Glasgow School and their group who called themselves the Immortal Artists. 'The Four' consisted of Charles Rennie Mackintosh, his friend of several years Herbert MacNair, and their wives Margaret and Frances MacDonald. Twining would already have been aware of Rennie Mackintosh's work – some had recently been exhibited in London – and would have found examples in Glasgow of his architecture, interiors, furniture and watercolours. His architectural work could already be seen in the first half of the Glasgow School of Art, interior designs in the Willow and the Ingram Street Tea Rooms, whilst Hill House at Helensburgh was completed not long before Twining left Glasgow. Did the things he saw have any influence on his own work? Or were they a factor in his brief attempt to earn a living as an artist? (2)

An equal, if not more, significant event in Twining's Glasgow period was meeting Alfred Rosling Bennett, like Twining an electrical engineer in the telephone industry, but better known in later years for his interest in railways. He completed his contract with the Glasgow Corporation Telephone Company in 1904, and moved to London, initially to prepare a proposal for a "Scheme for Improvements" for London County Council. Twining also moved south in this year, intent upon setting up his own studio, which was in Lavender Hill. Precisely why he left the telephone industry at this point there is no way of knowing; perhaps he could see no interesting future in it for him, perhaps he was unhappy at being so far from his family, or perhaps what he had seen of Glasgow's artistic world made him feel there was scope for him, at least for a trial period, in the corresponding field in London. Rosling Bennett presumably returned to London at this time specifically to work on the new scheme, and may well have been able to promise Twining enough work on this to get him established on his own.

The proposal was basically for a new Thames crossing, Temple Bridge, parallel to Waterloo Bridge, which would simultaneously provide an extra pedestrian and vehicle link across the river, connect the tramway systems north and south of the Thames, and provide a new City Hall, which was to be built on top of the bridge.

Twining's most obvious contribution was five of the seven watercolours used to illustrate the proposal document, although it seems clear from his papers that he also assisted with both calculations and architectural drawings. He also painted a further watercolour of the scheme for the Royal Academy 1906 exhibition; Catalogue No 1541 *Proposed new City Hall and Bridge over the River Thames* by EW Twining. (3)

Unfortunately London County Council adopted alternative solutions to resolve some of their traffic and accommodation issues and Rosling Bennett's scheme, and with it possible further work for Twining, was short-lived. His career might well have been affected more than that of most others involved by this, eventually following a completely different path from that which he might at that stage have anticipated. His friend did find him other work however, specifically the illustrations for his book *Historic Locomotives and Moving Accidents by Steam and Rail*, published in 1906. The ten watercolours for this book must have involved Twining in considerable research into both livery and technical details of the locomotives involved, as discussed earlier. The reproduction of the colour plates is excellent, as good if not better than any other colour plates which would appear in a railway book for the next 50 years, but still does little justice to the quality of the originals, four of which can still be examined at the National Railway Museum in York.

Above: View of proposed Temple Bridge and County Hall from Surrey side from Rosling Bennett's '*Proposal for London Improvements*', 1904. Twining family

Below: View of proposed County Hall from the Strand, from the same document. Twining family

By 1907 the Twining family had moved to Hanwell, Ernest setting up Alnwick (or Aldwick?) Studio. It is not known if he received any further commissions, either for individual works or for groups of paintings such as he had done for Rosling Bennett. What he had started by now however, were articles for *Model Engineer* with his own engineering drawings, sketches and watercolours; and articles for hobby magazines such as *Woodworker* and *Art Metal Worker*. He also prepared designs at this time for several household items and pieces of furniture, and for several interior design schemes. Some of these ideas remain in his papers but there is no indication of his intentions for them, although perhaps they were published in now forgotten journals or untraced issues of the *Woodworker and Art Metal Worker*.

He was clearly experimenting with a range of styles, some perhaps that he was asked to provide. "Art Nouveau" ideas appear in some schemes, notably the interiors, the polished steel coal scuttle and the pseudo-Mackintosh fire screen. Some of the proposed furniture however is quite ornately carved from dark wood, and with a very traditional appearance. Similar pieces remain with his family, although perhaps from a later period. One interesting idea is the telephone box, combining, as he so often did, experience from different fields in which he had worked. Whether this was a proposal for a public telephone is unknown, nor when it was designed, but it actually looks a lot more modern than our traditional red box. [Figs. c13, c14 & c15]

He continued to design utilitarian furniture and general wooden items for *Hobbies* and *Practical Mechanics* for many years, usually as "EWT" or "Handyman", but none of the items were of any artistic significance. One interesting thought however is that Charles Rennie Mackintosh undertook three commissions for W.J. Bassett-Lowke after Twining had started work at Northampton. In 1916 he designed the remodelling of No 78 Derngate, and its further redecoration in 1920; this has just been restored by the Derngate Trust with the help of the Town Council and the Heritage Lottery Fund. Rennie Mackintosh also provided most of the interior for a new house in 1925, *New Ways* on Wellingborough Road. There is no indication of any involvement of Ernest Twining in these but there is equally no doubt he would have jumped at the chance to supply a stained glass panel, painting or piece of furniture if given the opportunity.

OTHER APPLICATIONS

Twining now started to make much more use of his drawing and painting skills to illustrate his own articles (and later books) as well as various schemes and proposals. There are numerous examples, covering all the many areas in which he eventually worked. The use of his own sketches and watercolours for his *Model Engineer* articles on scenic features has already been mentioned and some are shown in the railway chapter. Other examples are the Chanute glider, drawings of his proposed Northampton Castle model, his illustrations for the *Pageant of English Naval History* and several paintings of miniature locomotive proposals; the 15in gauge 0-4-2 (1940), 7 $\frac{1}{4}$in gauge 2-4-2 *The Queen* (during WWII), and the 15in gauge 2-4-2 which eventually appeared as *Katie*.

Another important area was the preparation of advertising and publicity material, for his own companies (Twining Aeroplane Company and Twining Models), for Bassett-Lowke Ltd and eventually for a number of other companies in and around Northampton. His aeroplane company produced several catalogues during its brief life, using his drawings and photographs, whilst he was also helping Bassett-Lowke from an early stage; long before his covers appeared their model railway catalogues contain photographs of Twining's gauge 1 garden railway and no doubt other material from his studio. Most attractive in this line however are the covers for the Twining Models catalogues/brochures, especially the architectural and engineering model editions; and the range of Bassett-Lowke catalogue covers, especially from the 1920s but extending irregularly at least until 1951.

Interesting examples of his other advertising work are the Ironside window frame design; particularly

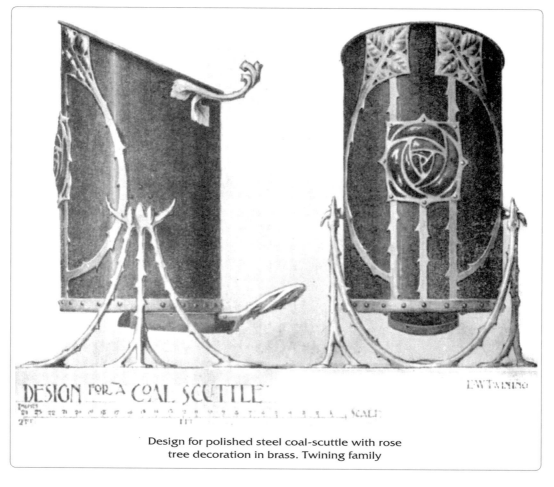

DESIGN FOR A COAL SCUTTLE

Design for polished steel coal-scuttle with rose
tree decoration in brass. Twining family

because his original oil painting of a Roundhead soldier on which this is based survives with his family; and the idea for an LMS centenary poster for 1930. The special interest with this is the later model which Twining Models made for the Euston Centenary. The two show that locomotive design had moved on considerably in the eight years from 1830 to 1838, but not the carriages or the dress of passengers. [Figs. c16, c17, c18 & c19]

PUBLICATIONS

This brief consideration of Twining's publicity work leads to his book on the subject, prepared with Dorothy Holditch and published in 1931. He had effectively been operating as a commercial artist in this area, covering most aspects of the design, illustration and production of publicity material. He denies this however in the book's preface, arguing that the term "commercial art" should really encompass all aspects of the application of art in commerce, from building design to office decoration. Perhaps he would have accepted the title "graphic artist" but it would be several more years before this came into regular use, at least in the UK.

Graphic design differs from art in that it is intended specifically to convey the message of the client, not that of the artist, and it has to be planned from the start for mechanical reproduction, even if the means of that have changed considerably over the years. The authors of *Art in Advertising* appreciated these distinctions and addressed their words to any existing trained artist "who proposed taking up this particular branch of art . . his thoughts must become . . more specialized" and "he must become acquainted with the requirements of advertising designs suitable for particular subjects and the mechanical processes of reproduction of his publicity material". Dedicated to "those who know a little of art in advertising . . and those who know everything but would hear the views of others." *The Northampton and County Independent* of 8 July 1932 claimed it was a volume which should be on the shelf of every advertising man . . "the book's purpose is made clear in the dedication." (4)

It has been said that Britain's lasting contribution to the appearance of the printed word was in the design of letterforms – the Arts and Crafts movement insisted on robust letterforms and Twining & Holditch devote a substantial chapter to the subject: "in the midst of so much printed matter it behoves an advertiser to strike a different note . . in the style and quality of the lettering. It is certain that it is a very important and most essential branch of art in advertising".

The Northampton and County Independent had previously (20 February 1932) carried a brief piece on Twining's co-author. Dorothy Holditch was then a young artist with locally based Bonaventure Press, an enthusiastic amateur artist and writer of children's books. She contributed many of the illustrations to *Art in Advertising* but it was not actually their first collaboration. Two years earlier they had produced *Heraldry and a glossary of heraldic terms*, Section VIII of a comprehensive six volume tome on painting and decorating, edited by Charles H Eaton. (5)

In this article they examined the origins and purposes of heraldic devices and their fundamental features and decorations. A considerable section is then devoted to layout and design, and finally it is shown how such devices should be painted, and how to achieve the correct traditional colours. Miss Holditch produced the vast majority of the drawings but the layout and style of the text is typical Twining; first background to the subject, then all relevant details and finally careful description of the practical aspects of producing the item involved.

One significant part of most, if not all, heraldic achievements is the "helm" on top of the shield, and Twining considers these in some detail. In fact from the amount of material on this and related subjects that he had filed away it is clear that he was considering a companion publication on arms and armour. He actually got as far as designing a title page, which is unfortunately in far too poor a condition to reproduce. He accumulated numerous sketches, tracings and drawings covering weapons and armour from early medieval times up to the restoration period, as well as buying a suit of armour

Above: Advertisement for *Ironside* window frames, based on Twining's painting of a Civil War soldier. from *Art in Advertising*

and several appropriate weapons. He also painted several different figures in period costumes and armour, typically recycling one of his Civil War paintings as the basis for Ironside advert. [Figs. c20 & c21]

LARGELY FOR HIS OWN PLEASURE

As well as his paintings or drawings for commercial purposes i.e. intended for publicity, illustration of an article or in support of a scheme or proposal, Ernest Twining painted throughout his life largely for his own pleasure, as well as taking a serious interest in the work of others such as Dorothy Holditch.

During his years at Northampton for example he seems to have been a member of the Northampton Town and County Art Society for around 20 years, exhibiting at least 16 works over the period from 1919 to 1937, as well as serving on the club's executive for a period in the 1920s and again around 1932. Most of these works seem to have been watercolours but *Windjammer in heavy weather* (1919) was an embroidery and *Come unto Me* was an oil painting. *The Northampton Daily Chronicle* of 1 December 1930 wrote of the latter that it was "a work of genius and extraordinary skill" which "makes the picture not unworthy of comparison with Holman Hunt's *The Light of the World*". *The Northampton Daily Echo* of the same date was equally impressed: "the picture that for emphasis we have reserved for mention last . . represents Our Lord after the Resurrection and . . Mr Twining could not have treated his subject with more care and reverence".

He maintained his interest after returning to Bristol and retained several catalogues from exhibitions by both the Clifton Art Club and the Bristol Savages. Only the Clifton exhibition of 1948 however seems to have had any of his work – *Frenchay Mill*. Twining's grand-daughter still has a painting with this title, but it was a favourite location, of which he took many photographs over the years, so the two works may not be one and the same.

Several other paintings have been kept by his family, although some of them were never completed, or if apparently complete he did not consider worth framing. It is worth reviewing his complete output and the range of subjects he tackled over the years. There are several historical (usually armoured) figures, and rural scenes with figures; but no portraits. His best known locomotive paintings are those he did for Rosling Bennett, but there are certainly others, all Great Western except some specifically commissioned like a pair of Highland Railway locos done in late 1952. Several marine scenes and seascapes exist; but all are sailing ships, never steam or motor vessels. The only aircraft views are those still at Sywell airfield, although it seems unlikely in view of his lifelong interest in aviation that these are the only ones. From the 1930s onwards he painted many watercolour landscapes, some extremely attractive, and also started to tackle religious subjects too. [Figs. c22 to c25]

TWINING'S METHODS

Ernest Twining collected and filed material from all kinds of sources – postcards, publicity material, his own photographs (especially of trees), commercial photographs and engineering drawings of technical subjects. All were regarded as potentially relevant to provide essential details at some future date, good examples of this are postcards received from his mother asking about Gilbert's childhood illnesses, which would hardly have merited keeping except that their photographs were worth adding to his reference files.

He also made numerous sketches of all sorts of subjects, some of them significant works in their own right, others just as a starting point. For example, he produced and filed a series of sketches of windmills, some identified, some not, some in ink, some just pencil. Sketches were useful as illustrations too in many of his articles or other writing, some have already been mentioned, of which those in a *Pageant on English Naval History* are perhaps most important.

Apart from these most of his finished works are watercolours up to the 1930s but with a number of oils thereafter. There are however experiments; a large charcoal drawing of a Civil War figure, the embroidery he entered in the Northampton Club's 1919 exhibition, and the oil on metal foil in the Northampton Museum which is discussed in the stained glass chapter.

As a chemical engineer, with painting skills limited to maintenance of doors and windows, and who has difficulty composing a photograph, it is not possible for me to comment on Ernest Twining's paintings except for those which seem particularly attractive, such as the landscapes, or where the amount of research and detail involved can be admired, such as those done for Rosling Bennett and for Sywell.

Fortunately others have done so. The newspaper reviews of his picture *Come unto Me* have been noted already but other religious works were well received; that for a new side altar at Hartwell Church near Northampton was specially painted, unveiled by Mary Twining and dedicated on 25 June 1938 to local approval, whilst a letter to Ernest Twining in 1951 expressed the gratitude of a Convent near Westbury for the gift of one of his paintings: "Reverend Mother and the Sisters are simply delighted . . it is quite the nicest painting of Our Lord they have ever seen". Perhaps not the epitome of artistic criticism, but none the less two satisfied groups of observers.

Another satisfied customer in the 1950s was a gentleman who commissioned paintings of two Highland Railway locomotives – a *Loch* and a *Skye Bogie*. He expressed himself well pleased with the results, writing of the *Loch* . . "I like it very much indeed"; and of the other . . "it is lifelike and has got the real feel of what I believe a *Skye Bogie* to be".

Perhaps the last word on the subject should be left to C. Hamilton Ellis, well known writer and painter of railways and especially those of Victorian and Edwardian Britain. In his later years Ernest Twining experienced problems with his eyes and Hamilton Ellis, friend of several years (in spite of Twining's criticism of his painting of *Liverpool*) wrote to him

Top: One of Twining's numerous drawings of windmills, unfortunately not identified.
Twining family
Right: Painting done especially for Hartwell Church, donated by Ernest Twining and unveiled by Mary Twining on 25 June 1938. Twining family

on 1 February 1956. "It is no consolation that trouble with the eyes not infrequently comes to great artists. For, sir, you are a great artist; your beautiful drawings will be priceless in years when we have all paid our accounts to the Supreme Artist, and I fear that is more than can be said of my own hurried and inaccurate chronicles of mechanical antiquities. I am glad . . several of the lovely watercolours you did for Rosling Bennett are in permanently safe keeping, including that one – a great favourite of mine – which shows a Brighton Jenny Lind in the snow". [Fig. c26]

1. *Annual Exhibition Catalogues, Bristol Academy for the Promotion of the Fine Arts, 1893, 1895,1899.*
2. *Baxter, C and McKeen, J: Charles Rennie Mackintosh – Lomond Books, Edinburgh, 2000.*
3. *Bennett, A R: Proposals for London Improvements – 1904*
4. *Twining, EW and Holditch, DEM: Art in Advertising – Pitman, 1931*
5. *Twining , EW and Holditch DEM: Heraldry and a glossary of heraldic terms p457-459 of: Eaton, CH. Editor: Painting and Decorating – Pitman, 1929*

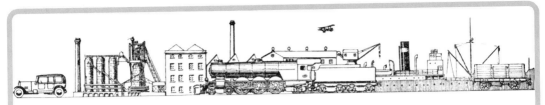

AERONAUTICAL INTERESTS

E rnest Twining traced his lifelong interest in flight and aviation to Jules Verne's tale *The Clipper of the Clouds*. Published in *Boy's Own Paper* in 1887, he later recalled anxiously awaiting each instalment and ". . young as I then was I never lost that thrill, nor the firm belief which it inspired in the possibility of mechanical flight". Verne's craft *The Albatross* was indeed a clipper, with a boat shaped hull supported by 37 pairs of contra-rotating rotors. This feature also encouraged in Twining an interest and enthusiasm for "helicoptere", as they were then described. He was still advocating their wider development and application in his last published articles on aviation more than 60 years later. (1)

Jules Verne also summarised the history of man's attempts to fly down to the 1880s and described some machines which had been tried, leading young Ernest to design a flying machine of his own. The further inspiration for this was the traditional kite, so it appeared with a pear-shaped main plane some 3ft long. This was made of paper (subsequently glazed linen) stretched over a cane frame and supporting a flat board intended eventually to have a steam engine and propeller. By early 1890 experiments showed it could be made to glide successfully once its centre of gravity had been adjusted with lead weights, ". . experiments conducted with much amusing secrecy in a disused stone quarry . . some miles from Bristol". However it clearly had insufficient lift for the proposed engine.

At this point the *Engineering Mechanic* carried a series of articles including the designs of the Australian Lawrence Hargreaves. Disheartened to find others so much further advanced than

Top inset: Twining's representation of Jules Verne's *The Albatross. Practical Mechanics*
Below: Ernest Twining's boyhood glider of 1890. *Model Engineer*

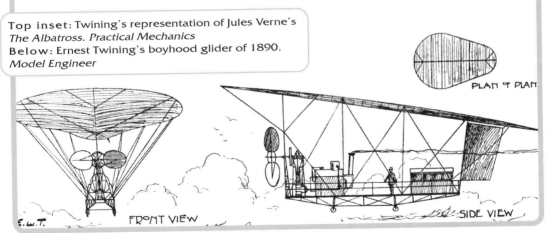

PLAN OF PLAN

FRONT VIEW

SIDE VIEW

E.W.T.

himself, Twining ceased his aviation experiments for a number of years, although not his reading and thinking on the subject.

After the first successful flights in Europe by powered man-carrying planes, in 1906 and 1907, Ernest Twining returned in earnest to the subject, carrying out considerable work on the design both of model aircraft and of screw propellers. This was subsequently detailed in a long series of articles in the *Model Engineer*, from 27 May to 4 November 1909, with a final part on propellers on 10 November 1910. By the time these articles appeared the Twining Aeroplane Company had been established and a booklet *Model Aeroplanes, how to build and fly them* had been written for Percival Marshall.

Successful models and further ambitions

When Twining resumed a practical interest in flying machines, early in 1908, it had already become apparent that, unlike his teenage glider, a high aero-dynamic efficiency required long narrow planes ("wings") of high aspect ratio. Little else however was generally agreed, with both model and full-sized aircraft being designed of many weird and wonderful configurations.

Using the materials then available – bass (American white wood), cartridge paper and Jap silk as a covering – he constructed a series of model gliders, both monoplane and biplane. Some were of what we would now regard as a conventional layout, but others had a leading elevator. These were subsequently described as tail-first or "canard", but with his usual desire for strict accuracy he objected to these titles as being incorrect.

At that stage of aircraft evolution he found that the leading elevator designs invariably gave the best glide angles, as well as having greater longitudinal stability. This was because, for a given length of longeron, this layout allowed elevator and main plane to be farther apart. (2)

By the autumn of 1908 he was satisfied that he had developed the best design then achievable and so modified this glider into a powered machine by the addition of a propeller driven by a skein of twisted rubber. This craft consisted of a wooden strut, with a wooden lower main plane above which were vertical divisions and an upper plane of cartridge paper. The forward elevator was also of wood, with an upper plane arched over (for strength) and supporting a vertical vane for directional stability.

It weighed only 2 $\frac{1}{2}$ ounces and was some 16in long by 13in span. It ". . flew very well, the distances covered varying between 46 and 172ft".

The next successful rubber-powered model was essentially a simplified version of the same aircraft, with a single plane replacing the biplane elevator and no vertical vane. This was regarded as "Number 2" in his own experimental series, but confusingly became No 1 in *Model Aeroplanes, how to build and fly them*.

It was followed by a radically different design, constructed entirely of wood, and as he says:

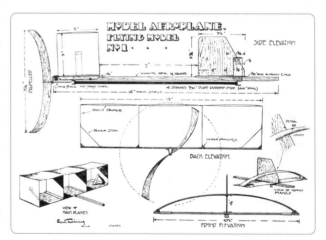

This page: Twining experimental model glider No 1. *Model Engineer*
Opposite top: Experimental glider No 2. *Model Engineer*
Opposite bottom: $\frac{1}{2}$in scale Wright Bi-plane. *Model Engineer*

" . . made immediately after the first pictures of the Wright Brothers were published last year (1908), and I was possibly influenced in the design, being prejudiced in favour of the Wright principle of main planes at the rear."

Trials with this were not altogether satisfactory, until an accident removed the upper elevator plane and its supporting struts. The craft now flew much better, and was still further improved when the remaining single elevator plane was made adjustable. This was No 3 in Twining's test series but did not form part of the later set, although No 2 of that series was a modified version with lighter section skids and shorter stays.

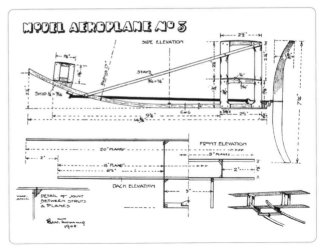

This was the position in late 1908 when Percival Marshall asked Twining to prepare the booklet *Model Aeroplanes, how to build and fly them*. Together with five sheets of drawings for three model aircraft this was first published in February 1909. Priced at one shilling (one and two-pence post free) it ultimately sold some 60,000 copies, a phenomenal number for the time. The drawings and instructions led to numerous requests for components from prospective builders of the models, so shortly the Twining Aeroplane Company was set up to meet the demand, selling roughly sized wooden parts and all other necessary materials as "parcels" or "packets" – the first model aircraft kits. Twining's stepson Cuthbert Davies was his partner in this enterprise, in a small workshop at 29b, Grosvenor Road, Hanwell, near to the Twining family home.

The final design in the booklet was a further variation on Twining's experimental model No 3, made to resemble more closely the Wright Brothers' aircraft. Twining then produced a yet further variation of this design, without numbering it in his own series, for the articles in *Model Engineer*. This was increased in size up to 20in wingspan, approximating to a $1/2$in to 1ft model of the 40ft span full size Wright plane. The model was not exactly to scale, hardly to be expected at such an early date, but in drawings and photographs it gives a good impression of its prototype and was also claimed to fly satisfactorily. (3)

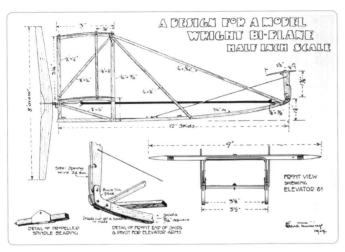

The Twining Aeroplane Company produced several catalogues over the period 1909 to 1913, of which the edition of October 1909, priced at 4d, is typical. It included both drawings and unfinished "parcels" of components for 5 different designs; the 3 listed in *Model Aeroplanes, how to build and fly them* and two larger designs. Sets of finished parts were also available for Numbers 1 to 3. Also included were seven complete models, ready to fly, of two different basic designs (a monoplane and a Wright biplane) and a large non-flying exhibition model of a Wright aircraft. This was priced at 12 guineas and was highly finished, with all moving parts functioning and propellers driven by an electric motor concealed in the dummy petrol engine. The complete flying models ranged from a 20in span monoplane at $^7/6$ to a 50in span, twin propeller Wright biplane at 7 guineas. Parcels of unfinished components were only 1/- or $^1/2$, finished sets of parts for design numbers 1, 2 or 3 from $^3/2$ to $^5/5$. Many, although not all, of these models were also offered via Bassett-Lowke, who briefly dabbled in the model aircraft world at this time.

Twining's own catalogue also offered propellers, wheels, all materials and tools, parts made to customer's own designs, and to quote for any full sized design. As far as their own full size designs were concerned, gliders were priced from £15 and ". .a speciality is to be made of small, low powered machines at a moderate price".

It is a very comprehensive range – although Twining later commented that most people wanted to build their own models, which of course provided a much smaller return to the company. Nevertheless he and Cuthbert soon needed help with the preparation, packing and dispatch of the "parcels" – help which then gave them time to work both on competition models and full size designs.

This work bore fruit next year. By early 1910 the Twining rubber-powered duration model consisted of a narrow v-shaped frame, almost 5ft long, with twin pusher propellers, a doped silk covered main plane and a forward elevator also of doped silk but on a wire frame. Twining and three of his colleagues from the Twining Aeroplane Company each entered such a craft for an August 1910 competition inaugurated for the longest flight. All did well but Ernest Twining himself won the silver challenge cup afterwards known as the Gamage Cup.

The following year the *Model Engineer* offered a further cup, this time for flight duration rather than distance, which Twining duly won on 14 June 1911, going on 3 weeks later to win the *Wakefield Cup* for which the aircraft had to take off under its own power rather than be shoulder launched. In fact he used the same 'plane for both competitions, apart from adding wheels and adjusting the skein

Below: West Middlesex Team for the Gamage Cup Competition of 1910. Ernest Twining on left, Cuthbert Davies kneeling. *Model Engineer*

Opposite page: Ernest Twining with his model which won both the Model Engineer and Wakefield Cups in 1911. photo – Twining family

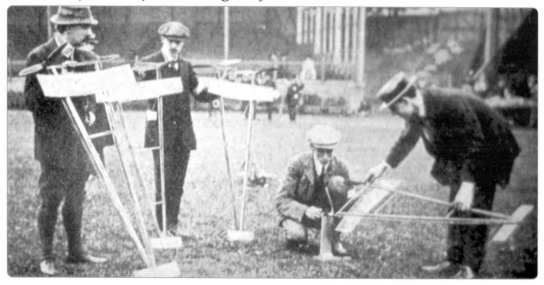

of rubber to correct the weight. The model was of especially lightweight construction, using a single slotted longeron with wire bracing. Many years later   F. J. Camm eventually prevailed upon Twining to write up the story, with a drawing of the plane, and had a replica made. (4)

Ernest Twining himself then gave up competing to join the council of the Kite and Model Aeroplane Association, but Cuthbert Davies continued to have success in the field. By this time however the Twining Aeroplane Company, as well as its existing catalogue range was selling designs and parts for competition replicas, and was also becoming significantly involved in full-size aircraft. Catalogues and advertisements include gliders in 1909 and powered aircraft in 1910 and 1911.

The newly established company exhibited some of its products and other models at the first Olympia Air Show in March 1909 and then at the Model Engineer Exhibition in October 1909. By early 1910 things had progressed considerably and at the second Olympia Air Show in March of that year they exhibited a powered man-carrying craft Twining Biplane No1. (5)

In Twining's usual manner however much of his company's progress with full size aircraft had meanwhile been recorded, notably in a series of articles for *Aero* magazine. These covered some of the designs in detail, including craft which were later advertised for sale in *Aero* in October 1910. The first type was a Chanute biplane glider of 22ft wing span, based on the ideas of Octave Chanute. Twining's sketch shows that its intended method of use was remarkably like the hang gliders of the present day, in that it would become airborne by the pilot running down hill or across a hilltop into a thermal updraft.

The article is quite detailed and several readers clearly followed the design. Twining followed it with a version modified by a Mr Maurice Wright, giving greater wing span and area to cope with the additional weight of a set of wheels. The unmodified design became the Twining Aeroplane Company's type 1, sold complete for 15 guineas.

The company then produced a tailless glider of 24ft span, based on the Wright Brothers layout. In fact Twining says he " . . submitted (the design) to Mr Wilbur Wright when he was at Eastchurch

recently, and he approved it entirely." This became the company's type 2 and in this case the articles were even more detailed, with dimensioned drawings of all major components and joints. According to the company's advertisements a 30ft span version was also available, and a further article mentions one was under construction. The same article shows photographs of a nearly completed type 2A, basically the type 2 adapted for an upright rather than prone pilot's position.

The company then moved on to powered aircraft, again derived from the Wright forward elevator layout, which Twining tended to prefer because it closely resembled his first successful models. Biplane No1, exhibited at Olympia, was of 28ft span and 14ft 7in length, compared with the 24ft and 30ft span respectively of gliders 2 and 3. It was therefore intermediate in size but of very similar layout, with no tail but a forward elevator. Biplane No2, built later in 1910, was larger and according to Lewis had both front elevator and a fixed aft tailplane. It was of 37ft wing span, with a 30hp engine compared with the 20hp of the earlier design. Finally a 40hp 2-seat design was proposed and advertised, but it would appear never to have been built; no drawings, photographs or details in any form have appeared. The subsequent history of any of these designs is unclear, how many were built or for whom, or how successfully they flew. This was however the end of full size aircraft production by the company. (6)

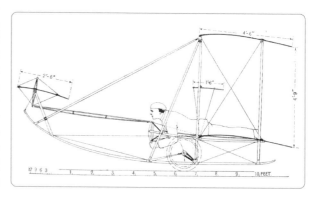

PERSPECTIVE

To appreciate the significance of Ernest Twining's early work with model and subsequently full size aircraft, it is necessary to examine what else was happening in the aviation world at this time.

Although the Wright brothers first flew in 1903, several years elapsed before this was emulated in Europe, first by Alberto Santos-Dumont on 23 October 1906 and then by Henri Farman on 10 November 1907. American Samuel Cody made the first flight in the UK, on 16 October 1908, sponsored by the UK War Office (who subsequently lost interest).

This was the start of a very intense period of activity. Wilbur Wright flew at Le Mans on 9 August 1908, whilst he and Orville were made honorary members of the Aeronautical Society of Great Britain (later the Royal Aeronautical Society) on 9 November 1908. Wilbur Wright also visited the Short Brothers factory on 4 May 1909, where six "Wright Flyers" were being assembled for UK customers. This was possibly the occasion on which Twining met him and gained his approval for the glider design based on the Wright machine.

Only weeks later, on 25 July, Bleriot crossed the Channel, whilst in the same year both Geoffrey de Havilland and J.T.C. Moore-Brabazon flew for the first time, the first Olympia Air Show was held, and the Handley-Page company was formed.

Several UK aviation pioneers, for example Frederick Handley-Page, Richard Fairey and A.V. Roe, started with model aircraft before moving on to man carrying machines, just like Ernest Twining. The closest comparison is perhaps with A.V. Roe, who won the *Daily Mail's* model aircraft competition on 6 April 1907 and a year later was making short hops with a full size craft at Brooklands. This was a scaled up version of the 8ft span model, made with the £75 prize money. Subsequently his brother was persuaded to invest in aviation, using the proceeds from his profitable business making gentlemen's braces.

Twining meanwhile had developed his own satisfactory powered model by 1908, and was later to claim that only Verdon Roe had beaten him to the production of a successful powered model aircraft in the UK. In fact Twining soon had considerable success in both competitions and sales, before moving on to man carrying gliders and eventually powered craft. So what led to the collapse of the company?

Perhaps the major cause was lack of resources, restricting their scope in keeping up with a period of intense technical development. A similar case would be Horatio Barber of the Aeronautical Syndicate who decided in April 1912 to retire from the active design and building of aircraft "owing to the cost of keeping up with the rate of progress being made in aviation". (7)

Between 1909 and 1912 well over 100 individuals or organisations in the UK made powered man-carrying aeroplanes, of which at least 90 actually flew; but few developed into significant or successful companies. Like many other pioneers in the early days of aviation Ernest Twining had neither the family finances nor the engineering or design resources enjoyed by de Havilland, A.V. Roe, Handley-Page or the Short Brothers, all companies which survived as household names in aviation until after WWII. These and other companies which now entered the field (e.g. Vickers, Sopwith, Bristol) in fact between them built several hundred civil and military aeroplanes before the outbreak of war. This provides a stark contrast with an eyewitness account of Twining Aeroplane Company's Hanwell facilities in 1910-11; a simple large room with only basic tools and machinery, staffed by Twining, Cuthbert Davies and a "hired lad".

Instead Twining's development of man-carrying aircraft ceased well before 1914, although model kits and drawings were reputedly still available into the early 1920s. In fact, in the last, 1913, Twining Aeroplane Company catalogue man-carrying aircraft are not mentioned. By this time Ernest Twining himself was already helping Bassett-Lowke Ltd with their architectural models, and Cuthbert Davies had started a motor-cycle repair business.

Years later, in 1949, F.J. Camm, another pioneer of model aviation and model making for whose magazine Twining had written many articles, wrote to him that he felt Ernest Twining's pioneering work should be recognised by the Royal Aeronautical Society and that he believed his brother Sir Sidney Camm would support such a proposal. Sidney Camm was by this time Hawker Aviation's Director of Design, having been responsible in one capacity or other for aircraft from the *Hawker Fury* biplane, through the *Hurricane* and other WWII machines, to jet fighters, such as the *Hunter*, then being considered.

A few days later Sir Sidney himself wrote to Twining. He did not mention his brother's idea but did stress the significance of Twining's early published model designs in encouraging his own interest in model aircraft; and subsequently aviation in general. The RAeS idea seems to have come to nothing, but it is not perhaps too far-fetched to suggest that Ernest Twining's greatest contribution to aviation development was not his few full sized craft but this interest which his model designs and experiments aroused and maintained in such a significant figure in British aviation history.

Opposite top: The Twining Aeroplane Company's type 1 glider, based on the ideas of Octave Chanute. *Aero Magazine*

Opposite bottom: Twining Aeroplane Co's type 2 glider. *Aero Magazine*.

SYWELL AND THE 1930s

Ernest Twining seems to have done little in the aviation field in the 1920s; apart from being very busy with the Twining Model Company and his two substantial books, the death of his partner in the company very early in the war may have influenced him. Twining Models did however make at least two glass case aircraft models at this time, a *North Sea* class airship (as used for maritime reconnaissance) now in the Imperial War Museum, and a Supermarine *Southampton* biplane flying boat.

Eventually however he returned to the field of aviation, with a series of articles for F.J. Camm's magazines, and involvement in the Northamptonshire Aero Club and the Northampton Model Aero Club, both with links to Sywell airfield, north-east of Northampton.

The Aero Club was founded in 1928, largely at the instigation of brothers Jack and Geoff Linnell. In 1933 it was taken over as an aircraft operator by Brooklands Aviation Ltd, a maintenance and training company which was the major operator for over 40 years. This included the wartime period

when the airfield was a significant location for aircraft repairs and pilot training, as well as for the Free French Air Force in the UK. In the 1970s the Northamptonshire Aero Club was bought from Brooklands to become the Northamptonshire School of Flying, the Aero Club title itself not being revived until 1999, by a combination of the staff of the flying school and members of the Sywell Aero Club. The Club House and other facilities have also now been revived, as the restaurant, bar and conference facilities of the Art Deco "Aviator Hotel", with a new accommodation block to match; Twining might have approved. (8)

What has this to do with Ernest Twining? Actually his links with the Aero Club are distinctly vague, because their early records are very incomplete. He was however definitely at the airfield on 29th June 1932 when the Prince of Wales called briefly, having been taken ill on a flight south from Nottingham. *The Northampton Chronicle and Echo* reported that only Ernest Twining and a ground engineer

Left: Northamptonshire's Aero Club's *Gypsy Moth* G-AAIE before Ernest Twining's flight on 6 July 1932.
photo – Twining family

Opposite page: Twining Models Ltd's *Supermarine Southampton*. photo – Twining family

Below: Sywell Airfield on 3 July 1932, with Gilbert Twining in the passenger seat of Mrs Deterling's *Gypsy Moth* G-AAWS. photo – Twining family

named Gallacher were at the airfield when the Prince landed. Unfortunately it did not say what they were doing.

A further link is provided by family photographs, all reputedly taken by Ernest Twining. An undated one shows an outdoor party at Sywell which includes Mary Twining and Gilbert with his wife. A second shows Gilbert in the passenger seat of a Gipsy Moth and a third shows another Gipsy Moth. The aircraft in which Gilbert is just about to take a flight, on Sunday 3 July 1932 (G-AAWS, construction No 1240), was the property of very active club member Mrs Deterling, whilst the other (G-AAIE, construction No 1094) belonged to the Club. Twining's note on the back of this picture says "I flew this aircraft on 6 July 1932" – not "I flew in this aircraft" This is the only clue as to him ever having taken a flight himself, so perhaps it means only that he was briefly allowed to take the controls.

The most significant link between Twining and the airfield is in fact still there. This is the two aviation pictures which he painted, and presented to the Club in May 1935. Both are now in the Aviator Hotel restaurant, and repay careful study, although their location makes them very difficult to photograph.

Each is almost 70in by 40in, and they represent respectively pioneers of aviation and the scene in the mid 1930s. The pioneer aircraft shown are those of the Wright Brothers, Bleriot, Santos-Dumont, Samuel Cody, A.V. Roe and Frederick Handley-Page amongst others, whilst the current scene includes a flight of Bristol Bulldog biplane fighters and several machines owned by club members, with another club Gipsy Moth G-ABJT prominent in the foreground. Twining regarded the gift of the paintings as a jubilee gesture, marking 25 years of successful flying in the UK, on the basis that anything before 1910 was essentially experimental. Reporting the presentation, the *Northampton Independent* of 17 May 1935 described Ernest Twining as an associate member of the Northamptonshire Aero Club, but this cannot be confirmed. [Fig. c27]

Twining was also closely associated with the early years of the Northampton Model Aero Club, which itself briefly had links with Sywell. Founder Harold Boys told the story of the Club's formation in the *Magazine of Antique Modellers*, reprinted in *Flying-in-formation*, the NMAC journal for January 2003. Apparently a newspaper article on his modelling had suggested that anyone interested in forming a model aircraft club should contact him, and this had produced replies from, amongst others, Ernest Twining and the Northamptonshire Aero Club.

The Aero Club later offered the use of Sywell Airfield for an inaugural meeting of aircraft modellers on 5 June 1932. Judges at the event included W.J. Bassett-Lowke and Ernest Twining. Twining then became the model aircraft club's first president at the subsequent meeting. The club continued to meet at Sywell, as well as other locations, for some years. Boys meanwhile worked for Twining Models Ltd in the early 1930s, specifically on the large Bournemouth model for display at Waterloo station.

This aerial activity actually coincided with a revival in Ernest Twining's writing on model aircraft

Above: A party at Sywell Airfield in 1932. Taken by Twining himself it shows Mary Twining and Gilbert with his wife. photo – Twining family

Above: One of the Sywell paintings when presented, essentially a landscape with a flight of historic aircraft. photo – Twining family

Below: Wright Biplane leading the chronological parade in the historic Sywell painting. photo - author

subjects, and with F.J. Camm he contributed a regular Model Aircraft Topics to *Hobbies* magazine throughout 1932 and 1933. This was later more or less repeated in *Practical Mechanics*. The articles included several on model aircraft wings; shapes, aerofoil sections and construction methods; all very comprehensive. Other series covered, in nine parts, the building of a full-size glider to Twining's 1910 design; and in completely different vein, possible alternative power plants for model aircraft, because the later universal supremacy of the small i.c. engine was not yet clear.

This series therefore started with a compressed air powered model, using a three cylinder radial engine originally designed by F.J. Camm, followed by a steam power plant and finally a 15 c.c. two stroke petrol engine, all in Twining's usual detail. In case the idea of a steam powered aeroplane causes amusement it should be remembered that in 1894 Sir Hiram Maxim's steam powered aircraft did succeed in taking off, development only being abandoned because it broke its restraining system and because the designer was ill. This was a slightly larger craft of course, weighing some 8,000lbs, with 104ft wing-span and carrying four people.

The Twining engines would have powered fairly large models, and would indeed have needed a large wing area to carry their weight, for example he estimated the steam plant (petrol fired flash-steam boiler and engine based on the compressed air unit) would have weighed 7lbs and generated 2 HP. For these designs he proposed a pusher biplane, with a wing span of 8ft and overall length of 5ft 6in; a substantial model.

Two particularly interesting articles were on Twining's own models, which had been successful in competition in 1910 and 1911. In *Hobbies* magazine on 11 & 18 June 1932 he gave a detailed design of the V-frame twin-screw design he and Cuthbert Davies had developed for flight distance competitions. This example was however only 34in long by 22in wing span, somewhat smaller than their actual successful machines but of identical layout. This was followed in *Practical Mechanics* for December 1933 by details of the duration design as used in the Wakefield Cup competition.

He certainly had not lost interest in full size aircraft however. Whilst there are no clues as to how far he proceeded with the design, a single drawing (numbered 9/A3) survives of parts (engine mounting, air-screw shaft and bearing) for a Twining High Wing Cabin Monoplane, dated 26 March 1936. Did he still have hopes of designing his own light aircraft or was it just a pipe dream?

BRISTOL AEROPLANE COMPANY

As noted elsewhere, in 1940 Twining Models Ltd was sold to fellow director Harry Clifton, Ernest and Mary Twining returning to Bristol, although it is not clear why. Mary must have been aware for some months, even years, of her serious illness, so perhaps this would bring her nearer to the rest of the family. Certainly Ernest

Twining's mother and younger sister were still in the Bristol area but Mary's sisters and three daughters have not been traced. Twining's technical abilities would naturally not long be wasted in wartime and he was soon working for the Bristol Aeroplane Company.

There is no surviving information on precisely what Ernest Twining did for the Bristol Company. It is however generally understood that he worked in one of the drawing offices, and the certificate of his second marriage describes him as a "draughtsman, aircraft". A further clue is the presence amongst his papers of parts of Bristol Aeroplane Company drawings recycled for his own use; for example with locomotive or other sketches on the reverse. Two intact drawings are both airframe components for the Bristol *Brigand*, dated 9 March 1944 and 30 June 1944. Finally there is a family story of him working on helicopters, an idea supported by a later *Practical Mechanics* article on the subject, which refers to a colleague in the field.

From these tenuous clues it is possible to outline what projects Twining might possibly have worked on during this period; possible but by no means certain! When he joined the company in 1940 they were already mass producing the Blenheim/Beaufort/Beaufighter family. Some 14,000 of these three were eventually delivered between March 1937 and September 1948, for roles varying from light or torpedo bomber to photo reconnaissance and night fighter. Numerous variations and improvements were designed and incorporated throughout the production period, making this a likely starting point for Twining in the company.

This series of aircraft was then developed into the Brigand, Buckingham and Buckmaster designs, although only the Brigand (Bristol type 164) actually entered RAF service. This project was initiated in July 1942, as a torpedo bomber replacement for the Beaufort and first flew on 4 December 1944. Eventually 147 were delivered up to 1950, mostly as light or torpedo bombers. It survived as the last piston engined attack aircraft in RAF service until replaced by the Canberra.

In mid-1944 Bristol formed a helicopter department, with a nucleus of people from the Airborne Forces Experimental Establishment. These were led by Raoul Haffner, a pioneer of rotor craft who had come from Austria in 1933. Development of the Bristol type 171 then started, although it did not actually fly until 27 July 1947, probably after Twining had left the company and returned to stained glass work. As the RAF's Sycamore the type 171 was in squadron service by 1953, whilst its twin engine/twin rotor derivative the type 192 first flew on 24 August 1952. (9)

Did Twining work on these projects? There is probably no way of ever knowing. However the timescales fit with the little available evidence and the first two must be regarded as probable, whilst the helicopter field was one in which he had always been interested and something he would have joined if he had been given the opportunity.

Opposite top: Twining's 3-cylinder compressed air engine for a model aircraft, based on a design by F.J. Camm. *Hobbies Magazine*

Opposite bottom: 3-cylinder steam engine and steam generator for a model aircraft. *Practical Mechanics*

This page above: Twining's 15cc 2-stroke petrol engine. *Hobbies Magazine*

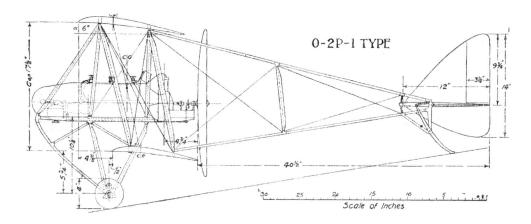

8ft wing span model aircraft for any of the above engines. Hobbies *Magazine*

LATER YEARS

After his spell with the Bristol Aeroplane Company, Ernest Twining returned to writing for *Model Engineer* and *Practical Mechanics*, for the latter producing several more articles on aviation or model aircraft topics. In his usual way of not wasting anything some of these were a retelling of earlier material, Camm's flash steam power plant for example. This makes interesting reading but it is difficult to believe anyone would have considered building their own as late as 1946. The *Model Engineer* did feature a steam powered lawn mower at about that time however so one never knows.

F.J. Camm, editor of *Practical Mechanics* and a long term friend of Twining's, having found a set of drawings for the 1911 Wakefield Cup winner, as well as a photograph of his own model, conceived the idea of having a new replica built and flown to demonstrate the abilities of such an early machine. Twining describes it in great detail and includes a photograph of himself with the replica. This was preceded by a comprehensive survey of *Early days of Model Flying;* more precisely his own early days of model flying as few of the many other, admittedly largely less successful, experimenters get a look in!

He then took the Wakefield Cup design configuration and produced an up-to-date version. Here a fuselage is fitted around the main spar and improved, more efficient wing sections are used. To permit a fuselage to enclose the two separate rubber skeins these are placed much closer together, with the two propellers overlapping as much as possible. (10)

He suggests his purpose in designing this is to produce a model of sufficiently modern appearance to persuade aero-modellers to try something different. He commented that nothing of this type, forward loaded elevator or "canard", had been built in the 15 years prior to his writing, either model or full size. No doubt he would be interested in the varying shapes and layouts of both model and full size aircraft built in more recent years. Airliners may all tend to look alike, apart from size, but both military and smaller civilian machines now use a wide range of layouts, some recalling those of the very early days of flying and some even the tail-first or tailless layout he espoused for so long.

His final articles on aircraft both relate to helicopters, Helicopters and their Development (*Practical Mechanics* June 1950 p296 et seq). The subject had long been an interest of his, perhaps influenced by his early reading of Jules Verne, and certainly in his 1909 *Model Aeroplanes; how to build and fly them* he expressed his firm belief that such a machine would ultimately be developed. This particular article does not consider the evolution of rotor craft, except through his Jules Verne comments, but does explain how they work by particular reference to two then current machines, the Westland-Sikorsky S51 and the Bristol type 171 Sycamore. Whether he at any point worked on the latter may be unclear but he was certainly at Bristol's when it was designed and the article implies he had colleagues in the Helicopter Team. He foresaw a considerable future for powered rotor craft; although he was wrong to predict the use of multiple rotors à la Jules Verne or that they would largely replace fixed wing aircraft.

Perhaps he could not have been expected to foresee the size, speed and numbers of jet air liners or that helicopters could grow so large and still use no more than two rotors. He was however correct about the use of gas turbine power plants in helicopters, the wide range of types which would be developed and the numerous tasks for which they would be used.

A year or so later (*Practical Mechanics* July 1951 p296 and August p346) he was scheming out model helicopters. He detailed a simple scheme, dependent on the stored energy of weights in the tips of its rotor blades. A ripcord was to be used to bring the rotor up to speed before it was released – such things are still in toyshops today. He then outlined a rubber powered design before moving on to both single and twin i.c. engined craft. These he envisaged as largely experimental, because at that date there was little hope of a radio control system for the engines and rotors adequate to give a scale model performance. Such models do exist now of course, both commercially available and scratch built. Another interesting feature of this article, written in his late 70s by someone born 28 years before the Wright Brothers flew, is that Twining not only envisages specific problems in the design of rotor craft; e.g the need for the rotors to freewheel if the engine stops or the need to synchronise the rotors of a twin rotor aircraft, but suggests solutions to these which look practical, at least on paper. Perhaps he really was, if only briefly, a member of the Bristol helicopter department.

There are few tangible remnants of Ernest Twining's interest and work in aviation. No models made to his design are known to survive, although there are likely to be examples in dusty attics. The only located Twining Models Ltd aircraft model is the airship in the Imperial War Museum; hardly representative when he made clear in very early days that he believed the future lay with heavier-than-air craft. The two Sywell paintings are the most readily accessible memoir of his work, especially that of historic designs which shows the depth of his knowledge of the early days of aviation.

An equal significance perhaps lies in the accuracy of some of his predictions – he may have been wrong about the general use of personal machines and multi-rotor helicopters but he certainly anticipated very early the wide use of heavier-than-air craft, large and very large passenger aeroplanes, gas turbine power plants and varied applications of helicopters.

The main value of his work is probably that illustrated by the letter from Sir Sydney Camm. Just as Jules Verne's ideas created and sustained Ernest Twining's early interest in aviation so, in turn, did Twining's early writings, experiments and designs for model aircraft encourage Sydney Camm and no doubt others, to believe that aviation had a future as an industry and livelihood, and that their own ideas and designs were worth trying.

1. *Practical Mechanics, June and July 1950.*
2. *Practical Mechanics, March 1949, p179.*
3. *Model Engineer, 26/09/1909, p268*
4. *Practical Mechanics, July 1950, p345-8.*
5. *Lewis, P.: "British Aircraft 1809 to 1914" Pitman 1962 – p500*
6. *As above.*
7. *As above, p46.*
8. *Sywell Magazine No 9, Winter 2002, p10.*
9. *Barnes, C.H.: Bristol Aircraft since 1910 – Pitman 1964.*
10. *Practical Mechanics, March 1949, March and July 1950.*

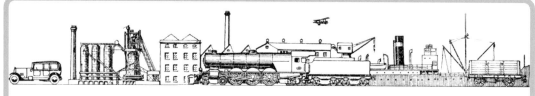

TWINING MODELS LTD

THE COMPANY

Twining Models Limited was formally established in 1920, but its origins go back several years to before the First World War. Ernest Twining first met W.J. Bassett-Lowke in about 1909, whilst promoting his Twining Aeroplane Company. Accounts vary as to whether the introduction was made by Henry Greenly (a long time friend of Twining) or by Percival Marshall, publisher of *Model Engineer* and later of *Model Railway News*. The meeting's initial importance however was that Bassett-Lowke's 1910 model aircraft catalogue included Twining models and sets of parts.

The association became more significant a couple of years later, by which time the Twining Aeroplane Company was going through a difficult time, with Twining himself taking on other work to help out. In 1912 Bassett-Lowke had started a major architectural model, a 40ft/1in representation of Blackpool seafront (with the tower, big wheel etc.) for the town's London Tourist Office in High Holborn (later in Regent Street).

At this point their architectural modeller, a Mr Audsley, told them he was going to emigrate to America, so to complete this urgent project Bassett-Lowke asked Ernest Twining if he would help with the work. The job was no doubt welcome, and made use of his engineering and artistic training, and his model-making abilities. The success of the model led to several similar commissions in the years before WWI. These included Port Sunlight (for Lever Brothers), Immingham Docks (for the Great Central Railway), the 1913 Mallerstang train crash (for the Board of Trade Inquiry) and Pullars Dye Works (Perth). For these jobs Bassett-Lowke established a large permanent studio in the yard at the rear of their Kerswell Street premises in Northampton. Twining then took control of their architectural work, although he was never part of the company. (1)

At this point the war intervened, with all Bassett-Lowke facilities rapidly being changed over to helping the war effort, and Twining apparently playing a major role in several aspects of this. The main task of their workshops was the production of precision gauges for the Ministry of Munitions, work which was reported to have been personally supervised by Ernest Twining. Another major field was the manufacture of ship recognition models, small waterline models of allied and enemy vessels to help in the identification of ships, especially by the new technique of aerial reconnaissance. This is also said to have been under Twining's supervision; actually he and Bassett-Lowkes were to put the techniques he devised for making these models to good use after the war, as noted in the ship models section.

Twining and his co-workers also produced training machine guns for sale by Bassett-Lowke. Described in *Model Engineer* of 11 November 1915 as made under Twinings direction these Instructional Machine Guns were also advertised in *United Services Magazine* for November 1915.

Finally it seems likely that Twining's studio was still making landscape models, but these were also for the war effort. A Bassett-Lowke scrapbook contains a newspaper cutting for 16th April 1917, referring to the Battle of Vimy Ridge, and acknowledging the tremendous benefit to military planning obtained from a model of the battlefield. One can only assume the presence of the cutting means Bassett-Lowke supplied the model, in which case Twining no doubt designed it and supervised its manufacture. One wartime model he definitely did make was an advertisement for the *Daily Mail's* Zeppelin Fund, showing a fully modelled airship above a low relief model and painted backcloth of a typical British townscape.

After the armistice Twining was soon back making landscape and factory models. Up to this point models are labelled E.W. Twining, Artist Model maker or E.W. Twining, Model Maker but this briefly becomes E.W. Twining, Son and Company. This was presumably going to be the new title for the organisation, but in 1920 it became Twining Models Limited, with directors R.V. Bailey and E.W. Twining (Managing). Work was soon underway on a large scale, with dioramas and architectural models but now also glass case models of locomotives, cars and military equipment. The studio rapidly seems to have been outgrown and by 1922 Twining Models had premises a few hundred yards away in Dychurch Lane, at the rear of Northampton Guild Hall; although there are still some small properties in this lane there is no evidence of the workshop. It is unclear whether all activities moved here or not, perhaps architectural work briefly remained in the studio with its large open space for such models.

By 1922 Twining Models had also moved into other activities, with an impressive catalogue of astronomical telescopes (astronomy was another of his lifelong interests) with a price range up to £740. This catalogue also carries an advertisement for Twining Models Ltd's modelling activities with

Twining's 3-dimensional advertisement for the *Daily Mail's* WWI Zeppelin Fund.
photo – Twining family

the note 'Sole concessionaires for models Bassett-Lowke Ltd'. Perhaps one reason for diversification was to find fields where Bassett-Lowke would not take so much of the profits! Shortly R.V. Bailey was replaced by E.H. Clifton as a director. Harry Clifton had joined Twining in 1914 straight from school, and had become a foreman by the time he was 19. He was to remain with the company until it closed down in 1967, taking over its control in 1940. Twining's son Gilbert also became a director in the 1920s.

After 1925 Twining Models moved again, this time to Pike Lane, fairly close to Northampton's present railway station. These premises are shown in their catalogues of the period and may previously have been a large warehouse or garage; it is shown as the latter on the 1925 25in/1 mile Ordnance Survey Map. In this case nothing whatever remains, the whole area having been cleared for housing after the factory closed (although post WWII Twining Models in any case had yet another home, in Nelson Street). Around this date the sentence 'sole concessionaires Bassett-Lowke Ltd' also disappears from the Twining letterhead.

A further diversification was the exploitation of another of Ernest Twining's personal interests, that of stained glass. This may not have lasted long, the depression of the 1930s was just round the corner, but examples remain in churches and elsewhere in the Northampton area, some of them included in special 1929/30 catalogues. A wide range of architectural and engineering models continued to be made however, although like other companies Twining Models had to lay off staff in the 1930s.

In 1940 Ernest Twining himself left the company, although it is not clear exactly why. His wife Mary was however terminally ill and perhaps wished to return to Bristol, where his skill at the drawing board soon got him work at the Bristol Aeroplane Company; he may well have been directed there of course once the war had started. Harry Clifton bought out both Ernest and Gilbert Twining, and took over the firm's goodwill. It traded as Twining Models (E H Clifton) Ltd, continuing in its original role as subcontractor to Bassett-Lowke. The company was also still undertaking work in its own right,

such as ship and aircraft recognition models (shades of WWI) and factory models for trials of alternative camouflage schemes. By the time Bassett-Lowke Ltd closed down Harry Clifton was past normal retiring age and Twining Models closed down too.

Top: Twining Models' Ltd's workshops in Pike Lane, Northampton.
photo – Twining family

Left: Ernest Twining's office in the 1920s. photo – Mrs Clifton

MODELS MADE BY ERNEST TWINING AND HIS COMPANY

Most of Twining Models early records seem to have been destroyed when the factory closed down, although photograph albums of some models survived. There are seven of these albums, which cover, albeit incompletely, the period 1912 to early 1938, of which the latest is numbered 11. The seven include well over 100 models so by extrapolation all 11 would have had around 180. Adding other known models the total for Ernest Twining's work in Bassett-Lowke's Studio plus that of Twining Models Ltd whilst he was with the company must be at least 200. Of these some 130 have been identified, but far fewer located. These include 23 locomotives, 24 factory models, 12 road vehicles, and 12 landscape dioramas.

Others include aircraft, military vehicles and various types of machinery; more unusual items in the albums, but not located however, were a Cornish druid circle (1912), a working model electric crane used by King George V to open an extension to Shrewsbury school (1914) and a mechanical golf swing figure (late 1930s).

In view of the construction methods used it is perhaps not surprising that none of the dioramas seem to have survived, and few architectural models. It seems likely however that most of the much more robust locomotive and machinery models still exist; but where? One problem is that of wrong attribution e.g. Acocks Green library believed that their Central of Brazil Railway Dining Car had been made by Metropolitan Cammell apprentices, until it was found in a Twining Models' catalogue. Similarly the Imperial War Museum's model *North Sea* class airship attributed to Bassett-Lowke is also in a Twining Models' catalogue. This has frequently occurred, although Janet Bassett-Lowke in her biography of W.J. Bassett-Lowke makes clear that from the early 1920s onwards most if not all landscape, architectural and one-off glass case models (except ships) ordered from Bassett-Lowke were sub-contracted to Twining Models, Bassett-Lowke at that point concentrating on marketing. Many models are no doubt also in private collections or museums. (2)

Twining glass case models, based on contemporary

This page: Twining Models' 1929 stained glass catalogue. Twining family.
Twining Models' telescope catalogue. Author's collection

descriptions and on those models which can still be examined today, all portray certain characteristics. These include strict attention to detail so that all externally visible features are included, as far as the scale of the model permits; detail which is largely but not entirely hidden is also included, such as inside valve gear and cab details on locomotive models or lifting car bonnets with engines inside. Finally a superb paint finish was applied, of microscopic thickness, which in his own words does not create fillets or blunt sharp edges. Unfortunately with the materials of his time this paint coat was not very robust, especially on wooden components, and several models have, albeit after 60 plus years, had to be restored.

Descriptions of a selection of models and other products are included, some still readily accessible, others based on technical or hobby magazine articles of the period. Finally Appendix 3 lists all models currently identified, plus a further 13 attributed to Bassett-Lowke but quite possibly made by Twining Models.

BLACKPOOL MODEL (1912)

Blackpool Corporation opened their Information Bureau in High Holborn in February 1912 and ordered this model as a window display. The Information Bureau later moved to Regent Street, taking the model along. It seems curious these days that Blackpool should have what was effectively a Tourist Office in London, but in 1912 of course a week in Blackpool was a much bigger step than a fortnight in Spain or the Canaries is today.

Built to a scale of 40ft to 1 inch the model was said to be 8ft wide, 5ft from front to back and 4ft high (from the bottom of the light wells to the top of the painted backscene). It represented about 2/3 mile of seafront and included the Pleasure Beach area with its Big Wheel, as well as the famous tower 13 1/2in high and with a working lift. A ferry was approaching one of the piers and a Bleriot type aeroplane circled overhead.

The buildings, and even a train in the station, were illuminated from below by low power mains voltage bulbs in light wells below them; Twining's standard system in early years. It is not clear whether this or any of the other ideas in the model were his or were inherited from Mr Audsley, who carried out a significant part of the construction before emigrating.

IMMINGHAM DOCKS (1912)

This was made for the Great Central Railway to mark the opening of their new Immingham Dock complex, aimed to increase freight traffic from Belgium and Holland. It was shown at a major exhibition in Ghent, to advertise the GC's improved continental links; and at the official opening of the docks by King George V.

Close-up of the 13 1/2in tall Blackpool Tower from the 1912 model. photo – Skinner Collection

Another section of the Blackpool model, largely complete apart from the backscene.
photo – Skinner Collection

Made to a scale of 33ft to 1inch it measured 14ft by 26ft (i.e. almost 1mile by 2 miles), representing an area of more than 2 square miles and had many scale miles of 3/16in gauge sidings, along with numerous railway wagons and ships. Much of the dock railway complex in fact still exists, now operated by Associated British Ports, with one of its major traffics being imported coal; ironic when the GCR used it to export coal.

MALLERSTANG TRAIN CRASH (1913)

This small landscape model seems to have been made for the Board of Trade Inquiry into the accident near Ais Gill summit, on the Midland Railway's Settle - Carlisle line, on 2 September 1913. The model was a simple landscape of the area slightly north of Ais Gill summit and was presumably used to explain the location of signals (the second train ran through signals), the position of the stationary first train and the difficulty of access in this remote area.

One source claims the model was made for the public prosecutor, but although the press became very indignant after publication of the inquiry report, which they regarded as a whitewash, no member of Midland Railway staff or management seems in fact to have been prosecuted. The accident was a rear end collision between two southbound expresses, with consequences seriously aggravated by the continued use of wooden carriages and gas lighting. This was the principal cause of the press agitation, as the MR had previously been criticised for an accident in which these features were implicated, only a year or so previously and in the same area. There is incidentally no longer the slightest evidence of these tragedies at the crash sites. (3)

LOCOMOTIVE MODELS (1920/21)

In May 1921 the *Locomotive Magazine* described several new examples of Twining Models' work. First of these were three pairs of contrasting 3/4in/1ft models for R&W Hawthorn of Newcastle upon Tyne. These were the Newcastle and Carlisle Railways 0-4-0 *Comet* of 1835, Hawthorn's first locomotive, and a recent example of their products in the shape of Caledonian Railway No 943 of 1915. This was in fact designed by F.G. Smith of the Highland Railway, intended to be their *River* class, but was rejected as too heavy by the HR's civil engineer. (4)

The pairs of models thus exemplified Hawthorn's earliest and most recent locomotive designs and were exhibited both at the Stockton and Darlington Centenary Exhibition in 1925 (where the *River* model was almost certainly seen by the prototype's designer) and at the 1924/25 British Empire Exhibition at Wembley.

The third pair was given to the Science Museum in 1924 and eventually reached the National Railway Museum at York. The Caledonian 4-6-0 had by this time been restored and repainted in a lighter blue livery (CR blue in any case varied markedly over the years, and with the paint shop applying it!) and renumbered 938. It was also fitted with a suitably modified chimney to represent the first of the class instead of the last. The pair of models which went to the North East are still there, now in store for the proposed Tyneside Museum of Science and Industry. They have now been joined by the third *Comet* but the whereabouts of the third 4-6-0 is unknown. [Fig. c28]

The model pairs demonstrate many fine attributes of Twining Models' skills, which have been enhanced rather than lost in the restoration of No 938, notably the fine detail such as worksplates, external pipework, brakegear and cab detail. The 0-4-0 *Comet* is noteworthy for a different reason; as discussed in the railway research section working out what was the proper design of the valve-gear was a good technical detective story, this valve-gear is fully modelled of course. In spite of its small size (for 3 $\frac{1}{2}$in gauge) it is a most attractive model in dark green, varnished wood and with red-brown frames.

The next model reviewed is the Great Eastern Railway's inside cylinder 4-6-0 of class S69, later better known as LNER class B12. The GER ordered a further batch of these after WWI, this time from Wm Beardsmore and Co Ltd of Dalmuir – their first venture into locomotive building. The makers celebrated by themselves ordering a 1in/1ft model of GER No 1541.

This model is now in the Glasgow Museum of Transport at Kelvin Hall and is a magnificent piece of work, with full inside valve-gear and cab fittings as well as all external detail. It is, however, in incorrect livery; presumably at Beardsmore's request it is finished in full GER lined blue. In fact this batch was turned out in GER wartime grey and the grouping of 1923 ensured the grey was replaced by LNER green rather than GER blue.

Last in the article is what is described as "perhaps one of the finest pieces of locomotive modelling produced by this Northampton company." The model is of a Lancashire and Yorkshire Railway 0-6-0, one of a class of 484 engines designed by Aspinall. The particular example is No 1249, built at the company's Horwich Works in 1894.

This 1in/1ft model was made by Twinings for the L&Y and there was certainly no penny pinching

Great Eastern Railway S69 class 4-6-0 made by Wm. Beardsmore. Later LNER B12.
photo – Skinner Collection

The magnificent 1in to 1ft Aspinall 0-6-0 model made for the Lancashire and Yorkshire Railway. photo – Skinner Collection

in the modelling and finish of the engine. Detail was complete even down to set screws in the wheel tyres, whilst all bright metal parts were plated, dull nickel for wheel rims, valve-gear, handrails, buffers, couplings etc. but gold plate for the brass cab fittings. Unfortunately the present location, or even the history, of this fine piece of craftsmanship is unknown.

KETCH NONESUCH (1921)

In 1670 or thereabouts the Hudson's Bay Company of Canada had its charter granted by King Charles II. The document was carried across the Atlantic by the two-masted ketch *Nonesuch*. For the company's 250th anniversary in 1922 they established a museum at their headquarters in Winnipeg, Manitoba. For this museum Twining Models made a $^1/2$in to 1 foot scale model showing many aspects of a typical small 17th-century vessel, from rigging to hull construction and with fully detailed fittings. The model was 4ft long by 3ft 9in in overall height.

The model is worthy of particular note as one of the few ship models made by Twining Models; Bassett-Lowke usually kept such jobs for their own large and active ship modelling department. Ernest Twining did however make and restore some wooden ship models at around this time, as noted in the ship models section, so he was almost certainly better able to understand the rigging and hull design of a period sailing vessel. In 1970 a full sized replica of the ship was built and subsequently both it and the, by now, major museum were handed over to the province of Manitoba.

ASTRONOMICAL TELESCOPES

In 1922 Twining Models Ltd produced a catalogue of astronomical telescopes. There were perhaps two reasons for this, one being a desire to use their skills and equipment to make things not covered by the sole concessionaires for models clause in their agreement with Bassett-Lowke. Probably more significant however was Ernest Twining's lifelong interest in astronomy, prompted in turn, like his interest in aviation, by his early reading of Jules Verne.

The catalogue was very comprehensive, including four different categories of telescope: a range of simple ones, a more sophisticated type on equatorial mountings, and High Class equatorially mounted

telescopes, both refractors and reflectors.

The simple units, types alpha, beta, gamma and delta, had from 3in down to 2in object glasses, hard wood tubes and pine tripods. They were also available as sets of parts for self-assembly, with prices ranging from the cheapest kit at £6/3/6 to a complete alpha at £22. The next category on full equatorial mountings, were the 4in epsilon, 5in zeta and 6in eta, ranging in price from £140 with a 4in object glass of basic quality to £284/10/- for the 6in with a Cooke object glass and driving clock.

The High Class equatorially mounted refracting telescopes were larger and more complex items, complete with clock drive and fittings for astro-photography. These were priced at £192 for a 4in type with ordinary object glass, to £740 for an 8in refractor with a Cooke Triplet. Numerous photographic accessories were also available.

The final category were High Class equatorially mounted reflecting telescopes, specifically for astro-photography – many years later Twining was to point out the merits of reflectors for this purpose. Prices for these ranged from £185 with a 6 $^{1}/_{2}$in mirror to £520 for a 15in mirror; again numerous accessories were available. It would be interesting to know how many of these telescopes were sold, especially the more expensive types; a figure such as £740 was a sizable amount in 1922. It would also be interesting to know how many survive.

The catalogue does not seem to have been repeated; Twining models were very busy with glass case

Above: Model of Ketch Nonesuch made for the 250th anniversary of the granting of the Hudson's Bay Company's Charter. photo – Skinner Collection

models in the early 1920s, especially for the 1924 Empire Exhibition at Wembley, and then moved into the production of stained glass. Ernest Twinings own interest in astronomy remained however and after WWII he wrote several articles on related subjects for *Practical Mechanics*. These included descriptions of several telescopes (and other optical equipment) and in particular how to make a 6 ^{1}/2in clock driven reflector. As usual Twining did not believe in wasting ideas or material and this was apparently identical to that shown in the catalogue of 28 years earlier. A final series was on astronomy proper as opposed to telescopes, the evolution of the solar system, a detailed description of the Moon, Saturn and its rings etc. (5,6)

Metropolitan Railway Bo-Bo Electric Locomotive

Twining Models made at least three models of electric locomotives, a large 2-Co-Co-2, No 8000, made in UK for Japan, North Eastern Railway 2-Co-2 No 13, and this one, smaller but much more familiar, because sister locomotive No 4 *Sarah Siddons* still survives in working order.

The prototypes were turned out in 1922 and were not technically new engines but drastic rebuilds by Metropolitan-Vickers of an earlier class. Twining Models made this ^{3}/4in/1ft model of No 2 in 1923, before it became *Oliver Cromwell* when the engines were named for London characters in 1927. The model spent many years in the Science Museum, where the wheels could be rotated by a motor inside the body at the touch of a button. Now at NRM York (along with the NER model) the original crimson lake livery has perhaps faded towards brown over 80 years but lining and detail are as usual superb. This is especially true of the hand painted Metropolitan Railway crests (two per side), bogies and pick-up shoes, and the lights, couplings etc on the cab ends. [Fig. c29 & Fig. c30]

Rolling Stock Models

Twinings also made models of railway rolling stock, of which excellent examples still survive. These include some made for predecessor companies of Metropolitan-Cammell, some of which were passed to Acocks Green Library when the company was reorganised and subsequently taken over by GEC (later GEC-Alsthom, now Alstom). Acocks Green is fairly close to the erstwhile Metropolitan-Cammell factory and claims to have the largest collection of railway books in any public library in the UK.

One example is a 1in/1ft model of a type KG open wagon, probably for coal traffic, made for the Bengal Nagpur Railway of India by the Midland Railway Carriage and Wagon Company in 1920/21. Recently restored and repainted the original fine detail survives, as does the Twining Models Ltd label inside its case. Noteworthy is that a coal wagon for India had continuous brakes many years before our own such trains in UK did!

Above inset: Twining Models Ltd's 6 ^{1}/2in reflecting astronomical telescope. Author's collection

The larger item is a Central of Brazil Railway Dining Car, made to $3/4$in/1ft scale and some 4ft long, the prototype was built by the Metropolitan Carriage and Wagon Company. The model is finished externally in varnished timber, in fact most of the model may well be wood. Detail on the underframe and 6-wheeled bogies is excellent, whilst the interior has ashtrays and table lamps on the dining tables and a kettle on the kitchen stove. Both models are to be found in some copies of the Twining Models' catalogue/brochure. [Fig. c31 & Fig. c32]

Acocks Green also have a magnificent 1in/1ft model of British Pullman Car *Hazel*. This has again been attributed to Metropolitan-Cammell apprentices, but according to the Bassett-Lowke booklet *50 years of Model Making* they supplied just such a model to the Southern Railway in 1932. This model poses two questions: firstly contemporary accounts say the customers were Metropolitan-Cammell; secondly had Bassett-Lowke started making such models themselves again by this time, or was it actually made by Twining Models?

Queen's Dolls' House (1924)

Designed by celebrated architect Sir Edwin Lutyens and made originally for Queen Mary, this was exhibited at the 1924/25 British Empire Exhibition at Wembley and is now on permanent display at Windsor Castle. Built to 1in/1ft scale the house is a substantial structure, fully fitted out by well known companies of the time who contributed model or miniature versions of their products to complete the household furnishings and fittings. In some cases the items were made by the companies in their own workshops, but others had the miniatures made for them by a number of model makers.

In her biography of her uncle W.J. Bassett-Lowke, Janet Bassett-Lowke says of this project that 'much work was done on the Dolls' House by Twining Models' which tends to confirm the suspicion that Twinings did more work on this than they have been credited with. Similarly Mary Stewart-Wilson in her comprehensive book about the Dolls' House wrote: "A distinctive feature of the Dolls' House was that almost without exception every item in it was specifically commissioned and an integral part of the whole gift . . Lutyens took control of the operation, artefacts were manufactured in the finest of UK workshops and factories of the era, and Twining Models Ltd was chosen to assist the manufacturers where necessary". In other words Twinings picked up the pieces for any company which wished to contribute but did not have the skills or facilities to make their own models, so who knows how many items in the Dolls' House did Twining and his men actually make? As with the heads of all the other participating companies Ernest Twining received from HM Queen Mary a personally signed letter of thanks for his company's work on the Dolls' House. (7,8)

Twining models certainly presented directly a miniature full-rigged ship, the *Royal George*, two globes of the world, a pair of tiny prams, bathroom, kitchen and working electric light fittings. They also made three cars for presentation by the respective car manufacturers, Lanchester, Rolls-Royce, and a Daimler Station Bus (estate car in modern terms). There are also three other cars, of which the Sunbeam was claimed to have been made in that company's own workshops. They even named the workmen; but Janet Bassett-Lowke attributes it to Twining Models and it appears in the Twining albums with the three they definitely made! These are extensively detailed, with fully equipped passenger compartments and opening bonnets which reveal detailed engines. The wheels of both prams and cars are interesting too, in that they are recognisable variations on the spoked wheels which Twining was to describe in his two series of articles on the making of wheels for models (see later).

Hypothetical Factory Model (mid 1920s)

This model, now in the reserve collection of the Northampton Central Museum, is one of the few Twining architectural models still virtually intact. It is labelled as made by Twining Models (E.H.Clifton)

Ltd, but must have been relabelled after 1940, because dating the model from its various railway items confirms construction in the mid 1920s. The numerous railway wagons in the factory sidings all have post 1923 LMS, NE, or GWR identities, whilst a passing express is hauled by a $1^{1}/2$in long Johnson single, ex-Midland Railway, and clearly identifiable in spite of its small size. The last of these engines was withdrawn in 1928, placing the model in the period 1923 to 1928. The railway track is about 3/16in gauge, with no detectable sleepers, but properly formed points with check rails, at the junction of the sidings with the mainline, which has its own signalbox.

The model is 18in by 38in, in a glass case giving an overall height of 18in, and is described as hypothetical as it is not known to represent any factory in particular, with various building styles both in the factory itself and adjacent dwellings. Nor does it seem to represent any particular type of plant, the yards include coal fuel stocks, and stacks of sawn timber in various forms as well as drums and barrels. With 1920s model road vehicles, cranes and barges as well as a large number of trees and the standard building lighting system it demonstrates most aspects of their architectural modelling skills. It seems possible that the model was intended for Twining Models Ltds own publicity. It is small enough to be fairly easily transported to trade exhibitions or even to individual potential customers. [Figs. c33 & c34]

MODEL GARRATT LOCOMOTIVE (1926)

Twining Models made several Garratt locomotives, for example a South African GA class 2-6-0+0-6-2 is in the NRM at York and a standard gauge industrial 0-4-0+0-4-0 in store for the South Wales Museum of Science and Industry. These are 1in or $^{3}/4$in/1ft scale models however whereas this example is completely different, being an O gauge working model (electric) closely approximating to the LNERs U1 class No 2395. The model was made for Mr G.P. Keen, then president of the Model Railway Club and operator of a substantial O gauge railway layout using freelance locomotives and rolling stock; freelance but often with a recognisable British or European prototype, as in this case.

The LNER U1 was unusual in being one of the only two standard gauge 2-8-0+0-8-2 Garratts ever built (the other was for the Ottoman Railway in Turkey). The model has similar proportions to the LNER engine but is numbered 2491; it is particularly unusual in that Twinings built very few models in this scale or for actual model railway operation. Also interesting is the presence in the National Railway Museum's model railway collection of an apparently identical model numbered 2492. Keen in fact commissioned such models from two sources, Twinings No 2491, and Rex Stedman (presumably No 2492). The latter ran more smoothly and reliably so the Twining model was not purchased. It is now believed to be in a museum in France. (9)

Above: Items from Twining Models' own contribution to Queen Mary's Dolls' House, including the Royal George, Twining's favourite wooden warship, and two globes of the world.
photo – Twining family

One of the 1in to 1ft model cars Twinings made for the Queen's Dolls' House, this one on behalf of the Rolls-Royce Car Company. photo – Skinner Collection

Sunbeam Car, also for the Dolls' House. photo – Skinner Collection

A pair of prams made on behalf of the Mamet Company for Queen Mary's Dolls' House. photo – Skinner Collection

LOCOMOTIVE VALVE GEAR MODELS

These became something of a speciality of the company in the 1930s; chiefly for overseas customers to go with British loco exports to India, Australia, South Africa, Rhodesia, Nigeria, Argentina and Egypt amongst others. Twining notes that the UK Big Four at this time never bought any, although several of the enginemen's Mutual Improvement Classes did so. These days it would seem absurd, given aircraft type simulators for our recent UK motive power, that as recently as the 1920s and 1930s enginemen were given no official training in many aspects of locomotive operation. MIC were voluntary training organisations attended in the men's own time, with the railways, sometimes grudgingly, providing facilities. The MIC often obtained demonstration models of other locomotive components, such as brake gear.

Valve gear models actually serve several purposes: very accurate ones were used in locomotive design offices to establish valve gear proportions in order to achieve desired performance from a particular design, others at workshop level to help maintain correct setting up of valves and valve gear, and finally so that enginemen could understand how the valve gear operated and how to obtain the best or most economical work from their machines.

The models made by Twinings varied, from one example incorporating both cylinders and all the driving wheels of an eight-coupled locomotive, down to the more usual left hand cylinder, valve gear and driving wheel. Models were usually in light alloys but other metals and even timber were occasionally used. For display to a large classroom audience some examples had to be large, up to $^1/4$ full size, but still light enough to transport. The most common design was therefore a flat model in aluminium alloy, using 10 gauge for most components and 12 gauge for the backplate.

There are several valve gear models in the NRM, some of them from Mutual Improvement Classes, but none which can be traced to Twining Models. At least one small flat model survives however with a private collector. (10)

O gauge model based on LNER U1 class Garratt. Made for Mr G.P. Keen but not purchased by him. photo – Twining family

Above: A very comprehensive $^1/_4$ fullsize valve gear model made for Sudan Government Railways. photo – Twining family

Below: Great Western Railway locomotive brake gear schematic, made for the enginemen's Mutual Improvement Class at Bristol. photo – Twining family

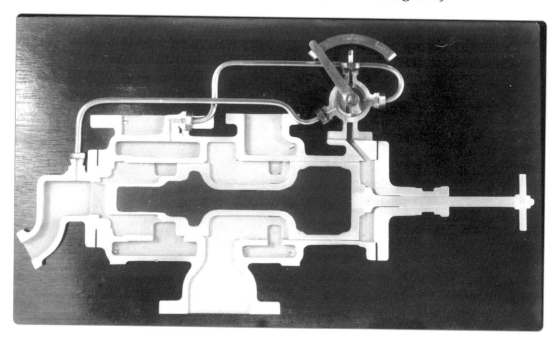

NORTHAMPTON CASTLE, THE ONE THAT GOT AWAY

In the latter part of 1936, the Industries and Development Committee of Northampton Town Council contemplated the construction of a publicity model of Northampton Castle, which for some 700 years occupied the site of what is now the railway station, goods yard and car park.

The castle's origins can be traced back to the first Norman Earl of Northampton, but it had probably passed into royal hands by 1130. Famous residents and visitors include Henry I, King Stephen, and Henry II at the start of his dispute with Thomas á Becket. King John is said to have visited the castle at least 17 times, whilst Henry VI stayed there before the battle of Northampton, which his Queen watched from the battlements. Some interpretations of Shakespeare locate the murder of the Princes in the Tower in Northampton Castle, and Richard III was certainly there in 1483.

Ernest Twining in his usual manner spent

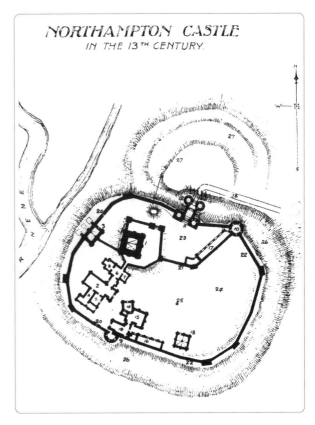

several months researching the history, layout and design of the castle, producing numerous plans and sketches. Unfortunately the Council decided not to proceed with the scheme, in spite of an offer from Twining to supply labour free and materials at cost. This left only £60 to be raised by a proposed public subscription, but the offer was not taken up. All that remains are Twining's designs and drawings.

He envisaged modelling the castle as it would have been in the 13th century, with a heavily fortified main gate to the north, the river on the west filling a moat around the other sides and a substantial wall with two major and six smaller towers. The area enclosed by the walls was some 500 by 300 ft and the massive bastion (or keep) was subsequently used for many years as a prison and assize court after the outer defences had fallen into ruins. The site was finally cleared by the London and North Western Railway in 1876, to permit enlargement of the station yard and other facilities. (11)

A PANORAMIC NAVAL REVIEW (1937)

For the Paris exhibition of 1937 it was desired by several UK government departments to demonstrate the recent progress in British shipping. There was not however a wide enough range of suitable models available to serve this purpose, so a rather ingenious exhibit was devised, which probably appealed to Twining's interest in unusual gadgets, so one wonders whose idea it was.

From the point of view of the observer this consisted of part of the inside plating of a ship, with two life-size sidelights or portholes. Beyond these Ernest Twining himself provided an artistic seascape/cloudscape, across which passed small-scale models of recent British ships. These consisted of 100ft/

Above: Twining's plan for a Northampton Castle model. Twining family

Above: Sketch of the intended Northampton Castle model. Twining family

Below: Visitor's view of the *Panoramic Naval Review* of British merchant ships of the 1930s. photo – Twining family

1in waterline models of all British merchant ships of over 20,000 tons built in the previous 10 years. A total of 24 ships was therefore covered, including Cunard-White Star's *Mauretania* and *Queen Mary*, Peninsular and Orient's *Strathnaver*, Union Castle's *Stirling Castle* and *Athlone Castle* and Canadian Pacific's *Empress of Britain* and *Empress of Japan*; an impressive array. The ship models were mounted on two separate chains, driven at different speeds, so that the observer saw a continuously varying display of shipping. (12)

South African Diorama (1938)

Probably the largest model ever made by Twining Models formed the centrepiece of the South African Pavilion at the 1938 British Empire Exhibition in Glasgow. The diorama measured 20ft by 40ft, was 6ft high to the top of the Drakensberg Mountains and according to different accounts weighed either 2 or 5 tons.

It was scaled from $1/24$th scale (i.e. $1/2$in to 1ft) at the edges to perhaps $1/2000$ at the 11-12,000ft mountain range; a true diorama with scale diminishing to emphasise and confirm the perspective effect. Whilst no particular features were precisely copied it was intended to show characteristic aspects of the scenery and living conditions, from native villages to a part of Johannesburg. Farms and orchards were modelled with accurate scale vineyards, tobacco plantations, sugar cane fields, bananas and paw-paws. Part of the Kruger National Park was also shown with elephants, rhino, lions and a selection of antelope and smaller wildlife.

Around the outer edge, and therefore to 1/2in scale, was a railway of $1\,3/4$in gauge, equal to South Africa's 3ft 6in. This was a two-rail electrified system (built just as Ernest Twining was advocating 2-rail in his model railway book) with engines each almost three feet long. These were a 16D class

The large South African diorama made for the 1938 British Empire Exhibition in Glasgow. photo - Twining family

Above: Details of the South African model. photo – Twining family

Below: Further details of the diorama. photo – Twining family

Pacific on a short passenger train and a 15CA 4-8-2 with mineral wagons.

According to *Practical Mechanics*, Ernest Twining, his son Gilbert and fellow director Harry Clifton all worked on different aspects of this mammoth project, which no doubt filled the Pike Lane workshop for some months. Twining Models had made a previous large South African Diorama, of Durban and its harbour, for the 1924/5 British Empire Exhibition, for which Gilbert Twining had spent five weeks in the country taking suitable photographs, and no doubt these would be put to use again. A permanent link actually seems to have been established, because Gilbert's elder daughter emigrated to South Africa after WWII. (13)

Euston of 1838 (1938)

This model is briefly mentioned in the historical railway section and was made for an exhibition held by the LMS. This marked the centenary of the opening of the London and Birmingham Railway, which operated its first through train on 17 September 1838.

The exhibition was held in the Shareholders' Meeting Room at Euston, with this model forming the largest and most prominent exhibit. The model had two components, both to $1/4$in to 1ft scale. These were a model of the original Euston Station, from the Doric portico to the two original platforms and short overall roof. Around this model, at a lower level, ran a modern train, a *Royal Scot* with six carriages. This was specially built by Bassett-Lowke, whilst Twinings designed and assembled the rest of the model.

At the departure platform was a five vehicle train, headed by a Bury 2-2-0 with 5ft 6in driving wheels. With typical Twining attention to detail the locomotive had proper inside bar frames and one of the vehicles was a carriage truck carrying 'a road vehicle . . of a new type 100 years ago . . known as a Brougham'. The other Twining touch was the presence of almost 100 model figures, each correctly costumed and painted, from the engine crew posed on their locomotive to the dappled grey horse and blue panelled carriage descending the station approach road. The surviving photographs do not show the train particularly well, but fortunately Twining's coloured sketches for the locomotive and carriages still exist. (14) [Figs c35, c36 & c37]

This is actually the only Ernest Twining model where any information survives as to costs or prices, and then only for minor parts of the work. The cost of the main structure for example is not known, but for the trestles and baseboards for the modern track, i.e. that carrying the Bassett-Lowke *Royal Scot*, Twinings charged the LMS £15/10/0, covering design, labour and materials. The model was initially set up at Euston for a Twining Models labour charge of £7/3/4 and subsequently moved to Birmingham and re-erected for £5/9/6. A further pair of the exquisitely detailed and painted first class carriages was charged at £3/0/0, or £1.50p each in today's money!

Twining Models (E.H. Clifton) Ltd

In early 1940, as noted earlier, Ernest and Gilbert Twining both sold their holdings in Twining Models Ltd to fellow director Harry Clifton, and the company then traded as Twining Models (E.H.Clifton) Ltd for a further 27 years. This book is really about Ernest Twining and his life, but summarising the later work of the company is an essential postscript to the Twining Models part of the story.

Over 140 models have been identified as having been made by Twining Models (E.H.Clifton) Ltd between 1940 and the company finally closing down in mid-1967, but there are only scanty records for the wartime period and none at all for 1948–51.

Assuming production rates were fairly constant until they tailed off in the 1960s, at perhaps 10–12 models per year, then the total production must have been around 200. This is similar to the 1914 to 1940 estimate for the period when Ernest Twining was in charge.

The company was already involved in priority wartime work for the government when Harry Clifton took control, in particular making factory mock-ups for trials of alternative camouflage schemes, and (reminiscent of their activities in WWI) the production of waterline models of allied and enemy warships for recognition and training purposes. This and other priority work was to have a significant effect on other projects, for example a model of Thurcroft Colliery, ordered in late 1941, was not actually completed and delivered until 1945. Correspondence of the period also reveals considerable problems in obtaining materials, especially anything even slightly specialised such as fine tinned wire. Certainly in the case of the Thurcroft and other models for subsidiaries of the United Steel Company items were often sourced by them and passed on to Twinings. Security was also sometimes a factor; Twining Models were not allowed to use pictures of many of their models for publicity purposes, although sometimes prospective customers were allowed to see photographs of their work but not the actual models.

Apart from specific war time activities the range of model types after 1940 was much the same as before, except perhaps for a greater bias towards architectural work. This may have reflected Harry Clifton's personal interests, just as the earlier prevalence of railway models reflected Ernest Twining's. More likely the post war reconstruction and redevelopment period encouraged the ordering of a higher proportion of such models. Appendix 5 lists identified work of Twining Models (E.H.Clifton) Ltd.

Significant amongst their architectural work were a model of Nottingham University and proposed town centre schemes for Bury (Lancs), Knutsford and Peterborough; whilst there were several models of hospitals, schools and housing estate schemes. The earliest of this type of model, and significant for their date, was a redevelopment proposal for Coventry, which Twinings worked on during 1942/43 (Coventry was heavily bombed in April 1941), and several for new houses and house interiors which they started in 1944. Such work of course continued into the 1950s, and included further ideas for Coventry for example.

Numerous factory models included four collieries for Rother Vale Mining, then a subsidiary of the United Steel Company, with ancillary factories and even parts of neighbouring villages. Later were Vauxhall's Luton and then Ellesmere Port Works, and a working model of Metal Container's plant for making oil drums. Also at Ellesmere Port this concern was later absorbed by Van Leer of Amsterdam. Another speciality of the period was the modelling of power stations or their components, including coal fired, nuclear and especially hydro-electric units.

Other models included cranes, ships, road vehicles and several locomotives, railway carriages and wagons. A significant part of their work may not in fact have been models at all, because throughout the 1950s and early 1960s there were steady orders for valves, of various types, for Hopkinsons Valves Ltd. Twinings made a model of J.Hopkinsons' Huddersfield factory in around 1920, refurbished it in 1955, and certainly made sectioned models of

Proposed 1950s development of shops and flats in Coventry. Mrs A.Clifton

several of their valve designs. However the sheer number of repeat orders suggests this may have been subcontracted work on actual valves rather than more models. There was also a similar period of work for the Clarendon Laboratory in 1960/63 which was invoiced against a long series of order numbers from the Laboratory without any other explanation.

As in the pre-war period, throughout this work the Twining Models' contribution to orders obtained and/or sold through Bassett-Lowke is not always acknowledged either in Bassett-Lowke publications or in periodicals of the time, leading no doubt to similar mistakes in attribution in museums etc. as has occurred with Ernest Twining's own work.

One thing that is available in records from this period is information on both the costing methods used by the company, presumably inherited from Ernest Twining, and actual prices charged for some of the models. Models were costed according to the man hours spent in researching, designing and making them; and testing them too if they were working models. This figure was then charged at a tariff, or charge-out, rate including a profit margin, some expenses and all overheads. Throughout the 1950s this hourly rate was 9/2d per hour, when workers were actually receiving only a fraction of this amount in wages. To this figure was added the cost of materials specific to a particular project (usually 20-25%) to arrive at a price to the customer. Where there had been a significant increase in costs compared with the original estimate this was not necessarily sufficient, and United Steel eventually reimbursed a significant loss in the making of their colliery models for example. Where items were sold through Bassett-Lowke they customarily added a further 33% for their own costs and profit. In fact Twinings often collected this fee and passed it back to Bassett-Lowke, often making payments on account when projects were paid for in stages.

Additions for special expenses were occasionally made, or sometimes submitted to customers as separate accounts, along with repair bills for models and the like. Other minor expenses seem to have been lost as overheads in the overall labour rate.

Considering the accuracy and amount of detail incorporated into most of the models it is worth listing a few examples of the prices actually charged for them:

Orgreave Colliery and By-product Plant (1943)	£352
Repairs to Bournville model – 132 buildings (1944)	£36/5/0
Model diesel loco for BTH (1952)	£246 (labour only)
Owen Falls (Uganda) Hydro-power plant	£224 (labour only)
Roxburgh (NZ) Hydro-power plant	£390 (labour, materials, Bassett-Lowke mark-up)
East African Railway steam loco	£220 (labour only)
Eildon power station	£1805 (labour, materials, B-L mark-up)
Modifications to GWR Cardiff Harbour model – 7 extra ships	£93 (including commission to Ernest and Gilbert Twining.)
Vauxhall Ellesmere Port factory	£1130 (labour, materials, B-L mark-up)

The payment of a small commission to the Twinings seems to have been associated with additional work done on models they had originally made, i.e. pre 1940. Even allowing for the general level of prices at the time, and subsequent levels of inflation, many of the models seem remarkably good value. It is perhaps not surprising that Twinings often supplied the display cases too, and that good quality ones cost almost as much as the models. This is apparently still the case.

Twining Models never seem to have had a large work force, tailing off from 7 or 8 in   the 1950s

Above: Down Shoes Ltd factory. Model made for Lotus and Delta Shoes.
Mrs A.Clifton

Left: Solway chemical plant, Marchon Products, Whitehaven. Made in 1962.
Mrs A.Clifton

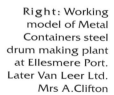

Right: Working model of Metal Containers steel drum making plant at Ellesmere Port. Later Van Leer Ltd.
Mrs A.Clifton

Hydroelectric generator for Roxburgh, NZ. Made for British Thomson Huston Ltd. Mrs A.Clifton

Restoration of part of Nottingham Castle. Mrs A. Clifton

Sectioned valve model for J.Hopkinson Ltd of Huddersfield. Mrs A.Clifton

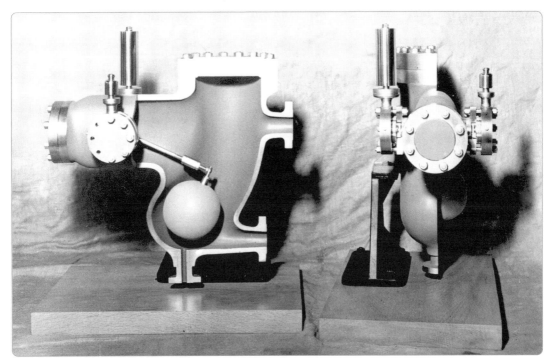

to Clifton himself and a couple of others by the time of closure in 1967. This was probably true in the pre-war period too; no workshop pictures ever show more than a handful of staff, whilst the big South African diorama of 1938 seems to have been largely made by the three directors of the time.

MODELLING TECHNIQUES – LANDSCAPE AND ARCHITECTURAL

It has been said that Twining nowhere described his modelling techniques. This is largely true, but there are clues and ideas, particularly in the architectural model catalogue/brochure, the model railway book and a couple of articles, as far as this area of his work is concerned.

He argues that a factory model forms the most striking and effective publicity for a company and hence its products with the added merit that a good model has its own fascination, which attracts interest that no advertising could bring. The particular superiority of a model over a two-dimensional illustration is its ability to convey a sense of reality as it is examined from every point of view.

Realism depends on a wealth of artificial detail; e.g. coal stock piles or timber seasoning sheds, but also natural landscape such as water features, grass, hedges and trees. In this respect trees must be recognisable as appropriate and correct species for the location; his surviving papers contain dozens of photographs of trees, which were also a major component of his landscape paintings. Likewise appropriate building materials and architectural designs must be used, down to the colour and design of masonry, doors and windows. Another important factor, of which use was made in some of the larger landscapes, is the perspective enhancing effect of deliberately reducing the scale of features or details in the model progressively from the viewing point towards the backscene. This was exploited

A post WWII housing project.
Mrs A.Clifton

especially in the larger landscapes made in the 1930s, such as that of Bournemouth, and the South African diorama for the 1938 Glasgow exhibition.

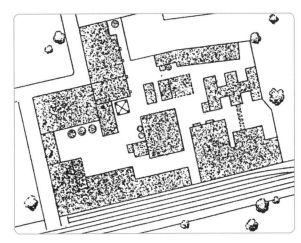

It is also essential that the model is to an appropriate scale for the space it is to occupy, whether for long term display or a specific exhibition; perhaps part only of a factory should be modelled but at a larger scale for example. Fitting the model into a specific space is also not straightforward; placing a rectangular group of buildings squarely and centrally into a rectangular space rarely gives the best effect nor is it most artistic. If the building (or group of buildings) is angled so that none of its lines are parallel to the base then the rigid symmetry of the whole is broken up and at least two sides of each building are visible wherever the model is viewed from, although to fit a given space a slightly smaller scale model might be called for.

The best source of Twining's thoughts on modelling landscapes, are to be found in Chapter 8 of *Indoor Model Railways*. This describes a timber and plywood framework, with cliffs and rock-faces made of pieces of coal in a plaster/gold size mortar. For the soil or grass he suggests several alternatives; plaster mixed with chopped hair, or sawdust mixed with plaster or cement, or just sawdust with a glue-and-water size. This should be keyed to the plywood slopes or shapes with protruding brads or tacks. This combination, albeit all that was available for the period when he was working, no doubt accounts in part for the survival of few if any of the landscape models. Many were of course made for specific, sometimes brief, exhibitions or displays, so long lives would not be expected. (15)

The basics of model building construction are also described in the same source (chapters 8 & 10) and, at least for civil engineering structures such as tunnel mouths and bridges, in the early *Model Engineer* articles (1905-8). Twining's main structural ingredient was necessarily timber, although occasionally other things found use, such as thin sheet lead for the battlements of gothic tunnel mouths which are for outdoor use. For indoor lines curved parts of modern station designs can be of cardboard, whilst windows and glazed roofs of celluloid or thin glass can have their frames painted on to the glazing material. Again these were the materials then available, although in spite of the wide spread use of plastics these days some features are still familiar; his baseboards for example

Top: Sketch from Twining Models' architectural model catalogue/brochure showing recommended plan of a typical factory model.

Right: Drawing for model of a modern large terminal station, from *Indoor Model Railways*.

resemble those of most model railways even today and many modellers still make wide use of cardboard.

He stresses the need for appropriate detailing, showing the correct amount of detail, neither too much nor too little, and that correct proportion for the scale of the model is vital to the overall impression, whether a building, locomotive or large diorama. The Bournemouth model is said to have had 2000 vehicles on the streets, and 4000 buildings each with an average of 10 windows. He is also especially concerned about trees in landscapes and architectural details on buildings. It seems an unfortunate fact that in making models of trees few people seem to realise that every species of tree has its own characteristics, chiefly of form. Looking at present day model railways, and architects' models to consider two completely different examples, it is all too obvious that this is still true; only hand made trees or the most expensive commercial products have yet overcome his strictures! He recommends using as many trees as practicable, compatible with the subject of course, but also that these should have individually carved trunks, with separately attached branches, twigs of shredded loofah and leaves of sawdust.

Buildings require equivalent effort in the detailing of roofs, cornices, arches, window lintels and sills. They may be finished in commercial brick or stone paper, where suitable types exist, otherwise in dove grey for concrete. Alternatively for any stone or concrete a flat white undercoat tinted with powder colour and/or artists' colours may be used, whilst brickwork, roads, paths and similar surfaces can be treated in the same way but it is essential that there must be no trace of gloss on any of these.

Doors, window-frames, and any visible metal structures should be painted with artists' colours mixed with gold size, or with enamel or cellulose enamels. Grass, vegetation and trees should be appropriate shades of green, although tree trunks are largely warm grey rather than the brown often used. He recommends round sable brushes (sizes 0,1,4,5), and writing in 1954, Ripolin paints as offering almost all the colours needed without any mixing except for blue bricks and blue or green slates.

The final concern in factory or other building models is that of effective lighting, a technique which Twining developed for his very first such model, that of Blackpool. (unless his predecessor Audsley devised the system). The method was to form all the buildings with largely open bases, standing them on ventilated light-tight troughs so that ordinary low wattage bulbs could be used, illuminating all the windows and roof lights and even things like trains and signals in some cases.

By the 1930s other methods were also being employed, for example where building interiors were detailed. He explains some of the miniature light bulbs then available and ways of making model light fittings in which they could be used. Twining Models had earlier contributed model light fittings for the Queen's Dolls' House so there was no doubt some spin-off from that development.

The final aspect of lighting a model is that of the whole environment, and certainly in the case of

Above: Modellers at work in the Twining Model shops. photo Tony Woolrich

the Bournemouth model (made for the town council and displayed at Waterloo Station for several years) there was a timed change-over sequence for its top lighting, white light for day time, orange for evening and blue for moonlight – together with appropriate interior lighting of buildings.

Modelling Techniques Engineering Models

Ernest Twining's philosophy on engineering models is well covered in a couple of articles. Broadly speaking, apart from differences of size models may be divided into three classes. 'First the perfect scale model intended for a glass show case . . next . . the working model . . modified to suit working conditions, and thirdly the freelance design. Each of these types of models have their purpose, but that of the perfect scale model is to hand down to posterity tangible records of what was done in engineering before steam locomotives became a thing of the past'.

In the case of locomotives Twining thinks ". . it is a great pity that reproduction of historic engines is so much neglected . . It is a deplorable fact that of dozens of famous locomotives not a single model exists . . What we need . . and should be in all museums is a collection of models of every noteworthy link in locomotive development for the benefit of the historian, the student . . and the public generally." He could not have been expected to anticipate the large number of fullsize locomotives which were eventually preserved but his comments are still valid for earlier periods and many other aspects of engineering sailing ships, even steam ships, trams, motor vehicles, fighting vehicles or aircraft, the list is endless.

Above: 1912 Blackpool model showing the light wells. The figure is Berthold Audsley, still in the UK although the model is clearly well advanced. photo – collection Ted Lightbawn

On locomotives in particular, Twining continues ". . Models of old engines are better not made to steam, because such ability to work involves modification to meet steam conditions and the truth to scale, and correct appearance is unavoidably spoiled even if a large scale is adopted. The cylinders should be internally correct, so that the wheels may be revolved by compressed air whilst the model is in its showcase, and that is the only extent to which it needs to work". One does not perhaps have to accept Twining's pedantic view on such issues, he was clearly a stickler for accuracy in most of his work, and one suspects in other aspects of his life, but if one does then these arguments are valid for all types of models which have, or have representations of, moving parts. Whether powered by steam or any other medium a perfect scale mechanical model either cannot work, or does so only at risk of damaging itself. (17)

Both Twining's own and his company's models, or at least those which can still be examined in museums, or in photographs, or which were reviewed in the contemporary journals, are all accurately detailed and proportioned, the amount of detail incorporated depending on the scale but for typical examples such as $1/2$in to 1in scale locomotives, rolling stock or road vehicles few external features were omitted. Locomotives have full cab fittings, and inside valve gear, cars have opening bonnets and externally detailed engines. Because he was an engineer, not just a model maker, all this detail was exactly to scale; none of the models has any components even slightly disproportionate.

Similarly all are as historically accurate as available information allowed, e.g. the pains taken over the Newcastle and Carlisle locomotives' valve-gear, or the upgrading to four wheel brakes of the Sunbeam car for the Dolls House when the prototype was altered. Exceptions exist, but always deliberately, such as the Beardsmore GER 4-6-0 in blue rather than grey livery, and the working model GWR *Gooch* with more visible and hence more attractive rear splashers than should be the case.

His painting, lining and lettering methods also produced excellent results, and in many cases are still near perfect after 50 – 70 years. One problem with some models was the use of timber for some components. After many years slight dimensional changes in this has sometimes caused crazing of the paintwork and restoration or repainting has been necessary.

Twining wrote several articles, or series of articles, on specific aspects of modelling, presumably based on his own or his company's methods. In *Hobbies* magazine in November and December 1932 and January 1933 there was a six part series 'Foundry Patterns for Models' covering features such as engine cylinders and locomotive chimneys. (He never wasted anything; some of this material turned up again in *Model Engineer* in 1954!) Whilst most relevant to the making of working models there would certainly be relevance to some glass case items, e.g. properly made cylinders would be needed for a locomotive or stationary engine intended to work under compressed air.

Of much more general value were two series of articles on the making of a wide variety of wheels for all types of models. The first was again in *Hobbies* magazine, a series of at least nine weekly parts from 7 January until 4 March 1933. The same material was expanded only five years later into a *Practical Mechanics* series, starting in December 1937 under the pen name EWT and continuing irregularly until at least December 1938, by then under the name Handyman.

Between them the series covered everything from making wooden wheels for (non-working) loco models to casting ones own proper wheels for railway vehicles; and from card or balsa aircraft wheels to wooden wheels for horse drawn vehicles, with the latter assembled exactly as miniatures of the full-size article. Much effort was also devoted to spoked wheels, whether for cars (as in those for the Queen's Dolls' House), model bicycles or prams (Dolls' House again) or colliery pit head gear. He also explains that traction engine wheels, in spite of their appearance are also spoked, and although the spokes are either flat or of a T-shaped cross section the principles of modelling are just the same.

Altogether these series provide a very useful and comprehensive coverage of an area of importance to many mechanical models; poorly modelled wheels can, and have, ruined the appearance of many otherwise excellent pieces of work.

The last useful article of this type appeared much later, in *Practical Mechanics* for June 1954 on 'Painting Models'. This covered locomotives, rolling stock, ships and architectural models, although his methods for the latter were described earlier. At this point most models were still brush painted and he explains the different brush sizes, bristle types and their uses. He advocates a flat soft haired brush such as No 6 for basic painting of $1/2$in or 1in scale models but up to No 10 size for $1^1/2$in or 2in scale.

Brushes such as No 0 or No 1 will be needed for lining out, whilst details such as boiler bands should be removed for painting, as must wheels and other components wherever convenient. He suggests painting tyre edges and any circumferential lining on wheels with them turning slowly in the lathe.

Coats of paint must be very thin; for non working models he advocates the use of artists oil colours, and the metal must be thoroughly degreased with turpentine, but he does not mention any priming coat other than a thin layer of the final colour. He repeatedly stresses the need for thin paint and varnish coats, if detail is not to be lost by . . rounding of corners and filling in all angles with fillets where everything ought to be sharp and clean.

He gives fairly comprehensive notes on the mixing of common pre-grouping liveries from artists colours and especially on lining and numbering. He used a draughtsman's ruling pen and compass for the lining out of smaller models but a striper brush (with long parallel bristles cut at an angle) for larger sizes . . a $1/2$in scale engine would call for the exclusive use of the pen for both thick and thin white or coloured lines, whereas a 15in gauge engine would not be taken to pieces, nor could it be turned on its side and all lining would be done with a striper. Here the broad lines would be $1/2$in to $5/8$in and thin lines $1/16$in to $3/32$in wide.

His comments on paint preparation may no longer be appropriate with modern materials, whilst use of airbrushes and transfers has much simplified work on the smallest models. His comments on painting techniques, brush selection and lining out for larger models, e.g. locomotives or other items from $1/2$in scale upwards are however still very relevant 50 years later.

1. Bassett-Lowke, J: W J Bassett-Lowke p137   Rail Romances, Chester, 1999
2. As above, p113
3. Baughan, P. E: North of Leeds p394 et seq Roundhouse Books 1966
4. Locomotive Railway Carriage and Wagon Review, 14th May 1921 p126-9
5. Practical Mechanics, Sept/Oct 1950 p22 et seq Astro-photographic Reflector Telescopes
6. Practical Mechanics, 9/54 p536, 10/54 p23and 11/54 p76 Astronomy
7. Bassett-Lowke, J: WJ Bassett-Lowke p139 Rail Romances, 1999
8. Stewart-Wilson, M: Queen Mary's Dolls' House Bodley Head, 1988
9. Model Railway News, April 1926 p98/9
10. Practical Mechanics, 4/52 p233/4 and 5/52 p277/8
11. Northants Mercury and Herald, January 1937- 8th,14th and 15th
12. Practical Mechanics, 8/37 p611 and 4/45 p242
13. Practical Mechanics, 8/38 p579/80, 9/38 p663
14. Practical Mechanics, November 1938 p88
15. Twining, EW: Indoor Model Railways – Newnes, 1937
16. Twining Models Ltd. Architectural Models Brochure/Catalogue 192?
17. Practical Mechanics, 5/34 p379 and 6/35 p428

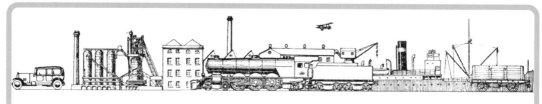

SHIPS & SHIP MODELS

E rnest Twining's work on ships and ship models is of much less importance than that in the railway and aviation fields, but is nevertheless worth looking at as yet another example of his interest in all things mechanical. There is in fact a range of models, photographs, paintings and designs showing his significant knowledge of ships and the sea, perhaps hardly surprising for someone with an abundance of engineering curiosity, who grew up in a major port such as Bristol. There seem however to be no nautical references from his childhood; no early visits to the vast array of docks in the area, nor to the Avon Gorge or Clifton Suspension Bridge where vessels could have been seen coming up river, nothing in fact corresponding to his early train watching or his experiments with model aircraft.

The earliest surviving material appears to be a collection of his own photographs, taken around 1902, of sailing ships in harbour (presumably in the Bristol area) and on the Avon. The pictures were apparently retained as reference material, perhaps for his painting, and few are labelled, nor are the ships or locations in them precisely identifiable. The only exceptions are three pictures of vessels being towed through the Avon Gorge in the Clifton Suspension Bridge area, all in 1902. These three are respectively *Cora*, a Norwegian ship of some 1300 tons, *Glen Doon* (1800 tons) and *County of Linlithgow* (2100 tons). By this time Twining was working in Glasgow so the pictures perhaps represent family outings during weekend or other visits home to Bristol.

WATERLINE MODELS

It was noted earlier, in the Twining Models Ltd section, that one of Ernest Twining's most important jobs for Bassett-Lowke during WWI was supervision of the manufacture of large numbers of small waterline models of warships, both allied and enemy, for recognition purposes. This conflict was the first time the British Navy had been involved in major battles since the change from sail to steam, and many things had changed. Larger navies meant more, and different, designs of ships had to be recognised, whilst higher speeds meant identification had to be carried out more quickly. The new technique of aerial reconnaissance however greatly increased the distance at

Ernest Twining's photograph of four masted ship *County of Linlithgow* being towed through the Avon Gorge sometime in 1902. Twining family

which vessels could first be sighted, partially compensating for the smaller silhouette of steam ships.

It was therefore essential to provide sailors and airmen with training aids to help their identification of naval vessels, either friend or foe. Many copies were therefore needed of each model – many, but far fewer than would usually be necessary for economic die-casting with low melting zinc based alloys.

In an article many years later Twining explained the methods used for this purpose, whereby the die was built up from hand-cut steel plates, laminated and bolted together. This is clearly much cheaper than machining the die from solid steel and although less strong and more subject to wear forms a perfectly satisfactory mould for the casting of a few tens or even hundreds of examples. This contrasts with the thousands of items needed to recover the much greater cost of the traditional die as might be used for die cast toys for example. (1)

Twining is at pains to stress the idea was not his own, and the article was actually prepared to show how the technique might be of value to the modeller with a requirement for a small quantity of identical components, e.g. lifeboats for a large passenger ship model. In fact he points out that if a very low melting alloy such as Rose's Metal (M Pt 212 °F / 100 °C) or even Wood's Metal (155 °F / 68 °C) was suitable for the desired object then hard wood or even varnished card could be used for a small production run.

The method (and possibly some of the actual dies) was further exploited after the war in several different ways. Bassett-Lowke's 1921 *Catalogue of model ships and accessories* comments "During

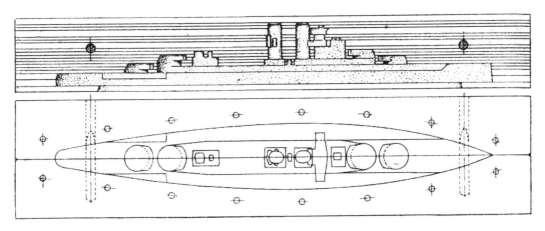

the war we supplied enormous quantities of waterline British, Allied and enemy warships to the Admiralty and have special facilities for producing accurate models of any ships required." Marketed under the collective title *A Fighting Fleet in Miniature* the catalogue contains page upon page of such models. Individual models, scaled at 100ft/1in ranged from 4/6 to 11/6 each, whilst smaller scale models were sold in sets. For example Set 131 *Dreadnought Squadron* consisted of 5 Dreadnoughts, 6 Destroyers and 2 Submarines for a total of 4/6, whilst Set 172 *Royal Spithead Review* offered 39 vessels for only eleven shillings. (2)

Above: Fabricated dies, as used for WWI ship recognition models and subsequently for Bassett-Lowke's *Fighting Fleet in Miniature*. *Practical Mechanics*

A Pageant of English Naval History

These models led in turn to the *Pageant of English Naval History*, 15 ship models covering 10 centuries from ships of the time of King Alfred to *HMS Queen Elizabeth* built in 1912, "modelled to a scale of 50ft to 1in, painted in correct colouring and with decorated sails, mounted upon a 'sea' of glass (giving) a realistic representation of the ocean covered by wavelets." This set was sold in a mahogany and glass case for £25, or £1/5/- extra if *HMS Hood* was included.

Most significantly this involved the largest piece of naval research undertaken by Twining, because each of the 15 vessels was intended to represent an important step in the evolution of British warships from the ninth to the early 20th century. This set was accompanied by an explanatory booklet (also available separately), illustrated with Ernest Twining's sketches. In this he explains his object was to design a set of models to illustrate the "History of the English Navy". He apologises for the use of the word "Pageant" in case it should be thought pretentious but says he wished the models to be of a uniform scale and therefore able to be properly compared. His first step had consequently been to use such information as he could glean to produce a set of modern drawings of each of the vessels.

His sketches in the booklet however are of uniform size rather than scale, and fortunately the original pen drawings have survived. The booklet and sketches are intended to provide "brief descriptions of the ships which marked particular epochs in England's Naval History". A few of the ships offer "perhaps, outstanding features of development, and . . mark practically new eras in policy and design."

The first two vessels in the set are very similar – one of King Alfred's time and one from William of Normandy's fleet 200 years later – both showing little progress from the popular image of the Viking longboat. By the 13th and 14th centuries however oars had disappeared and progressively larger fighting "castles" had been built upon the bow and stern of the ships. A further 100 years and the largest type was a caravelle, like Columbus' *Santa Maria,* and now carried guns in the form of iron or bronze cannons.

Henry VII gave considerable encouragement to the creation of an English fleet, and this policy was continued by Henry VIII (Twining calls him the "much married monastic despoiler"), some of whose ships may have exceeded 1000 tons for the first time in Britain. Typical was the *Henry Grace à Dieu* which is used to illustrate this stage of evolution; although he reported considerable confusion with period sources showing both different ships of the same name and different designs of the same ship. The next step was to *Ark Royal* of 1587, Howard of Effingham's flagship against the Spanish Armada. She was the newest large ship in the English fleet but at 800 tons smaller than some of her predecessors (only seven ships in the entire English fleet against the Spanish exceeded 600 tons).

Ships rapidly increased in size after this period, for example *Sovereign of the Seas* (renamed *Royal Sovereign* after the Restoration) of 1637 at 1683 tons, then *Royal George* of 1756 which Twining claims was one of the most beautiful ships ever built. Of 2047 tons the *Royal George* carried 100 guns, many more than ships of earlier centuries. She is unfortunately best known for her tragic end; careened (heeled right over whilst still afloat) for underwater repairs she capsized and sank virtually with all hands. Only nine years younger, launched in 1765, was *Victory*, Nelson's flagship at Trafalgar and fortunately preserved at Portsmouth. She is also marginally bigger at 2162 tons, measuring 186ft long at the gun deck and of 52 ft beam.

The next significant step was to auxiliary steam power whilst still retaining a wooden hull – represented in the "Pageant" by the last such vessel, the 3177 ton, 130 gun *Duke of Wellington* of 1852. Wooden ships were then rapidly replaced by iron ones, first by *Warrior* of 1861 (also preserved at Postsmouth) and then by the much superior designs of Sir E.J. Reed. Twining chose the *Bellerophon* type of 1865 (not to be confused with the earlier ship of the same name shown on the cover of the booklet), because it was the first class to have a double skinned hull of cellular construction as well as guns in a central battery rather than as a broadside. With a displacement of 7550 tons and overall length of 300 ft she represented a very major change in design, material and size in little more than ten years.

The final steps were to adopt breech-loading guns, place them in turrets and to abolish all masts and sails. This produced vessels such as the Majestic class of 14,900 tons laid down in 1893-5. *HMS Dreadnought* of 1906 introduced both steam turbine propulsion and an "all big gun" philosophy –

A ship of the 13th century; one of Twining's beautifully detailed pen and ink drawings used to illustrate Bassett-Lowke's *Pageant of Naval History*. Twining family

Ark Royal of 1587.

Duke of Wellington of 1852.

Bellerophon of 1865.

although the usefulness of secondary armament later became apparent and it reappeared in the *Queen Elizabeth* class of 1912; Twining's 15th and last example.

The booklet and set of models thus represented a comprehensive summary of the technical evolution of the English Navy down to WWI, and an excellent collection, even if £25 was a substantial sum in 1920/1.

Work in the 1920s

The early twenties seem to have been a particularly busy period for Ernest Twining and for Twining Models Ltd, and especially for things maritime. The *Pageant of English Naval History* is dated November 1920, and with the matching set of models and all the other small models for Bassett-Lowke was available the following year, although individual models may have been on sale rather earlier.

There is only one surviving maritime photograph from this period, showing however that he was still visiting Bristol, where his mother and at least one of his sisters continued to live. This was again taken in the Avon Gorge below the Suspension Bridge and shows paddle steamer *Lady Evelyn* with a large complement of passengers. The picture is not dated but must have been taken in the summer of 1919, 1920 or 1921 because the ship's history is well documented. *Lady Evelyn* was built in 1900 for the Furness Railway's service across Morecambe Bay, which lapsed with the outbreak of war. The service was not revived when hostilities ceased and the vessel was sold to the Tucker family of Cardiff, sailing for three seasons in the Bristol Channel. The company was then taken over by the much larger P & A Campbell organisation who transferred the ship to their South Coast operation as *Brighton*

Another of Ernest Twining's photographs in the Avon Gorge. Paddle steamer *Lady Evelyn*, taken in the summer of 1919, 1920 or 1921. Twining family

Above: Model warship of the Napoleonic period, made by French prisoners. Owned and restored by Twining.
Twining family

Left: Wooden warship model restored by Ernest Twining for W.J.Bassett-Lowke.
Twining family

Belle. She was sunk at Dunkirk on 28 May 1940. This is the only illustration of any kind of a paddle steamer amongst Twining's papers, perhaps it was the idea behind his 1954 model design for *Practical Mechanics*.

Further work at this point was the production by Twining Models of one of their few ship models, ketch *Nonesuch* for the Hudson's Bay Company. This is considered in the Twining Models Ltd section however, and noted here just for completeness. Much more significant are Twining's two articles at this time for the *Model Engineer* on 'Old Battleship Models'. He comments that model ships have existed at least since ancient Egypt and so are well established as toys, souvenirs, artistic artefacts and engineering tools. In this light he considers some of the highly detailed wooden warships then in the Science Museum collection, covering five models, all $1/4$in or $1/2$in to 1ft scale. These are the 100 gun *Royal Charles* of 1672, frigate *Juno* of 1757, *Triumph* (74 guns, 1764), an unnamed 64 gun ship of 1780 and finally *Ajax* (1795, also 74 guns). He explains how the models demonstrate detailed changes in construction methods, equipment and colour schemes; especially how the latter was progressively simplified from the elaborate detailing of earlier years to the plain black of Nelson's time, relieved only by yellow bands marking each row of gun ports.

The articles conclude with a look at the small models made by French naval prisoners during the Napoleonic Wars – admiring the ingenuity, perseverance and skill of the "humble Frenchmen, who through many years of captivity . . . kept their hopes alive and their spirits from breaking down in despair . . . by making these beautiful little ships." He believes the models are rarely freelance, usually representing an actual prototype and probably the familiar vessel in which the patient craftsman had served.

His illustrations are two such models which he himself had restored and re-rigged. Firstly a 24ft/1in model of an un-named 80 gun ship; un-named but almost certainly *Tonnant*, taken from the French at the Battle of the Nile on 1 August 1798, and which belonged to W. J. Bassett-Lowke. The second was his own, a somewhat larger, 14ft/1in (16in overall) model of *Le Sanpariel*, another 80 gun ship captured from the French navy at the Battle of The Glorious First of June, off Ushant in 1794. The excellent hull design of this particular ship was later extensively copied by English Dockyards. (3)

Working Models

After a gap of many years, Ernest Twining eventually came round to ships and ship models again, first with a large yacht and a cargo vessel in 1939/40 and then a series of models in1955/6, all for *Practical Mechanics* magazine.

The first article was a 40in long by 9in beam two masted schooner, with a planked hull carefully built up on a series of frames just like the full-size vessel. This was written up by "Handyman", Twining's usual nom-de-plume for articles about woodwork or joinery; he used it for articles on both household and garden furniture for example. In this case he claimed the model "puts up a very good performance, and has surprised several experts by its ability to sail close to the wind."

Certainly the general arrangement, sketches and photographs of the finished planking show his typical thoroughness and attention to detail. For example each plank, $1/8$in thick by $9/16$in wide, pine or mahogany has to be screwed to every one of the frames, being shaped to its specific location where necessary. He specified the purchase of four gross (i.e. 4 x 144) of $1/4$in long counter sunk No 0 brass screws for this purpose! One might wonder how robust the boat would be if regularly sailed, but regardless of how well it performed on the water, its construction would have been a fascinating exercise in woodwork and the result highly decorative and attractive in appearance. (4)

Twining followed this a year later with a large model cargo ship scheme – strictly a joint effort with Harry Clifton who designed and wrote up the hull and superstructure while Twining concentrated on the machinery. In November 1939 Twining had drawn a simple, single acting, single cylinder steam engine, intended as a beginner's model. The simple principles of such a design: fewer parts, the need for much less accuracy in making most of them and in fitting-up the engine, led him to propose its use for a model steamship. Here the model is out of sight and is required only to do useful work; there is no need to copy a more complex prototype.

For this job the engine proposed has four such cylinders in a flat-four arrangement, and it is claimed it can be made entirely from sheet, rod and tube without needing any castings. This might have been a significant feature at the time, certainly "LBSC" suggested ways of making many components for some of his wartime locomotive designs with few if any castings. Twining also claims reduced labour

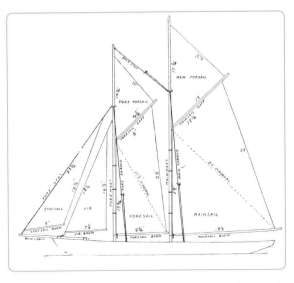

in making his ship's engine design, as well as improved lubrication. The flat-four layout would certainly help give a low centre of gravity. The only disadvantage he admitted for the design is the more complex steam and exhaust pipe-work needed.

His drawings offer engines of either $^3/_4$in bore and stroke or 1in bore and stroke, for a ship model of 5ft or 6 to 7ft in length (Harry Clifton was already using metric dimensions, his corresponding ship designs being respectively 1.5 metres and 2 metres in length). Twining's boiler, in contrast to the engine, is a fairly complex semi watertube type, with large steam drums, water drums and steam generating tubes, heated by a methylated spirits burner or by a vaporising paraffin burner for the larger version. Curiously, in view of his aversion to brazed or silver-soldered locomotive boilers, he recommends this method of construction, in case the model ship becomes stranded out of reach and the boiler runs dry and over-heats. Perhaps Harry Clifton persuaded him this would help protect his hull and upper works. (5)

Ernest Twining's final ship model articles, in fact his final articles of any sort, for *Practical Mechanics* covered five designs published between November 1954 and October 1956, the last actually appearing after his death. None of them had any unconventional design features but they cover a wide range of types. The first was a paddle steamer, followed by a Bermuda sloop, Drake's *Golden Hind* in three sizes – the largest intended to sail – and two battery powered vessels, a tug

Top: Design for sailing model 2-masted schooner. *Practical Mechanics*

Left: Individual planking of the model schooner. *Practical Mechanics*

and a large cargo /passenger ship.

At the time he was writing, the Model Yachting Association had adopted five sizes of model yachts as standard for their competitions, and his design is for the smallest of these, the 36in class, which was then popular with clubs sailing on smaller stretches of water. The MYA rules controlled only certain hull dimensions: maximum length 36in, maximum beam 9in, maximum depth 11in, and an all-up weight including sails and fittings of 12lbs. Because there is therefore no restriction on mast height or sail area, Twining

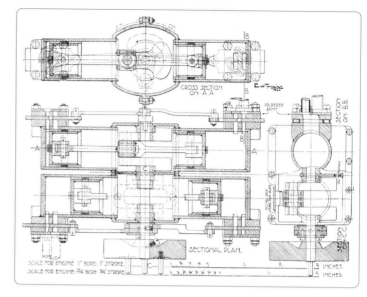

emphasises the importance of keeping down the weight of the hull and spars, so that a heavier keel can be used to permit a greater sail area. He covers, in detail, construction of the hull (from 1in planks, bread and butter fashion), mast, sails, lead keel and self steering gear; then final rigging and finishing off. (6)

Later in the year he produced a design for a series of models of Drake's *Golden Hind*, in sizes from 12in to 24in length on water line. Whilst all were potentially capable of floating and sailing he stressed that the largest version would have much the greatest directional stability and should be the one built by anyone wishing to actually sail their model.

As with the yacht and the earlier paddle steamer, the hull is of bread and butter construction, in this case using just six planks, of a thickness depending on the size of model being made. If the model is actually to sail then the hull needed to be hollowed out and then ballasted to the correct waterline when masts, spars, sails and all accessories have been fitted, or at least completed so their weight can be taken into account. As he felt it impractical to devise any form of self steering gear (compared with the yacht's much simpler sail plan) he recommends rigidly fixing the rudder. He does however comment that the rudders of model powered craft can be radio controlled but this would not be practical for this square rigged ship; no doubt someone has subsequently achieved this.

Again he concludes with details of masts, spars, sails and rigging, much more complex in this case of course. It would be interesting to know how many such models were built, and how well they sailed. It would certainly have made a very attractive model actually on the water. (7)

The last two ship models were a complete contrast, both battery electric powered and with soldered tinplate hulls, of very different prototypes but similar sized models. The first was of a tugboat, modelled at $1/4$in/1ft to give a model 28in long. It was based on the *John Payne* of Avonmouth, but he would not claim it was a scale model as he had no proper dimensions, presumably working from photographs.

Modelling a tug or similar small prototype gives the advantage of a large scale and therefore large, easily handled components, and no minute detail. By comparison his other model, Cunard's SS *Media* is only $1/16$in/1ft scale but still 33in long and would need much more detail, for example eight lifeboats instead of just two for the tug. Modelling this ship seems to have been prompted by Bassett-Lowke

Above: Fabricated flat-four single-acting steam engine, for the Twining/Clifton model cargo ship. *Practical Mechanics*

being asked to make a $^{1}/4$in/1ft glass case model of *Media,* some 13ft long. He had maintained his connections with Bassett-Lowke as well as Twining Models (E.H.Clifton) Ltd and presumably had ready access to information and photographs. (8)

None of these five late model ship articles are highly detailed; a prospective builder would have a lot to work out for him/herself. It is also unlikely that the Twining's flat provided room for a workshop suitable for him to make this sort and size of model, although he did still have what he termed his studio. As with the late model railway articles one is drawn to the conclusion that his friend F.J. Camm needed articles for his magazine and Ernest Twining obliged, no doubt finding the money useful. His writings on ships and ship models were as always interesting, and some of the models, especially the schooner, paddle steamer, and *Golden Hind* most attractive, but his most significant contribution to the maritime field was undoubtedly the *Pageant of English Naval History* and the research on which it is based. It is fortunate that the original sketches for the accompanying booklet still survive.

1. *Practical Mechanics: May 1951 pp 224-6.*
2. *Bassett-Lowke Ltd: Ship models Catalogue 1921.*
3. *Model Engineer: 17th January 1921 p 415 et seq, 24th November 1921 p445 et seq.*
4. *Practical Mechanics: February 1939 p248-50 and March 1939 p320-2/6.*
5. *Practical Mechanics: March 1940 p267 et seq, May 1940 p360 et seq, July 1940 p453 et seq.*
6. *Practical Mechanics: March 1955 p256-8, April 1955 p251-2.*
7. *Practical Mechanics: December 1955 p142-5, January 1956 p193-4.*
8. *Practical Mechanics: February 1956 p254-256, October 1956 p30-3.*

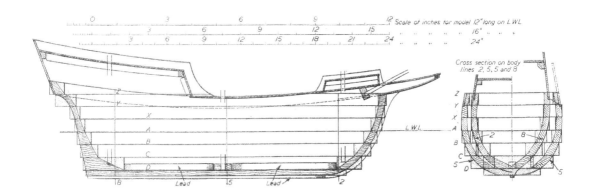

Scale sailing model of Drake's *Golden Hind,* sheer
plan and body plan. *Practical Mechanics*

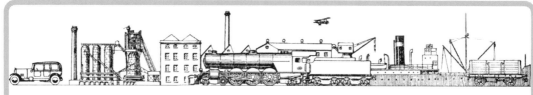

Stained Glass

Family links

t is far from clear when, or even if, Ernest Twining undertook any formal training in working with stained glass. His obituary, in the *Journal of the British Society of Master Glass Painters*, claims "his work in stained glass began much earlier (than his commercial modelling activities) in Bristol, where he was connected with the firm of Joseph Bell". (1)

Twining actually left Bristol in 1901, aged 26, to work in Glasgow. The above statement is consequently difficult to reconcile with his engineering apprenticeship, presumably from about 16, and formal artistic training starting in his late teens. His maternal grandfather William Jones (to whom his book on stained glass is dedicated – see later) and his uncle William Gilbert Jones were however both long term employees of Joseph Bell and Son, ecclesiastical glaziers.

Joseph Bell started stained glass work in Bristol in 1840, and Twining's grandfather must have been one of his earliest employees; born in 1826 he eventually worked for the company for 54 years according to his son. He presumably started with them in the 1840s and so may well have worked on the restoration of 14th–century glass from Bristol Cathedral, a task Bell's performed between 1847 and 1852.

Joseph Bell subsequently purchased 12 College Green, Bristol in 1857 and this remained the company's studio and workshop until 1933, when the area was cleared to make way for new municipal buildings. Ten years earlier, in 1923, Fred Bell, son of the company's founder, had sold out to Arnold Robinson and it was he who now transferred their activities to 68 Park Street. Arnold Robinson died in 1955, leaving the company in the hands of his son Geoffrey, who later recalled Ernest Twining working in the studio when he was a boy. The company finally closed down in 1978. (2,3)

In July 1935, William Gilbert Jones was interviewed by the *Bristol Evening Post* about his almost 60 years with Joseph Bell and Son. As he was then 72 years old this means that he worked, in some capacity, in the glass industry from the age of about 12, probably the age at which he left school. This provides the clue as to how Ernest Twining might have gained early experience in the field, because when he was a child, full time schooling was still only compulsory up to the age of 12. So he could have worked with his grandfather in his spare time whilst still at school, or attended school only part time and worked part time at Bell's, or even worked there full time for a brief period.

Whenever or wherever his early knowledge of the craft was gained he subsequently built upon it sufficiently that, by 1925, the British Society of Master Glass Painters was prepared to make him a fellow of their organisation, and for him to produce only three years later a substantial book on the practical aspects of the craft. A further year on, in late 1929 or early 1930, Twining Models issued a catalogue (brochure might be a better term) of their stained glass work, including pictures of several items completed or in hand. Two of the completed items, which are not dated, appear also in the book, so perhaps these had been finished early enough to influence the BSMGP decision.

A further uncertainty is the reason why Ernest Twining started making stained glass panels and windows on a commercial basis. Throughout his career however, he was always willing to exploit any of his (many) artistic or technical abilities which might provide an income for his family or his companies and, perhaps not accidentally, give him an opportunity to express those talents.

Twining Models had already diversified into items of church furniture – a reredos, illuminated candlesticks and religious paintings for example – as natural developments of their model making skills. Stained glass, drawing once again on Ernest Twining's own skills, experience and possibly equipment must have seemed a natural step, especially if demand for architectural models had fallen away.

Presumably in this case, as with Twining Models' earlier foray into making astronomical telescopes, these products were outside the "sole concessionaires for models" agreement with Bassett-Lowke, with a useful bonus for receipts. Those windows which can readily be closely examined are labelled E.W. Twining, not Twining Models Ltd, like the models from the early 1920s onwards. This may simply mean that he thought of himself as the artist regardless of any input from his staff. On those labels where Pike Lane is mentioned, rather than just E.W. Twining, Northampton, the premises are described as "The Studio" – just further to confuse locations with his much earlier studio at the Bassett-Lowke offices! Harry Clifton, writing in the 1970s, actually remembered only one window being handled at Pike Lane, so were the others made elsewhere?

Art or Craft?

In the introduction to his book, Twining agrees with the oft repeated adage that no art can be taught through the medium of a text-book. "The fact is that an artist, whether his talents lie in the direction of literature, painting, sculpture or music, must be born – he cannot be made; and if art is not born in him it cannot be developed." However there is, he believes " no reason why instruction cannot be given. . . in the practical application of an art." It is after all the knowing how to do a thing which is significant, enabling one to develop and apply one's inherent aptitudes and abilities.

In many aspects of his life Ernest Twining very much reflected the Victorian age into which he was born – and perhaps that is apparent in the character of his stained glass work. His BSMGP obituary suggests he was content with quiet, unspectacular effects of tone and colour and was not much attracted by the novelties and experiments of the early 20th–century. If correct this would echo most of his watercolour paintings, but it is not entirely in line with his own view "my tastes are distinctly modern, but I do maintain that there should be delicacy and beauty of line and colouring." He avers that some modern work " is far finer in the glass, in the design, and in the painting, than anything which has ever been done before." (4)

He was far less sympathetic to those modernists aiming to shock rather than to soothe – " there is too great a tendency to be merely eccentric . . I think it behoves every artist . . to keep constantly before him what will be the value which posterity will set upon my work?"

Ernest Twining's own talents were however largely as a practical man and he was not an innovator in any artistic sense. His stained glass work is pleasing to the eye and filled with interesting detail, often reflecting significant research on his part, such as the numerous musical instruments in the *St Cecilia* window for Semilong Church, Northampton. Although he clearly admired some of the new work which was being done at this time, as evidenced both by his comments and his choice of illustrations for his book, he was not prepared to emulate these trends.

This is reminiscent of certain aspects of his model engineering work, and particularly his small locomotive designs. In the inter-war period for example, miniature locomotive boiler designs and boiler making techniques moved on considerably. In this case too Twining's writings make clear that he was aware of progress around him. His own designs however by and large did not pick up on this progress and thus appear distinctly old fashioned as far as their boiler construction is concerned.

He points out that, at least in modern times, " the painter of pictures is usually a painter only . . he does not . . prepare his own canvases . . grind and mix his own colours, and then fix the pictures in the frames." The designer and painter of windows on the other hand must know how to design, what is possible or impossible in glass, and must be able to execute the whole work. In other words he is a mechanic as well as designer and painter. "If he is not all these, then he is not a craftsman in stained glass (and) it was due to this lack . . that some eminent painters of pictures in the past . . failed (in attempting to design for stained glass) because they themselves (were not) craftsmen and did not understand the limitations of the media." (5)

For example in achieving the detail of a picture by painting the glass with enamels or stains: " in no way whatever does working upon stained glass . . resemble either picture painting or any other form of pictorial or decorative art." An entirely new technique will be required of any painter of pictures, however experienced in other fields.

"It has been said, and I think truly, that stained glass is either a trade or an art, according to whether the various portions of the craft are divided up amongst a number of operatives or whether it is carried through by one brain and pair of hands." (6)

The Art and Craft of Stained Glass

Regardless of any evidence as to where, or how formally, Ernest Twining undertook any training in the practical or craft aspects of stained glass work, whether from other family members, periods at Joseph Bell's, or from the careful study of any relevant literature which was his norm in fields new to him, by the mid 1920s he was making stained glass panels and windows.

Having by then perfected practical methods which suited his own artistic interpretations of the medium, Twining produced *The Art and Craft of Stained Glass* (Pitman, 1928), dedicated "to the Memory of my Grandfather, glass painter and craftsman, from whom, through my mother, I have inherited a taste and love for art."

Following the view that no art can be taught, but its practical application can be developed he makes clear that he is not pretending to teach the art of stained glass but providing " the young craftsman . . with a lamp to light him along the rough road of technicality"; in other words how to apply his artistic talents to the "art and craft of stained glass". In particular " there is no modern book, and no book whatever which is still in print and obtainable, which describes in detail the (crucial) process of firing painted glass. I have therefore attempted to fill what I believe to be a long felt want."

Another of the objectives he had "in mind in compiling this book is to assist those whose ambitions would lead them to become masters of this, the noblest of the decorative arts and to practise in their own homes, studios or wherever possible so as to become proficient in all aspects of the craft." In other words he is far from advocating "one man – one job" and is endeavouring to assist the young craftsman to learn how to perform all the portions of the work, from original design to final installation.

This is in contrast to what he sees as modern commercialism, which often requires the various phases of the work to be split up between different operatives and workshops. Whilst it may be unlikely that (say) a firing kiln operative would become an artist it is clearly feasible for a draughtsman, painter or cartoonist to learn the more practical aspects, from glass cutting to glass firing. Eventually he might " be able to design for glass . . a well balanced composition . . then carry the design through to its ultimate end through a series of steps which laces the artist at the very front rank of his profession."

The book was highly thought of in its day. "Northampton's book of the year? "To the uninitiated this book will be a great revelation".(7) "It is very difficult to write about one's ordinary work, yet every glass painter knows how difficult it is for the ordinary person to comprehend the difficulties of working in a material such as glass . . Mr Twining writes in such a lucid and clear manner that . . one might imagine the designing and painting of a stained-glass window was one of the simplest things in the world; so . . it is to the craftsman who knows what he is about . . I feel the whole thing has been so carefully thought out and arranged by the author – a straightforward story by a man who knows how to do his job." (8) "This beautifully produced book fills a long felt want. The task . . has been so well done on the whole that the highest compliment a reviewer can pay to the author is to mention points in which an excellent book can be made better."(9)

Certainly the book seems to have proved of considerable practical value; it was still being cited as a source of ideas, methods and techniques in 1981, after 53 years. In addition a substantial portion was reprinted in 1978 as *Painting and Firing Stained Glass,* with a further printing now said to be in hand.

Twining divides the task of the stained glass artist into 14 processes:
- Making the Sketch, the original watercolour drawing which the layman might call the design
- Taking templates, or assessing the opening in the stone-work which is to be filled
- Cartoons, scaling up the sketch to the full-size figures and details of the window
- The Cut-line, transferring the cartoon to the different colours of glass to make the image
- Cutting the Glass – the frightening part for the inexperienced layman!
- Embossing or etching, using hydrofluoric acid to reduce the density or intensity of colours and achieve other effects, especially with "flashed" glass
- Waxing-up. Prior to painting, analogous to the masking process familiar to modellers
- Painting, with enamels to provide detail and subtle colour effects
- Silver staining, adding a yellow stain to provide a variety of effects
- Firing of the glass so that the enamel and silver stain react with and bond to the glass
- Leading-up, or assembling the finished glass pieces into the final picture
- Cementing, in effect "gluing it all together"
- Banding, or attaching the supporting framework
- Fixing, or installing the window into the building.

In addition he devoted a section to window design – assuming his readers were competent artists but stressing the significant differences required for an image which is to be rendered in glass. The basic materials and processes of stained glass were also covered, as was photography of the final product. Finally the book includes designs for a glass painter's easel and for a pair of gas-heated glass firing kilns. All in all "an exceptionally complete directive to workshop practice, which describes every process of technique and some principles of design," to quote DW's obituary of Twining in the BSMGP Journal. (DW was Edward (Davie) Woore, a one-time pupil, with Arnold Robinson, of Christopher Whall, at the Royal College of Art.)

As examples of the detail in which he covered his subject it is worth examining a few areas more closely. It is perhaps important to mention that "painted" glass, in this context, does not mean what the term implies to the layman. The light, colour, texture and detail of a stained glass window or panel are achieved by a combination of coloured glass and materials fired onto that glass, either enamels (which are themselves a special kind of glass), or silver stain.

The term "glass" strictly refers to any solidified liquid which has no crystalline structure, and even in the more specific daily usage of the word compositions vary widely as between, say, window panes or the optical glass of a camera lens. Chemically speaking window glass is a sodium calcium silicate, made by fusing sand (silica) with sodium carbonate (soda ash) and calcium hydroxide (lime). Proportions vary but at least 10% lime is needed if the product is not to be readily attacked by moisture – a common problem with old stained glass.

For windows, and indeed other uses, the glass is coloured whilst in the molten state by the addition of metal oxides. Not only do different metals give different colours, but many elements used alone can give a range of colours depending on their oxidation state. For example copper can give blue or green depending on degree of oxidation, but if severe reducing (i.e. oxygen scavenging or removing) conditions are created it forms sub-microscopic colloidal particles of elemental copper which give a rich ruby red colour. By adding different metal oxides and varying the conditions in the melt it is thus possible to make glass of almost any colour or tint.

A variation is "flashed" glass, obtained by dipping a lump of molten glass of one colour into another, so that when the lump is blown or worked a thin coat of, for example, blue or red will remain on the surface of a sheet of glass which is either clear or of a different colour. Later removal or partial removal of the coating by etching with hydrofluoric acid allows effects of varying colour intensity to be created, such as draped clothes or tree bark or foliage.

Enamel "paints" are basically metallic oxides again, this time fused into a lead silicate glass (which melts at a lower temperature than a sodium calcium silicate glass) and then finely ground so they can be used as pigments to be painted onto the glass and then fired, providing variation in shadows, subtle changes in colour from that of the basic glass and the considerable detail which is too small to be achieved with separate pieces of glass. A further variation is provided by "silver stain", also painted and fired onto the glass giving a deep yellow stain which provides a further change to the colour or shading of parts of the scene.

It was noted earlier that Twining gives as his main impetus for writing the book the absence (in 1928) of any modern literature on the firing of painted glass. These days, kilns for such purposes are available off the shelf, either gas fired or more commonly electrically heated. When he was writing however kilns were generally gas fired, and experience with coke fired ones was not far in the past – he records his grandfather's many tales of work broken or spoiled in these inconsistent and unreliable units, and thus having to be redone.

He therefore felt it very important to provide the design of a satisfactory piece of equipment for firing glass. He describes in detail, with proper engineering drawings in his usual style, the design of two sizes of modern glass kiln, both suitable to be made and used by any individual wishing to pursue the craft as either hobby or occupation. In fact electric kilns were also just becoming available and he illustrates and briefly describes the first example on the British market. He then goes into considerable detail on all aspects of the use of the kiln; without which after all the "Art and Craft" could not be practised.

Another area which exemplifies the book's attention to detail, is the glass panel *Sir Galahad's Visionne of ye San Grail*. This is a design he "prepared specially as an example for the young craftsman to use . . for the purpose of copying and executing in glass." Throughout the book he refers to the design and it is illustrated at various stages of production. It thus appears as original sketch, as monochrome cartoon and finally as mounted glass panel. In between it is used to demonstrate most of the processes of making a stained glass panel or window. Preparing the cartoon from the sketch, developing the cut-line (i.e. which parts are in which colour of glass and their actual shapes), dealing with difficult cuts, waxing-up for (enamel) painting, and details of the picture after painting and firing.

Finally the parts are leaded-up, cemented and framed; a very detailed account and strongly reminiscent of the "how to make . . " articles which he wrote on many model engineering subjects, although in fact these were rarely in such detail. Fortunately his own version of this panel survives, now in the reserve collection of the Northampton Central Museum and Art Gallery.

Opposite top: Stages in the making of a stained glass panel, from *The Art and Craft of Stained Glass*. a) The cut line. **Opposite middle:** b) Ready for firing. **Opposite bottom:** c) Panel completed and leaded-up.

STAINED GLASS WINDOWS AND PANELS MADE BY ERNEST TWINING AND HIS COMPANY

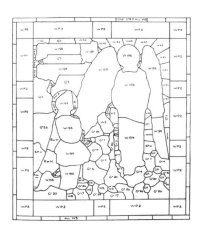

It is far from clear just how many windows were actually made by Ernest Twining, and equally unclear when he first undertook such work on a commercial basis. His obituary in the BSMGP Journal claims most of his work is in churches in the West Country, but none of this has in fact been located. However this comment may well relate to his post WWII period with Joseph Bell and Son of Bristol.

On the other hand a *Northampton Independent* report of 17th May 1935 (actually on one of his many other activities) claimed his company "had made most recently installed windows in the Northampton area". This does accord with known facts at least in part, all identified windows or panels are in or near Northampton. The timescale also fits because in late 1929 or early 1930 Twining Models Ltd published a catalogue or brochure of their stained glass and other items of church furnishings. (The catalogue is dated February 1929, but contains a picture of a window with the note that it was dedicated in November1929)

The brochure includes five windows, of which two, at Hardingstone and Holy Trinity (formerly Semilong) can still be readily examined. A further one is still with his family but there is no trace of the others, although one also appears in *The Art and Craft of Stained Glass;* albeit only as a monochrome cartoon. Additionally Northampton Central Museum has two Twining glass panels and the Catholic Church in nearby Wolverton has four Twining windows. These latter however are WWII Memorial windows, made during his renewed association with Joseph Bell and Son, rather than by Twining Models Ltd.

Museum panel – Sir Galahad's Visionne of ye San Grail

This was the panel, made in 1928 to illustrate, for his book, the various steps and processes involved in making a stained glass window. It is labelled "Presented by the artist, July 1940", presumably when Twining left Northampton for Bristol. The subject is a favourite of his, tales of King Arthur and his Knights of the Round Table and especially their adventures in search of the Holy Grail. This particular scene was invented to make up the design and shows Sir Galahad kneeling before the Angel of the Holy Grail; Sir Galahad according to legend being one of only three persons to experience a vision of the Grail. These are accompanied by symbols of the particular virtues of Sir Galahad; Love of God, Faith and Purity, represented respectively by the rose, the passion flower and the lily. This symbolism is repeated

around the border, leading from the cross and chalice at the bottom to the crown of life at the top.

Twining notes in his book (p71 and p207) that his uncle (William Gilbert Jones, of Joseph Bell's) had commented on the design "that it would be better if the border were of uniform design in each of the sections". Ernest Twining agreed, so the leaves of the three flowers are intertwined into a single design; the final panel differs from the original sketch and its cartoon in this respect. [Fig c38]

Museum panel - Angel of the Holy Grail

This is unusual in that the museum have not only the finished panel but also its original sketch and the painting on which it is based. This has been described as a cartoon, but is actually a same size painting of the same subject, painted in oils on tin-foil to increase its lustre; an experiment he did not repeat. The sketch is dated 1932 but its original label "The Studio, Pike Lane, Northampton" has been altered, in Twining's hand, to read "The Studio, 1 Iddesleigh Road, Redland, Bristol 6". Clearly these items were also donated at about the time of the move to Bristol.

The subject relates to the same Arthurian legends, a single figure, with halo, chalice and angel's wings. There is considerable variation between the three images, with the final panel following the sketch in terms of the colour of the wings (blue) and light background, but having the red and purple robes of the painting. The figure in the final glass is perhaps also more masculine, with stronger chin, more prominent Adam's apple and squarer shoulders than either sketch or painting. The intended destination for the panel is unknown, but if he still had it in 1940, although the sketch is dated 1932, perhaps it was made largely for his own pleasure, like several of the locomotive and other models. [Figs. c39, c40 & c41]

St Edmund's Church, Hardingstone – St Edmund and St Dorothea

This two light window was dedicated on 20 November 1929, a bequest under the will of Mary Caroline Freeman in memory of her father John Stevens Freeman and her aunt Annie Shaw, both regular worshippers at the church who are interred there.

The two lights represent St Edmund, to whom the church is dedicated, and St Dorothea – the reason for this choice no longer being known. St Edmund holds an arrow, the weapon with which his life was taken as was customary in the depiction of martyrs, and his light is headed by his shield of arms. St Dorothea rests her hand on a sword, with which she was killed, and has at her feet the legendary fruit and roses of paradise. The arms of the See of Peterborough are at the top of the light.

Unfortunately this window has suffered in a number of ways in its 70 plus years. Comparing present day photographs with that in the 1929/30 catalogue (albeit in black and white) and with Ernest Twining's original sketch which survives, several changes are apparent. These seem to be due to different causes over the years.

Firstly some panels seem to have been broken and replaced with plain glass, with changes to the leading in some places e.g. St Dorothea's sword and the lower part of St Edmund's cloak. Secondly considerable detail has been lost in some areas although the original glass has survived, e.g. the dedication where some 97/98% has gone, and the background and border of the St Dorothea light. This has been blamed on poor workmanship by Twining but his other windows are unaffected, so inappropriate cleaning techniques seem more likely. A further possibility is the generally damp environment of the church – damage to an earlier window in the same church has been attributed to this cause. Finally the Twining window has received some poor restoration work, particularly repainting of St Dorothea's dress. This is ivory/cream in the original sketch and off white in the black and white brochure photograph of the newly installed window, but it is now crudely painted blue/green except for the lowest part, which seems unchanged. [Figs. c42, c43, c44 & c45]

St Paul's Church, Semilong -
St Catherine and St Cecilia

This two light window was erected by friends and pupils of Charlotte Elizabeth Ward, who was for 35 years principal of Somerville House School, Northampton, and died on 2 January 1927. Although a contemporary of the Hardingstone window it has suffered little damage over the years and any cleaning or restoration has been carried out sympathetically. It has had its problems however, because in the 1990s St Paul's was declared to be structurally unsound due the inadequacy of its foundations. The parish was then amalgamated with the adjacent parish of Holy Trinity, but before the church was demolished this window was removed and is now displayed in Holy Trinity church hall, Edinburgh Road, Northampton.

The saints portrayed relate to Miss Ward's particular interests, literature and music, and the St Cecilia light (patron saint of musicians) contains numerous references. Twining was not a musician, nor had any particular musical interests, but as was his custom he expended considerable effort to get details correct. His papers include numerous small drawings of musical instruments, exactly as shown in the St Cecilia panel. As well as the organ pipes beside her (an instrument she is supposed to have invented) smaller instruments appear in the border,

on her belt and on the clasp of her cloak. These include a harp, lute, violin and horn amongst others. St Catherine supports the spiked wheel by which she was martyred and carries a book symbolising literature in her other hand. [Figs. c46, c47 & c48]

The Good Shepherd and St Cecilia

These windows have not been located, but photographs of them appear in the 1929/30 Twining Models' Ecclesiastical Catalogue, whilst the first appears in Twining's book as a cartoon. The St Cecilia panel is described "as executed to private order" and is simpler than the Semilong image, without the musical symbols apart from organ pipes in the background.

The cartoon for the *Good Shepherd* shows only the central section of a tall single light – designed for a 15th century baptistry according to the brochure which shows the completed item. In *The Art and Craft of Stained Glass* Twining comments that, if designing a window for a church, or part of a church, where the architecture is 15th-century then one should design accordingly with a 15th-century canopy to the window (the canopy is the upper part of the window, above what a layman might regard as the actual picture). He includes in the book a drawing (fig8 p27) of a very similar design to that used for the *Good Shepherd* window.

Above: Ernest Twining's own photograph of the
Hardingstone window as originally installed. Twining family

Sir Galahad and the Quest for the Holy Grail

This appears as a photograph in the catalogue and as a cartoon in the book. The window returns to his Arthurian legends, with Sir Galahad on his horse with accompanying angels. This window has remained with Ernest Twining's family and is still in a private house. It is not very large, perhaps 6ft by 2ft but it is a more complex design than any of his other windows, with four figures, Sir Galahad's horse and a highly detailed canopy. [Fig c49]

St Mary's, Fawsley

Perhaps the most historically important stained glass job that Twining Models undertook was not new work but restoration of several windows for the Knightley family at this church close to the family seat at Fawsley. St Mary's windows contain several 16th– and 17th–century roundels depicting both scriptural subjects and heraldic achievements of the Knightley family. Twining's reorganised these in their appropriate genealogical sequence and releaded and replaced the windows – the only stained glass job which Harry Clifton remembered being done at Pike Lane. (10) [Fig c50]

Roman Catholic Church of St Francis de Sales, Wolverton – WW II memorial windows.

These four windows, placed high in the east wall of the church, were installed early in 1948, and dedicated on 2 May in memory of three servicemen of the parish who died in the war. The choice of St George, St Francis and St Bernard reflects their names; Sergeant-Navigator George Sigwart, Flying Officer Francis Morris and Seaman Bernard Hobin respectively.

Twining at this point had not produced any stained glass for some years, but his second wife was a Catholic with family connections in Wolverton. After the war Joseph Bell and Son (by now the property of Arnold Robinson) would have had much restoration and replacement work in hand at the same time as Ernest Twining found himself without a job at the Bristol Aircraft Company (he would have been 70 when the war ended); so his stained glass skills would have been valuable to them. Geoffrey Robinson, who later took over the company on his father's death, believed Ernest Twining worked with them from perhaps 1946 to 1949, and undertook his own

commissions in their workshop, whilst helping with their work. This would seem to be one of those commissions.

The four windows certainly make an impressive effect above the altar in this relatively small church; its layout and hemmed-in location would have made taller windows impossible. They represent, from left to right, St George, Christ and Mary, with St Francis and St Bernard together in the fourth window. Close examination is impossible without scaffolding but all seem in excellent condition, having recently been properly cleaned by an artist working elsewhere in the church. [Figs. c51 & c52]

Twining used this job to illustrate a *How to Make Stained and Painted Glass* article in the May and June 1949 editions of *Practical Mechanics*. Other illustrations were taken from his book, but figs. 5 and 6 of the article are portions of a window, or windows, which are not otherwise known – another little mystery!

Summary and significance

There is no doubting the attractive and handsome appearance of Twining's windows; the set of four in St Francis de Sales, Wolverton, being particularly striking. All are colourful and detailed, and present their subjects well, backed up like all his work by significant research into relevant historical or fictional background, and include appropriate specific items and details. The identified windows or panels (of which the Hardingstone and Semilong windows are each of two lights) however do not represent a large amount of work in this field, but it was of course just a sideline, a personal interest of Ernest Twining's, exploited for his own and his company's benefit.

It seems clear however that Ernest Twining's greatest contribution to the art and craft of stained glass was his book of that name. Its importance is in its gathering together of all the practical aspects of the trade and explaining them in useful detail for a potential craftsman in the field. This of course is something he did in many different areas: model aircraft before WWI and model railways in the 1930s for example. In this case the significance was that his work was sufficiently comprehensive that no one else felt the need to revisit it for many years. Twining's book therefore continued to be cited as a source of information for practical glass making and was partially reprinted after 50 years.

1. *Journal of the British Society of Master Glass Painters: Volume XII No 2 p153.*
2. *Bristol Evening Press, 23rd July 1935.*
3. *Western Daily Press, 15th March 1944.*
4. *"The Art and Craft of Stained Glass": p xvi.*
5. *"The Art and Craft of Stained Glass": p12.*
6. *"The Art and Craft of Stained Glass: p13.*
7. *Northampton Herald: 7th September 1928.*
8. *Bell, Reginald: BSMGP Journal, Volume III No1 p43-4.*
9. *Knowles, JA: Journal of the Society of Glass Technology, Volume XII No 47 September 1928.*
10. *"Northampton County Magazine", September 1930.*

Opposite page: Cartoon for *The Good Shepherd*, from *The Art and Craft of Stained Glass*.

ERNEST TWINING: AN APPRECIATION

$\mathcal{S}$everal photographs of Ernest Twining exist – some reproduced in this book. Most are from the middle period of his life and confirm the much later recollections of a youthful visitor to the Twining Aeroplane Company at Hanwell " . . of average build, and height average or slightly above, hair fairish rather than dark, with a generally thoughtful or studious appearance", and usually smoking a pipe, although this is less apparent in the photographs.

He was unfailingly courteous and considerate – reflected in his cordial relations over many years with three proverbial "firebrands", F.J. Camm, Henry Greenly and W.J. Bassett-Lowke – but also with Percival Marshall, Alfred Rosling Bennett, Trevor Guest and C. Hamilton Ellis. Some of his workmen may have found him difficult to work for, but he no doubt expected the same dedication and meticulous standards in others that he worked to himself. His gentle nature however clearly helped him to get on well with women, notably the wives of his staff and later his grand-daughters. Like many people who are shy with adults, he also seems to have got on well with younger people: stepson Cuthbert Davies, the young visitor to Hanwell, encouraging Harry Clifton into a model-making career, helping the youthful founders of the Northampton Model Aero Club, encouraging Harry Clifton's young son to sit in his office and read *Model Engineer,* and after WWII with his second wife's niece.

This same reserved, retiring side of his nature had however the disadvantage of allowing him to be overshadowed by more assertive colleagues and contemporaries, so that his part of any sort of collaboration or co-operation with Henry Greenly or with W.J. Bassett-Lowke's company has long been overlooked. Similarly his solitary inclination and preference for working alone led some of his workers to regard him as standoffish, whereas his family were accustomed to his "studio" or workshop being "out of bounds" with an unwritten "do not disturb".

He seems to have developed in middle age, if not before, a serious interest in religion, which first became apparent in his stained glass and associated paintings from the 1920s. Numerous religious drawings and several paintings survive with his family and at least three in churches or religious foundations – one was at the time compared favourably with the work of Holman Hunt. Whether his increasing religious interest was in any way influenced by the tragically early death of his stepson Cuthbert Davies, who was clearly also a close friend, it would no doubt be reinforced by the slow and painful death of his first wife Mary. His subsequent marriage to a lady who was herself a Roman Catholic presumably made the final step of his own conversion almost inevitable.

Technically he showed considerable curiosity in all manner of things (for example astronomy) and interest in new developments such as gas turbines. He was certainly receptive to some new ideas, for example fitting roller bearings to all axles of his final 15in gauge design just as our full size railways were making the same step; but he avoided other innovations he was clearly aware of, for example not brazing small locomotive boilers or using modern designs in his stained glass windows or panels. However he was not short of creative initiative or imagination, shown clearly in his early views on the potential of heavier than air aircraft and subsequently of helicopters.

He also showed what is perhaps another characteristic of many shy or reserved people in that they may be overlooked and have their ideas or the credit for their work stolen but they are ultimately both determined and independent. Once Ernest Twining had completed his apprenticeship and early years gaining experience with various telephone companies, he never subsequently worked directly for anyone else except for his WWII period with the Bristol Aeroplane Company. Apart from this he was running his own companies, Twining Aeroplane Company or Twining Models Limited, or what would now be called a self employed contractor, e.g. preparing drawings for Rosling Bennett, early architectural models for Bassett-Lowke, or helping Bells of Bristol with their post WWII boom in demand for stained glass work.

He was also sufficiently independent and self sufficient as to be prepared to undertake considerable research for his projects. In the workshop this included for example techniques for mass producing ship models, various aspects of stained glass work and of course his very significant pioneering work on both model aircraft and screw propellers. Largely documentary studies were the uncovering of technical details of numerous early locomotives, from Newcastle & Carlisle's *Comet* to the slightly later Cramptons; and on ships from the Saxon period right up to the early 20th century. His work on locomotive valve gears also deserves to be much better known.

His designs for modellers and other hobbyists were intended to be as practical, reliable and straightforward to make as he could arrange – for example, his efforts to clarify many areas of stained glass window design and production, his furniture designs, and his small steam locomotives. However he himself was a skilled, careful and meticulous worker, paying immense attention to detail; there are of course many examples but those which come immediately to mind are his *Hirondell*e model; his paintings especially of technical subjects and flowers; his two-masted schooner design and his rebuilding of French prisoner of war models. He was also highly organised and systematic in all his activities, for example carefully filing source material for potential projects, and attempting to get established a standard notation for aircraft types akin to the Whyte system for steam locomotives – he actually proposed a classification of types of models, but this proved even less popular!

Clearly a man of many parts, and of many talents, he was proficient with the tools and the workshops of a joiner, glass worker or metal worker. He was equally versatile and adaptable with drawing board or artist's palette, and readily prepared to transfer ideas from one field to another. For example he used his electrical training and skills to build one of the very first OO gauge model locos, routinely used his artistic talents to illustrate proposed models or designs, and adapted the skills of his Twining Models' staff to make first of all telescopes and later stained glass windows.

He was prolific too with both camera and pencil. Papers surviving with his family are undoubtedly only a small fraction of his work but contain dozens of small photographs, e.g. of windmills and of trees, apparently retained (perhaps taken) as potential information for future models or paintings, and hundreds of pencil sketches. These clearly used whatever came to hand when he had an idea, from notepaper with the letterhead of his apprenticeship company through to scrap copies of Bristol Aeroplane Company drawings. Most of us doodle on scraps of paper but Twining did something much more positive, some sketches deserve to be framed in their own right.

Some people may ultimately choose to remember Ernest Twining for the output of his model company, some 200 items whilst he was in charge. Perhaps half or two thirds of these were glass case models of locomotives, vehicles or other technical equipment and most of these probably survive even if they have not been traced. It is however important to summarise the whole of his large and diverse output.

He personally made at least six large locomotive models, ranging from a gauge one model of a GWR single driver up to two very much larger specimens: Midland Railway 0-4-4T No 1830 for 7 ^{1}/4in gauge and his 1in/1ft GWR *Hirondelle*. All except the last were working models. Apart from his 15in gauge and above locomotive schemes, of which there were at least six, although only the "scale" 4-6-0/4-6-2 and "narrow gauge" 2-4-2 were built, he also designed for *Model Engineer* or *Practical Mechanics*, at least six miniature steam locomotives, seven ship models (steam, electric and sail) and five model aircraft. His pioneering aircraft work included numerous models, at least six of which were described in print, and led to five full size craft – assuming the final two-seater, powered machine, was not actually built. How many pictures he painted is completely unknown, but between 40 and 50 are believed to survive, covering landscapes, ships, locomotives, aircraft and religious subjects. Many are with his family but others in museums and churches, and with private collectors. During his lifetime they were hung in numerous exhibitions, including the Royal Academy in 1906. Similarly 12 stained glass window lights or panels have been located, made largely by himself but probably with some input from Twining Models' craftsmen. A personal sideline was the making of furniture, some highly carved and ornamented, of which several specimens remain in the family and others may have been described in now defunct periodicals.

Finally he wrote, or co-authored, three substantial books, two very detailed booklets, and numerous articles for at least ten magazines between 1906 and his death 50 years later. *Art in Advertising* reflected his own current practice, designing advertising material for local Northampton companies. Best known are the range of catalogue covers he did for Bassett-Lowke; mostly in the 1920s but in later years too, because one signed "EWT" includes a *Duchess* Pacific in the British Railways green livery that was only applied to this class from 1951. His photography was not just for his own amusement either, it seems likely that most early pictures in the Twining Models' albums were taken by Ernest Twining himself or by Gilbert, whilst several pre–WWI articles in *Model Engineer* contain his photographs, as do early Bassett-Lowke catalogues.

Any examination of Ernest Twining's overall work reveals four themes or principles underlying much of what he did, or at least how he presented it, even in such apparently different fields. These are: encouraging others to take up that particular hobby, field of work or design principle; the idea of basic practicality, providing sound practical advice based on his own experience or research together with practical designs and solutions; striving to achieve realism in all forms of art or of modelling; and lastly the related but not always compatible issue of obtaining the highest possible degree of accuracy.

There are numerous examples of each of these throughout both Twining's own work and that of his companies. For example the idea of encouraging new workers into the field is a stated objective of *The Art and Craft of Stained Glass*, specifically to show how a craftsman from one part of the industry might become conversant with all the other steps and thus become a stained glass artist. As a more specific example consider the case of Harry Clifton, who joined Twining more or less straight from school, was sufficiently encouraged in the model making industry that he became a director of Twining Models Ltd in his early 20s and eventually took over the company. Other examples concern the model aircraft field; helping to establish the Northampton Model Aero Club, and perhaps most important of all, the effect of his early model aircraft experiments and articles on Sidney Camm and others. After all if Camm had not first developed an interest in aviation and then decided upon it as a career we would never have had the Hawker Hurricane.

In terms of practicality, *The Art and Craft of Stained Glass* is again relevant, because its greatest value proved to be the gathering together of all the practical aspects of the craft so comprehensively that this did not need to be done again for over 50 years. A different case is that of Twining's model aircraft, developed by his experiments into robust, practical and successful competition craft. In a different field, the methods he described for baseboard construction for model railways, based on the experience of many Twining Models' dioramas, are also robust, eminently practical, and remarkably similar to designs in use 80 years later. Finally we can return to the last large scale locomotive design, 2-4-2 *Katie* of 1951, simple but elegant, robust yet easy to maintain and operate, i.e. practical.

Achievement of the highest possible degree of realism, consistent with the type of models and the modelling methods available, Twining thought was essential in any working model, railway, ship or other. This extended to the architectural models and landscape dioramas made by his company – appropriate layout of the whole model, arrangements for viewing and level of detail in terms of, for example, figures, cars, trees and other surrounding features. He clearly also felt the need for a high degree of realism in many of his paintings and went to great lengths especially in landscapes and seascapes, making considerable use of photographs of, e.g. trees and waves on which to base his work. A similar underlying principle was applied to his stained glass work – any persons depicted appear as lifelike as permitted by their role in the scene and by the medium – his horses are especially realistic.

Finally accuracy – not always compatible with achieving realistic operation in a working model – for example where absolutely scale dimensions would make something too delicate or fragile for regular use. This is not of course relevant in static or glass case models and all those made by himself or his company are supremely accurate in proportion and detail, just as he insisted was essential in any work intended to preserve for posterity the appearance of a locomotive or other machine. A similar principle applies to his paintings of technical or highly detailed subjects such as locomotives, sailing ships, flowers or men in armour, everything is in its precise location and proportion. Excellent examples can be found in the locomotive paintings for Rosling Bennett's *Historic Locomotives and Moving Accidents by Steam and Rail*, and Twining's early studies of passion flowers, completely different subjects but both exquisitely detailed and coloured.

The basic philosophy behind all his work therefore, whether consciously recognised or not by later workers, is: that it is important to draw new blood and new ideas into any field, and that one can never anticipate how significant these may eventually become; that practical experience needs to be recorded and drawn upon in any new design and construction to ensure robust and reliable operation; designs of models (systems or individual items) should be realistic whether they are to operate or not, and finally where the application permits extreme accuracy this should be followed, if necessary at the expense of operability, if the object or painting is intended as a historical record.

Between 1904 and 1914 Ernest Twining changed careers three times, from electrical engineering to art and design, then to aviation and finally to model making. Perhaps in many ways he was a frustrated artist – certainly his second wife Edna thought of him as such, and on his death certificate recorded his occupation as "Artist, Retired". However he deserves to be remembered for these basic ideals in all his work, for specific examples of the work itself, such as his paintings of technical subjects and the quality of his own and his company's models, and also for the influence of some of his ideas, for example on early aviation workers such as Sidney Camm, on many aspects of railway modelling, and the long term effect of his larger locomotive designs on the policies of passenger-hauling miniature railways.

Appendix 1

Ernest Twining Chronology

Date	Event
29 March 1875	Born Ernest Walter Twining, 20 Mina Crescent, Bristol.
1880-90	Educated St Marks School and Dr Abel's Academy. Living at 19 Wood St.
1891-96	Apprenticed as electrical engineer to the Western Counties and South Wales Telephone Co.
1893-99	Studying at the Bristol Academy of Fine Art (now the Royal West of England Academy).
19 July 1898	Married – from 'Rockleigh', Daisy Road, Easton to – Mary Ethelfreda Davies (widow, 28, with son Cuthbert 10, and 3 younger daughters) of No 2, Westbourne Park, Bristol.
26 July 1900	Gilbert Ernest born – only child.
1901	District Superintendent with Glasgow Corporation Telephone Co.
16 Sept 1902	Birth of Edna Alice Lane, later EWT's second wife.
1904	Set up commercial art studio in London at Lavender Hill, SW (home and studio).
1904-08	Stepson Cuthbert Davies apprenticed to H. Greenly at Watford.
1904-06	Assisted Alfred Rosling Bennett with *Proposals for London Improvements,* then illustrated his *Historic Locomotives* book. RA 1906 Exhibition,No 1541 *Proposed New City Hall and Bridge over River Thames* by E.W. Twining.
1906-08	Moved to Alnwick (or Aldwick) Studio, Hanwell. 1907 Illustrated ARB's *Railway Magazine* article on continental Crampton locos. Probably first met Henry Greenly during this period. Began writing for *Model Engineer.*
1909	Twining Aeroplane Co, partnership with Ct Davies, workshop at 29B, Grosvenor Rd, Hanwell. *Catalogue* and *Model Aircraft* book published. Introduced to W J B-L by Percival Marshall.
1910-12	Man - carrying gliders and man - carrying powered aircraft built. Twining Aeroplane Company eventually folds-up.
1912-13	Sub-contractor to B-Lowke, initially for Blackpool model. Sub-contractor to Henry Greenly for Class 60 4-6-2.
2 Sept 1914	Stepson Cuthbert Davies killed in France.
1914-18	Models for War Department/Admiralty – training aids – ship models, training machine guns.
1915	3 $\frac{1}{2}$in gauge loco designs for *Model Engineer.*
1919	Joins Northampton Town and County Art Society. Twining Models Ltd established.
1922	*Pageant of English Naval History* produced.
1920 -30	Busy period for Twining Models – initially still in 'Studio' but also Dychurch Lane. Miscellaneous writing for *Model Engineer.*
1925	Twinning models moved to Pike Lane. Home: Duncan House, St George's Avenue, Northampton.
1928	Publishes *The Art and Craft of Stained Glass.*
1929	Substantial article on Heraldry with Dorothy Holditch.
1932	Own glass panel The Angel of the Holy Grail presented to Northampton Museum 1938.
1930s	Writing for *Practical Mechanics* and for *Hobbies.* Associated with Northants Aero Club and Northants Model Aero Club. 1931 *Art in Advertising*, also with Dorothy Holditch.
1934	*Locomotive* magazine article advocating designs for the job for pleasure lines, 20in – 22in gauge 0-4-2 and 0-6-2.
1937	Publishes *Indoor Model Railways. Who's Who in Model Engineering No 44 – Ernest Twining* in *Model Engineer* volume 77 p 610.
1938	Model of original Euston for LMS *Century of Progress.*

1939	10^1/4in gauge 4-6-0 completed for Trevor Guest.
1940	Gives up Twining Model interests and returns to Bristol (455 Fishponds Road, Later Iddesleigh Rd). Starts work with Bristol Aeroplane Co. 15in gauge version of the 0-4-2 illustrated in *Model Engineer*. Twining Models Ltd sold to E. H. Clifton.
July 1940	Glass panel *Sir Galahad and the Holy Grail* donated to Northampton Museum.
26/10/1940	Mary Twining dies.
24/5/1941	Marries Alice Edna Lane, 38, Northampton librarian.
194?	7 ^{1}/4in gauge (?) 2-4-2 idea.
1946	Retired from Bristol Aeroplane Co.
1946-9	Work for ecclesiastical glaziers, Joseph Bell of Bristol, including Wolverton Church windows.
1947-8	Designed 15in gauge 4-6-0's for Trevor Guest. Writing again for *Practical Mechanics*, for rest of his life.
1949	Major article for *Locomotive* magazine, including first reference to, and design of, his own valve gear. No 5751 completed – first Guest 4-6-0. Second loco altered to 4-6-2 during construction.
1950	No 57512, Guest 4-6-2 completed.
1951?	Narrow gauge outline 2-4-2 proposed to Guest.
1952	*Model Engineer* article on foundry work – illustrations include the cylinder design used on all five of the 15in gauge locos.
1953-4	*Model Engineer* Crampton articles (11).
2/12/54	Last *Model Engineer* article – on roller bearings – illustrations include *Katie's* front truck, a design subsequently used for *Siân* and *Tracey–Jo*.
1956(?)	*Katie* enters DZR service.
10/9/1956	Died at 1, Iddesleigh Road, Bristol.
October 1956	Last *Practical Mechanics* article – SS *Media* model.
1957	*Katie* sold to Capt. Hewitt.
1960	No 5751(4-6-0) loaned to Fairbourne Railway.
1961	No 57512 loaned to Fairbourne and named *Ernest W Twining*. No 5751 leaves at end of season.
July 1963	*Siân* delivered to Fairbourne.
1964	*Tracey-Jo* completed as a steam-outline 2-6-2.
1967	Twining Models closes down.

Appendix 2

Accessible work of Ernest Twining and Twining Models.

ITEM	LOCATION in 2003
15in gauge locomotive designs:	
Narrow gauge 2-4-2	Windmill Farm Railway, Lancashire
Siân & Katie	
'Scale' 4-6-2	
Prince William	Evesham Country Park
Ernest W. Twining	Shuzenji, Japan
10 ^{1}/4in gauge locomotive	
4-6-0 *Hampton Court*	Stapleford Miniature Railway.
Glass case models	
NER 2-Co-2 electric loco No 13	NRM, York
Metropolitan Railway Bo-Bo No 2	

Caledonian 4-6-0 (HR River class)
Newcastle & Carlisle *Comet*
South African GA class 2-6-0 +0-6-2

GER 4-6-0- (S69, later B12 class)   Glasgow Museum of Transport

GWR 4-2-2 *Hirondelle*   National Museum of Scotland, Edinburgh

Bengal Nagpur Rly coal wagon   Acocks Green Library, Birmingham
Central of Brazil Rly Dining Car

Austin Whippet tank   Imperial War Museum
Mark V tank
Gun carrier tank
AEC Type 'B' bus (LGOC troop transport)
North Sea class dirigible airship

Rolls Royce Car   Queen Mary's Dolls House, Windsor
Sunbeam Car
Lanchester Car
Daimler Car 'Station Bus'
Mamet baby carriages
Ship model, globes, kitchen fittings etc

Architectural Models

Bournville Factory and village   Cadbury World
Hypothetical Factory   Northampton Central Museum

Paintings

Aeronautical, pioneer aviators   Aviator Hotel, Sywell, Northampton
1935 scene

Religious subject   Hartwell Church, Northampton

Locomotives, four originals for   NRM, York
Rosling Bennett 1906 book

Stained Glass windows or panels

St Edmund and St Dorothea   Hardingstone Church, Northampton

St Catherine and St Cecilia   Holy Trinity Church Hall,
                                                     Northampton

Four WWII Memorial Windows   St Francis de Sales, R. C. Church,
                                                     Wolverton, Milton Keynes.

Two panels   Northampton Central Museum

Aircraft and Model Aircraft

None of his flying models or man - carrying aircraft is known to have survived.

Please note some of these items are not currently on display, and may be viewed only by prior arrangement. These include *Hirondelle*, the paintings in NRM archives, and all the items in the Northampton Museum.

Appendix 3

Models made by Ernest Twining and by Twining Models Ltd whilst he was in charge of the company. Except for the locomotives made for Hawthorn Leslie only one-off items are included. Items are in approximate chronological order, with actual dates where these are known or can be estimated. Information on the whereabouts of these or any further models would be much appreciated by the author and publishers.

Model	Date	Customer	2003 Location
1in scale freelance 4-4-0	1906	E.W. Twining	Not known
Blackpool Seafront	1912	Blackpool Corporation	Not known
Druid Circle (Cornwall)	Early?	Not known	Not known
1/4in scale house with garden railway	Not known	Bassett-Lowke Ltd	Not known
Austin Factory, 16ft/1in	1912/13	Austin Motor Co.	Not known
Immingham Docks 33ft/1in	1912	Great Central Railway	Not known
Rudge-Whitworth Cycle Factory	1912/13	Rudge-Whitworth Company	Not known
NCR Factory, Dayton, Ohio, USA	N/k	National Cash Register Co.	Not known
Mount Austin rubber plantation, Jahore, India	N/k	Not known	Not known
Port Sunlight, first model, 32ft/1in	1913	Lever Brothers	Not known
Working electric crane	July 1914	Shrewsbury School	Not known
Model gas retort	N/k	Not known	Not known
Pullar's Dye Works (Perth)	1914	Pullar's	Not known
Port Sunlight, second model, 60ft/1in	1913/14	Lever Brothers	Not known
Midland Railway 2 Sept.1913 accident at Mallerstang	1913	Board of Trade Inquiry	Not known
Panels of Knots	Early?	Bassett-Lowke	Not known
Daimler Factory and airfield	Not known	Daimler Company	Not known
BSA Works, Sparkbrook	N/k	BSA Company	Not known
7 1/4in gauge Midland Railway 0-4-4T No1830	1915	Private customer	Private collector in the Midlands
3 1/2in gauge GWR 4-4-0 *Gooch* No 8	1915	E.W. Twining	Not known

The Gramophone Co.'s factory, Hayes	1919/20	The Gramophone Company (HMV)	Not known
Trueform Factory	1919/20	Trueform Boot Co.	Not known
Hopkinson's Factory, Huddersfield	1919/20	J. Hopkinson and Company	Not known
Cardiff Docks	1920	GWR	Not known
Newport Docks	1920	GWR	Not known
Broughton Hall, Staffs	1920?	Not known	Not known
Boots' Factory, Nottingham	1922	Boots' Pure Drug Company	Not known
Cadbury Works and Bournville Village	1920	Cadbury Company	*Cadbury World*
9 cylinder aircraft radial engine	1919/20	Vickers Ltd	Not known
16th Century Ketch *Nonesuch,* $^1/2$in/1ft	1921	Hudson's Bay Company	Company H/Q, Winnipeg
Newcastle and Carlisle Railway 0-4-0 *Comet* (3 copies)	1920	Hawthorn Leslie	NRM York (1 copy) Proposed Tyneside Museum (2 copies)
Caledonian Railway (ex Highland) River class 4-6-0 (3 copies)	1920	Hawthorn Leslie	NRM York (1 copy) Tyneside Museum (1) Not known (1)
Hopkins portable road bridge	1920/21	E.C. & J Keay Ltd Co.	Not known
South African Railways *GA* class 2-6-0+0-6-2 Garratt	1921	Beyer Peacock	National Railway Museum, York
Bengal Nagpur *KG* class coal wagon	1920	Midland Railway Carriage and Wagon Co	Acocks Green Library, Birmingham
Great Eastern Railway *S69* class 4-6-0	1921	Wm Beardsmore and Co.	Glasgow Museum of Transport
Lancashire & Yorkshire Railway 0-6-0 No1249	1921	LYR	Not known
Ship section showing flue layout	1920	W.H. Allen, Son & Co., Bedford	Not known
Ship section showing furnace air supply layout	1920	As above	Not known
As above, but for a different type of ship	1920	As above	Not known
Handley Page biplanes,	1920?	Handley Page	Not known

types O/400 and V/1500		Aeroplane Co.	
Durban (SA) Town and Harbour	1922	Town Corporation	Not known
North Eastern Railway 2-Co-2 loco No 13	1922	NER	NRM, York
Blackpool South Shore Open Air Baths	1923	Town Corporation	Blackpool Civic Society
Metropolitan Railway Bo-Bo electric No 2	1923	Metropolitan Railway	NRM, York
Three different stationary boilers	1920	Duncan, Stratton & Co., Bombay	Not known
Domestic hot water schematic	1921?	Not known	Not known
Sectioned model of locomotive superheater	Not known	Not known	Not known
W.D. 3 ton lorry	1920?	Daimler Co.	IWM?
London Bus, *Type A* (^{1}/5th full size)	1920/1	London General Omnibus Co.	Not known
London Bus, *Type K*	1920/1	LGOC	Not known
WWI Ambulance	1920/1	Daimler Co.	Imperial War Museum?
Daimler built aircraft, types BE 12 and RE 8	1919/20	Daimler Co.	Not known
Mark IV Tank	1919/20	Not known	IWM
Engine and transmission of Mark IV Tank	1919/20	Not known	Imperial War Museum
London Bus, *Type B Warbus*	1922	LGOC	IWM
Oil-well boring plant	N/k	Oilwell Supply Co.	Not known
Model Biplane for Wind Tunnel trials	1919/20	Not known	Not known
28 gun frigate, ^{1}/2in/1ft	1923	Not known	Not known
Dining Car for Central of Brazil Railway	1922/4	Metropolitan-Cammell	Acocks Green Library, Birmingham
2-Co-Co-2 electric loco No 8000, for Japan	1924	North British & English Electric	Not known
SAR class *FC Modified Fairlie* (2-6-2+2-6-2)	1924	North British Locomotive Co.	Not known
Grain Elevator	Not known	Henry Simon (Manchester)	Not known

Colliery Winding Equipment	Not known	Fraser and Chalmers (Erith)	Not known
Cement Making Plant	1922	Ernest Newall	Not known
Whiskey Distillery	1925	Jamieson's of Dublin	Not known
Paddle Steamer *Westward Ho*	1925	P&A Campbell (Bristol Channel)	Not known
Unspecified model for Rhodesian Railways	Not known	Rhodesian Railways	Not known
Intercepting Valve Schematic	Not known	Unspecified Argentinean Rly	Not known
Yarrow Water Tube Boiler	1922	Yarrow and Co. Ltd	Not known
fullsize locomotive superheater &c	1922	Marine and Loco. Superheater Ltd	Not known
Fairfield Yard Shipyard Gantry	1922	Redpath Brown and Co. Ltd	Not known
Whippet Tank	1922	IWM	Imperial War Museum
Sectioned Mark V Tank	1922	Daimler Co.	IWM
North Sea class Airship, 1/50th scale	1920/1	Not known	IWM
3 1/2in gauge GWR *Gooch* to 1915 design	1922	Indian Customer	Not known
6 in gun-carrying tank	1923	IMW	Imperial War Museum
Steam working model of Grab Crane	1923	Priestman Bros. (Hull)	Not known
Leyland Truck with oil tank	Not known	Shell Oil Co.	Not known
Rolls Royce 40hp Laundalette, 1in to 1ft	1923/4	Rolls Royce Co.	Queen Mary's Dolls' House, Windsor Castle
24hp Sunbeam Car	1923/4	Sunbeam Motors	As above
Lanchester Saloon Car	1923/4	Lanchester Co.	As above
Station Bus (Estate Car)	1923/4	Daimler Co.	As above
Model ship, globes and other items	1923/4	Twining Models Ltd	As above
Pair of Baby Carriages	1923/4	Mamet Co.	As above
Hypothetical Factory	1923	Twining Models Ltd	Northampton Museum

Locomotive Valve Gears	1920s?	GWR Enginemans M.I.C.	Not known
Stone Crushing Machinery	1920s?	John Marsden & Co., Leeds	Not known
Humber Car model 15.9 1 1/4in to 1ft	1923	Not known	Private collector in the East Midlands
8 cylinder Marine Diesel Engine	1924	North Eastern Marine Engineering	Not known
Salt Union Works, Winsford, Cheshire	1924	Salt Union Group	Not known
Standard gauge industrial Garratt 0-4-0+0-4-0	1924/5	Vivian & Sons (Hafod Copper Works)	In store for S. Wales Museum of Science and Industry
Exide Factory	1925	Chloride Electrical Storage Co.	Not known
Great Northern Railway Stirling 7ft 2-2-2	Not known	Private customer	Private collector
Swansea Docks	1925	GWR	Not known
GWR 7ft Gauge 4-2-2 *Hirondelle*	1907/25?	E.W. Twining	Scottish National Museum, Edinburgh
O gauge working Garratt (2-8-0+0-8-2)	1925	G.P. Keen	Believed to be in a French Museum
Indian Railways Class XC, Standard 4-6-2	1930	East Indian Rly, Chaudausi Training School	Not known
Buenos Aires Great Southern Railway Class 12E 4-6-2	1930	Vulcan Foundry	Not known
Killingworth Colliery Locomotive	1926	Science Museum	Believed <u>not</u> to be the model in NRM, York
Ford Factory at Dagenham	1929	Ford Motor Co.	Not known
Dundee wharf and Limehouse	Not known	Dundee, Perth and London Shipping	Not known
Sectioned 1/10th scale *Junkers Monoplane* metal wing	1931	Ford Motor Co., Aviation Division	Not known
Wickstead Memorial Pillar	Not known	Gotch and Saunders	Not known

Golden Acre Park Diorama	1934/5	F. Thompson Esq. Leeds	Not known
$1/6$th scale Lighthouse for Golden Acre Park	1935	As above	Not known
$1/2$ size railway signals for Golden Acre Park	1935	As above	Not known
Dining Car for Golden Acre Park Railway	Not known	As above	Not known
Paper making machinery	Not known	Walmsbury's (Bury) Ltd	Science Museum?
Tientsin Pukow Railway 4-6-2 to Alco design (Chinese National SL14)	1934	North British Locomotive Co.	Not known
Ship's turbine, gearbox and propeller	Not known	Parsons Marine Steam Turbine Co.	Not known
Proposed house at Harrogate	Not known	P.B. Armistead	Not known
Proposed Hotel	Not known	Northampton Brewery	Not known
2 $1/2$in gauge working model 4-6-0 Windsor Castle	1934/5	E.W. Twining & Practical Mechanics	Not known
Supermarine Southampton flying boat	Not known	Supermarine Co.	Not known
Ruston Bucyrus Excavator	1932?	Ruston Co.	Not known
Locomotive Vacuum Brake Schematic	1932?	Engineman's MIC, GWR, Bristol	Not known
French Line Historic Ships	1932?	French Line	Not known
Modern Cowhouse	N/k	Not known	Not known
Concrete City of the Future	1932/3	Cement & Concrete Association	Not known
Automatic Winding Shaft	Not known	Not known	Not known
SAR signalling demonstration layout	Not known	South African High Commission	Not known
Complete 0-8-0 valve gear model	Not known	Sudan Government Railways	Not known
Royal United Hospital, Bath	1935	Alfred J. Taylor (Architects)	Not Known
GKN Cardiff Works	1935?	Guest, Keen and Nettlefolds Ltd	Not Known

Proposed Hotel	1935	F. Thompson Esq.	Not known
Indoor Welfare Centre	Not known	J. Templeton (Glasgow)	Not known
Mechanical golf-swing figure	Not known	D.S. Thyne (Edinburgh)	Not Known
Bournemouth, with back scene and lighting	1934	Town Corporation	Not known
Sectioned 1 ^{1}/2in to 1ft *Rocket* as built	1937	Royal Scottish Museum	Scottish National Museum
King George V 4-6-0	1937	GWR	Not known
Panoramic Naval Review	1937	UK Board of Trade	Not known
Butterley Ironworks, By-products plant	1938	Butterley Ironworks	Not known
Euston in 1838	1938	LMS Railway	Not known
10 ^{1}/4in gauge 4-6-0	1939	Trevor Guest	Stapleford Miniature Railway

The following models were supplied by Bassett-Lowke during and slightly after the period in which, according to Janet Bassett-Lowke, Twining Models Ltd were making almost all their glass-case, architectural and one - off working models; except for ships. These items have not been confirmed as having been made either by Twining Models or by Bassett-Lowke, although Harry Clifton's son believed that his father had worked on several of them, including the train ferry and canal models.

Model	Date	Customer	2003 Location
^{1}/2in to 1ft Burma Railway 4-6-0	1922	Burma Railway Locomotive Dept.	Not known
1/4in to 1ft scale section of London Underground	1924	London Underground	Not known
1in to 1ft 2-8-2 for Nigerian Railways	1925	Not known	Not known
King Arthur 4-6-0 for Southern Railway	1925	Not known	Not known
Harwich-Zeebrugge Train Ferry Dock	1925	LNER	Not known
^{1}/2in to 1ft 4P 4-4-0	1926	LMS	Not known
^{3}/4in to 1ft *Royal Scot*	1928	LMS	NRM?
Working Model of a Train Ferry Dock	1930	LNER	Not known
1in to 1ft scale Pullman Car *Hazel*	1932	Metropolitan Cammell	Acocks Green Library, Birmingham
Unspecified aircraft	1933	Imperial Airways	Not known
1 ^{1}/2in to 1ft scale	1933	Robert Stephenson	Not known

Locomotion		& Hawthorns	
¹/4in to 1ft working model of a flight of canal locks	1934	Grand Union Canal Company	Not known
Working model of coal mine surface machinery	1938	Mining Association	Not known

Appendix 4

Ernest Twining bibliography.

The following listing is all material identified during the preparation of this book. It seems certain that there are other magazine articles, especially from the 1905 to 1912 period, which have not been located and which may subsequently come to light.

4.1 Books, booklets and contributions to other works.

1904	*Proposals for London Improvements.* Illustrations by Ernest Twining, written by Alfred Rosling Bennett. Pub: author.
1906	*Historic Locomotives and Moving Accidents by Steam and Rail.* Illustrations by Ernest Twining, written by Alfred Rosling Bennett. Pub: Cassell.
1909	*Model Aeroplanes; how to build and fly them.* Text and illustrations by Ernst Twining. Pub: Percival Marshall
1910	*Model Gliders; how to make and fly them.* Text and illustrations by Ernest Twining.
1912	Chapter on Model Aircraft in *The Boys Book of Aeroplanes.* Authors: Hubbard and Turner. Pub: Grant Richards.
1920	A Pageant of English Naval History. Text and illustrations by Ernest Twining. Ed: Bassett-Lowke Ltd.
1928	*The Art and Craft of Stained Glass.* Text and most illustrations by Ernest Twining. Pub: Pitman. (Partially reprinted in 1978 as *Painting and Firing Stained Glass).*
1929	Chapter on Heraldry and a glossary of Heraldic Terms. Jointly with D.E.M. Holditch, from p457 of *Painting and Decorating.* Pub: C.H.Eaton. Pub: Pitman.
1931	*Art in Advertising.* Written jointly with Dorothy M.E.Holditch. Pub: Pitman.
1937	*Indoor Model Railways.* Written and illustrated by Ernest Twining. Pub: Newnes
1954	*How to read workshop drawings.* Revision by Ernest Twining of an earlier work by W. Longland

4.2 Patents

1905	No 7203	With A. Rosling Bennett *Lining Railway Tunnels.* Application 5 May 1905, accepted 6 July 1905.

1910	No 2094	*Screw Propellers.* Application 27 January 1910, accepted 22 July 1910.
1907	No 3590	) These five applications were made but subsequently
1909	No 8407	) abandoned, all for matters relating to railways
1910	No 2095	) or aviation
1910	No 17638	)
1912	No 22235	)

4.3 Magazine articles on Railways or Model Railways

MODEL ENGINEER

Vol.13 Jul – Dec 1905	Picturesqueness in Model Railways (3pts). pp202, 249, 298.
Vol.14 Jan – Jun 1906	Model Railway Tunnels. p109
Vol.15 Jul – Dec 1906	Letter from Twining re. proposed SMEE track. p426. Review of *Historic Locomotives* book. p532
Vol.16 Jan – Jun 1907	Letter suggesting companion volume on railway carriages.
Vol.17 Jul – Dec 1907	Letter from Twining on model railway track. p354 Engineering Works and accessories for model railways. (17 parts) pp391, 476, 492, 551, 592, 616.
Vol.18 Jan – Jun 1908	Engineering Works cont. pp86, 106, 160, 251, 464, 505.
Vol.19 Jul – Dec 1908	Engineering Works cont. pp155, 208, 244, 300, 446.
Vol.29 Jul – Dec 1913	Article on Bassett-Lowke Class 60 *Gigantic*, designed by Twining and with signed drawing. p326
Vol.31 Jul – Dec 1914	Trials of the Class 60 at *Staughton Manor* p241. Letter from Twining on broad gauge locos. p578
Vol. 32 Jan Jun 1915	A $^3/_4$in scale GWR 4-4-0 No 8 *Gooch.* (5 parts) pp198, 221, 243, 263, 286.
Vol.33 Jul – Dec 1915	A Maximum loading gauge $^3/_4$ in scale locomotive. (3 parts) pp9, 31, 55.
Vol. 47 Jul – Dec 1922	Letter from Twining re solid or liquid firing for locos. p 283.
Vol.54 Jun – Dec 1925	p680 model of same and letter.
Vol. 61 Jul – Dec 1929	Letter about building a Twining locomotive. p283
12 October 1939	Large Scale Locomotives, p438. Reaction to Twining's ideas as expressed in the *Northampton Independent* of 25 August 1939.
21 December 1939	Large Scale Locomotives, p688 Twining's reply.
12 March 1953	First part of British Crampton Locomotives, p332 (11 parts) subsequent parts: 26 March p383, 23 April p496, 21 May p619, 30 July p133, 22 Oct. p478, 5 Nov. p550, 24 Dec. p738, 14 Jan 1954 p38, 11 Feb p149, 25 March p322.
2 December 1954	Roller bearings for narrow gauge locomotives and rolling stock. p644

PRACTICAL MECHANICS

| October 1933 p31 | $^1/_2$in scale GWR Castle Class |

January 1934 p185	4 $^3/_4$ in gauge Garden Railway locomotive (4 parts) Also: Feb.1934 p 229, March p273, Jan.1935 p189.
March 1935 p273	Permanent Way for 4 3/4 in gauge. (for the above).
May. 1934 p379	Modelling Historic Locomotives. (7 parts) Subsequently: June 1934 p427, July p473, Aug. p519, Sept. p569, Oct. p29, Nov. p75.
April 1935 p321	Model electric railway automatic control and signalling system. (2 parts) also May 1935 p379.
June 1935 p427	Early OO gauge loco design, but adapted to 4-6-2.
August 1935 p519	Model Railway Construction for beginners. Also Oct. p51
November 1935 p101	A model Electric Garden Railway (2 parts, mains voltage 4 $^3/_4$in gauge). Also December p190
March 1936 p351	Adapting the Twin-Train table railway. (5 parts). Subsequently April p411, May p485, July p597, November p105.
December 1936 p144	An OO gauge railway station.
January 1937 p229	A Model GWR broad gauge loco. (6 parts, steam in 3 gauges). Subsequently: February p281, May p 456, June p516, November p115, September 1939 p642.
April 1937 p405	A new Twin-Train railway unit. (Adapting a Trix motor into an electric train motorcar).
February 1938 p271	Milestones in the progress of British Steam. Written by W.J. Bassett-Lowke, illustrated by Ernest Twining, (5 parts). Subsequently: March p335, April p403, May p441, July p541.
January 1950 p130	Locomotives for narrow gauge railways. (Re-use of earlier *Locomotive* and *Model Engineer* material).
October 1951 p22	A Passenger Hauling Model loco. (3 $^1/_2$in gauge 0-6-0) Subsequently: Nov.p55 and Dec.p89.
February 1952 p166	A miniature scale indoor railway. Also March p207
January 1953 p155	Model locomotive boiler mountings. Written as *Engineer*). Also February 1953 p 199.
May 1955 p341	Outdoor O gauge model railways. Also June p391
August 1955 p483	A gauge O steam loco. (For the above, also September p544).
November 1955 p95	O gauge coaches and rolling stock. (For the same railway).
HOBBIES magazine	
30 January to 26 March1932 and 9 April to 28 May 1932	Model Railways and how to make them, which evolved into Realistic Model Locomotives and how to make them. 17 parts consecutively, in weekly issues No 1893 to 1901 and 1903 to1910.
RAILWAY MAGAZINE	
April 1907 p303	Crampton Locomotives on the Continent. Written by Alfred Rosling Bennett, illustrated by Ernest Twining.

LOCOMOTIVE magazine

15 March 1934 p67	Small power locomotives for narrow gauge railways. (Twining's original scheme).
15 October 1940 p253	Locomotives for public miniature railways. DZR No 3 and better alternatives for the job.
15 November 1940 p297	Critical letter re the above from J.N. Maskelyne.
15 December 1940 p322	Supportive letter from J.W. Smith.
15 February1941 p?	Further letter from J.N. Maskelyne.
15 June 1949 p83	Locomotives for Narrow Gauge Railways. (30in gauge 2-6-2T with Twining valve gear &c).

NORTHAMPTON INDEPENDENT

25 August 1939.	Northampton engine at Dudley Zoo. Article on DZR No 3, but also spells out Twining's design philosophy as in *Locomotive* magazine.

4.4 Aviation

MODEL ENGINEER

Vol. 20 Jan – Jun 1909	My Experimental Work in connection with Flying Machines. (10 parts) pp483, 569, 581. Note on Twining Aeroplane Co. Kits & Designs. p575
Vol. 21 Jul – Dec.1909	My Experimental Work cont. p50, 101, 197, 266, 439. Letter re. Twining Model Aircraft p 210. Account of Twining Aeroplane Company's stand at the Model Engineer exhibition.
Vol. 22 Jan – Jun. 1910	My Experimental Work cont. p232
Vol. 23 Jul – Dec 1910	My Experimental Work concluded p437 Note re Twining's entry in Crystal Palace competition p323.
Vol. 24 Jan – Jun 1911	Twinings Gamage Cup Monoplane p297. Cuthbert Davies Twin Propeller Winder p375
Vol 25 Jul – Dec 1911	Account of *Model Engineer* Challenge Cup and Ernest Twining's success p68. Note about Twining's Aircraft models p95. The Screw Propeller simply explained p278. Note about Twining Co. at *Model Engineer* Exhibition p402. Note about awards in the aircraft section of the exhibition, including Twining and his company p444. Twining became an Official Observer for the Kite and Model Aeroplane Association p576.

FLIGHT magazine

19 March 1910	Review of Olympia Aircraft Exhibition, with picture of Twining Biplane p 206.
25 March 1913	The Twining Propeller p316.

CATALOGUES of the Twining Aeroplane Company

October 1909, November 1909, January 1910, May 1910, January 1913

AERO magazine

May 1909 p59	The Construction of a Chanute or modified Chanute glider. Subsequently: June p88, July p119, Dec. 1909, Jan 1910 p26

August 1909 p148   A Tailless Glider continued Sept p207

November 1909   Letter from Twining on Rotary Gliders.
p480

March 1910   Twining Co's Biplane at the Olympia Exhibition.
p177 & p206

HOBBIES magazine

11 June 1932 p286   A twin-engine racing monoplane Also 18 June p303.

6 August 1932 p479   A compressed air model aeroplane plant. Subsequently: 13 August p507,
                          20 August p529.

27 August 1932 p561   A compressed air model aeroplane. Also10 September p610.
                          17 September 1932 p648   All about model aeroplane wings.
                          Subsequently: 24 September p663, 8 October p33, 29 October p129.
                          (The August to October articles are all numbered as one series, parts I to
                          IX).

15 October 1932 p64   A steam plant for model aeroplanes. Cont: 22 October p88, 29 October
                          p111, 5 November p138, 12 November p169.

11 March 1933 p605   A 15cc two-stroke aeroplane engine. Subsequently: 18 March p634, 25
                          March p657, 1 April p?

6 May 1933 p124   Design for a primary Glider (11 Parts). Continues: 20 May p172, 27
                          May p199, 3 June p223, 10 June p246, 17 June p274, 24 June p293, 1
                          July p319, 8 July p345, 15 July p365, 22 July p393.

PRACTICAL MECHANICS

December 1933 p145   Model aircraft of the flying spar type   cont: January, 1934 p193
February 1934 p213   Power driven model aircraft cont: March p279
September 1945 p405   High flying kites.
October 1946 p6   F.J. Camm's Flash Steam Plant (for aircraft)   cont: November p 46.
March 1949 p179   Early days of model flying.
March 1950 p192   A model aircraft of the loaded elevator type cont: April p235
June 1950 p296   Helicopters and their development.
July 1950 p345   A notable model aeroplane.
July 1951 p296   Modelling Helicopters cont: August p346.

4.5 Ships and Boats

MODEL ENGINEER

Vol.43 Jul – Dec.1920 p354 A Pageant of English Naval History.

Vol.45 Jul – Dec.1921   Old Battleship Models.
p425 and p445

PRACTICAL MECHANICS

August 1935 p499   Rubber powered model boats.

February 1939 p248   A model plank built schooner yacht cont: March p320.

March 1940 p26	A model of a cargo vessel. (with E.H. Clifton, steam powered). Subsequently: May p360, July p453.
November 1954 p72	A model paddle steamer – cont: December.p121, January 1955 p161 (by *Designer*).
March 1955 p256	A 3ft model yacht cont: January 1956 p192
December 1955 p143	A sailing model of the Golden Hind cont: January 1956 p192
February 1956 p 254	Modelling a Tugboat.
October 1956 p30	Modelling Cunard's *SS Medea*.

4.6 Twining Models Ltd

MODEL ENGINEER

Vol. 26 Jan – Jun 1912	Note about the Birmingham model p460
Vol.28 Jan – June 1913	Note about Immingham Docks model p47
Vol.29 July – Dec 1913	Account of Immingham Docks model p84. Immingham model at Ghent Exhibition p403. Account of Bassett-Lowke, stand at Model Engineer Exhibition with Port Sunlight model.
Vol.31 July – Dec 1914	Note on Pullars Dye works model p393.
Vol. 44 Jan – June 1921	Presentation of Bus Models to Science Museum.
Vol. 45 July – Dec 1921	Scale models, their classification, construction and uses. pp133, 147,171.
Vol.47 July – Dec 1922	3/4 in scale GWR loco model for an Indian customer p435.
Vol.48 Jan – July 1923	Twining Models Ltd at the Model Engineer Exhibition p117.
Vol.49 July – Dec 1923	Some recent Work of Twining Models Ltd p619.
Vol.50 Jan – June 1924	Some commercial engineering models. p59. Models at the Wembley Exhibition. p650.
Vol.51 July – Dec 1924	Twining models at the Wembley Exhibition pp272, 276. Note about Twining Models brochure p277.
Vol.53 July – Dec 1925	Commercial models by Twining Models Ltd. p590.
Vol.55 July – Dec 1926	Note about Twining Valve gear models. p41.
Vol.56 Jan – June 1927	Twining Models *Killingworth* loco. p531.
Vol.62 Jan – June 1930	Sectioned locomotive by Twinings. p9.

LOCOMOTIVE magazine

14 May 1921 p126	Some interesting locomotive models.

HOBBIES magazine

19 November 1932 p?	Foundry patterns for models (6 parts). Subsequently: 26 November p223, 3 December p253, 10 December p? 7 January 1933 p391.
7 January 1932 p389	Wheels for models (11 parts). Subsequently: 14 January p412, 21 January p441, 28 January p464, 4 February p488, 11 February p512, 18 February p535, 25 February p559, 4 March p585.

PRACTICAL MECHANICS

April 1935 p329	Electric lighting for models.
August 1937 p611	A panoramic Naval Review (Twining exhibit).
December 1937 p174	Wheels for models (5 parts, by *Handyman* and *EWT*) Subsequently: January 1938 p231, February p297, May p 443, December p161.
August1938 p579	South Africa comes to Glasgow (Twining diorama), Cont: September p663.
November 1938 p88	Euston Station 100 years ago.
April 1945 p242	World of Models.
April 1952 p233	Locomotive Valve Gears Cont: May p277.
June 1954 p385	Painting Models.

TWINING MODELS, brochures and catalogues

1922	Astronomical Telescopes
1923/4	Models for Advertising (Engineering models)
1923/4	Architectural Models (Landscape or factory models)
1928/9	Stained glass and other church items
1929/30	Stained glass, new edition

BASSETT-LOWKE Catalogues

These featured the work of Twining Models Ltd for several years, including 1922, 1924 and 1930.

MODEL RAILWAY NEWS

April 1926 p99	Model Garratt locomotive. (No2491, in O gauge).

NORTHAMPTON AND COUNTY INDEPENDENT

2 November 1934	Northampton made model at Waterloo. (Twining's Bournemouth model).

NORTHAMPTON MERCURY AND HERALD

8, 14 and 15 January1937 Stronghold of Kings in turbulent days. (Account of the proposed Northampton Castle model).

4.7 Miscellaneous Subjects

PRACTICAL MECHANICS

August 1934 p527	Hints on mechanical drawing. (By *Draughtsman*).
September 1937 p669	Garden Woodwork. (By *Handyman*).
December 1938 p135, p162	An electrical game of chance. (By *Handyman*). Painting on Glass. (By *Handyman*).
November 1939 p72	A horizontal steam engine.
January 1940 p163	Boiler for the above.
May 1949 p244	Stained and painted glass windows. Cont: June p269.

Sept. Oct. 1950 p22	An astro-photographic reflector telescope.
May 1949 p244	Casting soft metals.
September 1951 p382	Telescope object glasses and eyepiece lenses.
June 1952 p298	A simple telescope. Cont: July p342.
August 1952 p379	Making a telescope eyepiece.
October 1952 p21	Lead Glazing.
November 1952 p60	A model of Trevithick's stationary engine.
January 1953 p142	Making a microscope cont: February p192
March 1953 p230,	A pantograph for copying drawings p246 Making Kaleidoscopes.
April 1954 p279	Periscopes.
May 1953 p334	Making stereoscopes.
June 1953 p379	Making a stereo magazine camera.
April 1954 p296	Polar telescopes – cont: May p352.
July 1954 p431	Making lay figures.
August 1954 p471	Soldering and brazing.
September 1954 p536	Astronomy. Cont: October p23, November p67, December p115.
January 1955 p55	Show cases for models.
November1956 p69	Obituary.

MODEL ENGINEER

23 December 1937 p610	*Whos Who in model engineering* No 44 Ernest W. Twining
July 1952 p59 & p85	Making small-scale foundry patterns
October 1956 p542	Obituary.

JOURNAL OF THE BRITISH SOCIETY OF MASTER GLASS PAINTERS

Vol.III No 1 july 1940 p43	Review of *The Art and Craft of Stained Glass*.
Vol XII No 2 p153	Obituary.

JOURNAL OF THE SOCIETY OF GLASS TECHNOLOGY.

Vol. XII No 47 p267 (September 1928)	Review of *The Art and Craft of Stained Glass*.

WOLVERTON EXPRESS

14 May 1948	Dedication of the War Memorial window in St. Francis de Sales, Wolverton.

HOBBIES magazine

June? 1932	The *Hobbies* model making lathe. (5 parts, concluding 16 July. p407 and 30 July.p467)
19 November 1932 p192	Mr E.W. Twining a brief biography.

PRACTICAL ENGINEERING

10 February 1940 p104   Drawing Office Practice. Subsequently: 17 February p145, 24 February p188, 2 March p222, 9 March p256, and 16 March p311. (The series was taken over by another author from 23 March).

WOODWORKER AND ART METALWORKER

October 1907 p8   A modern Grandfather's clock.
          p18   A coal scuttle in wrought and beaten metal

NORTHAMPTON DAILY CHRONICLE

1 December 1930   Review of Twining's painting *Come unto Me*

NORTHAMPTON DAILY ECHO

1 December 1930   Review of *Come unto Me*.

NORTHAMPTON HERALD

7 September 1928   Review of *The Art and Craft of Stained Glass*

NORTHAMPTON COUNTY MAGAZINE

September 1930   Description of Twining's restoration of the windows of St. Marys, Fawsley.

WORLD LOCOMOTIVE MODELS

Author: George Dow. Pub: Adams and Dart, 1973.   Contains descriptions of several Twining Models Ltd locomotives and their prototypes: Metropolitan Railway Bo-Bo No 2. Newcastle and Carlisle Railway *Comet*. Highland/Caledonian River class. Lancashire and Yorkshire Aspinall 0-6-0, Hafod Copper 0-4-0+0-4-0 Garratt. South African Railway *GA* class. North Eastern Railway 2-Co-2 No 13. Great Eastern Railway *S69* class 4-6-0.

Appendix 5

Models made by Twining Models (E.H. Clifton) Ltd between 1940 and the company's final closure in mid 1967. As with the models listed in Appendix 3 the author and publishers would be pleased to hear of the present locations of any of these models, and of any other models which can be positively traced to Twining Models (E.H. Clifton) Ltd.

Model	Date	Customer
Warship recognition models	1940/44?	Admiralty?
Factory mock-ups for camouflage trials	1940/43?	UK Government
Orgreave Colliery and By-product plant	1940/41	Rother Vale Collieries (United Steel Company)
Treeton Colliery	1941/2	As above

Brookhouse Colliery	1941/43	As above
Thurcroft Colliery	1941/45	As above
Redevelopment proposals for Coventry city centre	1942/3	Not known
Repairs to Bournville factory model 132 buildings repaired/replaced	1944	Cadbury Ltd
Waste treatment plant, Paliser Works	1944	Refractory Brick Co. Hartlepool
New kitchen and house interior layouts by Jane B.Drew, F.R.I.B.A	1944	British Gas Association
Proposed Hebrew University	1944	British Association for a Jewish National Home in Palestine
New house designs	1944	Not known
Experimental House	1944	D.E.E. Gibson, A.R.I.B.A
A1 House of British Steel Homes Ltd, by Frederick Gilberd A.R.I.B.A	1946	*Daily Herald, Modern Exhibition Homes 1946*
Bradford Sewage Works	1946/7	Bradford Corporation
Lotus and Delta Factory – Stafford	1947/8	Lotus Shoes
Nottingham University, 1/800 scale	1949	The university
Dockside buildings at Liverpool	1949	Bibby Line?
Mitchell Memorial Youth Club	1950s?	Not known
Down Shoes Factory	1950s?	Lotus Delta Company
Edwardian Car Model	1950s?	Not known
Unidentified Factory	1950s?	Not known
Knutsford Town Centre Development by Brian O Rorke F.R.I.B.A and W. Dobson Chapman L.R.I.B.A	1950s?	*News Chronicle*
Cotton Mill, $^1/_{10}$in to 1ft	1950s?	Stotts & Co, Oldham
Cotton Mill?	1950s?	Pine and Co.
1in scale railway carriage	1952	Metropolitan Cammell
Set of $^1/_4$ scale lawnmowers	1952	Atco Co.
Diesel Locomotive (BR No 10800)	1952	British Thomson Houston
Metal Drum making factory at Ellesmere Port	1952	Metal Containers Ltd (later Van Leer of Amsterdam)
Sheerwater Housing Estate	1952	Sir Lindsay Parkinson

Unidentified model	1952	Shell-Mex
Factory of W. Pearce & Co.	1952	W. Pearce
Pneumatic Grain Elevator	1952	Not known
Bradford Gasworks	1952	Bradford Corporation
Assorted valves	1952	J. Hopkinson, Huddersfield
Greenwich Power Station	1952	British Thomson Houston
Proposed Royal Palace for Baghdad	1952	Not known
Tyre factory model	1952	John Bull Tyres
Three historic South African locos	1952	South African Railways?
South African Railway carriages	1952	South African Railways?
Fire Engine	1952	Not known
Butter Factory (NZ)	1952	Not known
Modern Ambulance	1952	Lancashire County Council
Sewage Farm	1952	Not known
New South Wales Locomotive	1953	Not known
Two railway carriages	1953	Gloucester Railway Carriage and Wagon Co.
Owen Falls Hydro-electric Power Station (Uganda)	1953	British Thomson Houston
Cresswell Laboratory	1953	Not known
Lindley School	1953	Not known
Assorted valves and gauges	1953	J. Hopkinson & Co.
Unidentified Harbour Model	1953	Trinity House
Motor coach for Indian Govt. Railway	1953	English Electric Co.
Point of Ayr Power Station	1953	Fairclough of Wigan
Twin generator hydro power station	1953?	Not known
Locomotive Model	1954	Bengal Govt. Railway
Valves etc.	1954	J. Hopkinson & Co.
Bungalow model	1954	Mr Miller
Hydro-electric Power Station, Roxburgh, New Zealand	1954	British Thomson Houston
Fairhurst Research station	1954	Not known
Dutch Locomotive	1954	Not known
Repairs to Van Leer Ellesmere Port factory model	1954	Van Leer

Factory Model	1954	J.D. Sturge & Co, Birmingham
Loco for Peru (Andes type 2-8-0)	1954	Beyer Peacock Ltd
South African locomotive	1954	Not known
Factory repairs and alterations	1954	Marchon Products, Whitehaven
Southern United Cables	1954	Southern United, Dagenham
Factory Model?	1954	Northrop Looms, Blackburn
Railway carriages and wagons	1954	Metropolitan Cammell
Railway wagon	1954	Gloucester Railway Carriage and Wagon Co.
Iron Ore model (handling?)	1954	United Steel Co.
Model of Beyer Peacock's first loco of 1855 (GWR Std Gauge 2-2-2)	1954	Beyer Peacock Ltd
Eildon Power Station	1955/57	Not known
$3/4$in scale East African Railway locomotive (29 or 30 class)	1955	North British Locomotive Company
Repairs and alterations to Hopkinson's factory model of 1919/20	1955	J. Hopkinson & Co of Huddersfield
Extensions to chain(?) factory	1955	Reynolds Co.
Four apartment house	1955	Mr Miller
Factory model(?)	1955	Babcock and Wilcox, Renfrew
Grudie Bridge power station	1955	Not known
Castle Donington (power station?)	1955	Not known
Confectionery Factory	1955/57	Pascalls Confectionery
Newport Docks updating (made 1920)	1956	BTC, originally GWR
Aylseford Paper Mills	1956	Reeds paper
Railway luggage van	1956	Metropolitan Cammell
Paper mill extensions	1958	Reeds paper
Kariba Dam project	1958	Not known
Hinkley Point Nuclear Power Station	1958	CEGB (?)
Valves/valve models	1958	J. Hopkinson & Co
Bradford factory	1958	Richard Johnson & Nephew
Bournville modifications (originally 1920 and 1944)	1958	Cadbury Ltd
Staythorpe Power station, $1/64$ scale	1958	British Thomson

		Houston
Blakeboro Colliery	1958	National Coal Board (?)
Update to Orgreave By-products plant (originally 1941/2)	1958	United Steel Co (?)
Brookhouse By-products plant up date (1941/3)	1958	As above
Alterations to Treeton Colliery (1941/2)	1958	National Coal Board (?)
Package Boiler	1959	Babcock and Wilcox
Notting Hill Gate Station	1959	Not known
Bungalow	1959	Odhams Ltd
Nigerian Cement Works	1959	Not known
Luton Car Plant 1/500th scale	1959	Vauxhall Ltd
Assorted Valves	1959	J. Hopkinson & Co.
Seven extra ships for GWR Cardiff Docks (original model made in 1920)	1959	British Transport Commission (?)
Basildon Road Bridge	1959	Not known
Vauxhall Road Bridge	1959	Not known
Factory(?)	1959	Evans Medical Supplies, Liverpool
Two tea processing Factories for India	1961/2	Not known
Solway Chemical Plant	1961	Marchon Products, Whitehaven, Cumberland
Police Headquarters	1961	Bedford
Valves	1961	J. Hopkinson & Co.
Cabin and library interiors for *Transvaal Castle*	1961	Union Castle Line
Unspecified work	1961/3	Clarendon Laboratory
Bradford Iron Works	1962	Richard Johnson and Nephew
Ambergate Factory	1962	As above
Severn Crossing for High Tension Cables	1962	Central Electricity Authority (?)
Valves	1962	J. Hopkinson & Co.
BBC Madin (?)	1962	BBC (?)
Bus Garage at Vauxhall	1962	London Transport
Tormore Distillery factory 20ft to 1in, interior features $1/32$nd scale	1963	Scotch Whisky Distillers Association
Cosmetics Factory	1963	Avon Cosmetics
Modern Church and Hall	1963	Howitt & Partners

Index

Fig. c1 Watercolour of Caledonian Railway Connor 8ft 2-2-2 from Rosling Bennett's *Historic Locomotives and Moving Accidents by Steam and Rail.*

Fig. c2 Twining Models' Newcastle and Carlisle *Comet*
in the National Railway Museum, York. Author, courtesy NRM

Fig. c3 No 1830, Twining's 7 ^{1}/4in gauge Midland Railway Johnson 0-4-4T of 1915.
Well-detailed for a working model of the time apart from the overscale boiler.
photo – author's collection

Fig. c4 No 5751 *Prince Charles* on the Fairbourne Railway. photo – G.A. Barlow

Fig. c5 No 5751 as 4-6-2 *Sir Winston Churchill* at Blenheim Palace. photo – N.R. Knight

Fig. c6 4-6-2 No 57512 as *Ernest W Twining* at Shuzenji in Japan. photo – Hiroshi Naito

Fig. c7 2-4-2 *Katie* on the Fairbourne Railway, summer 1971. photo – N.R. Knight

Fig. c8 *Siân* on the Bure Valley Railway in 1994 waits for proper steam 2-6-4T *Wroxham Broad*, rebuilt from steam outline *Tracey-Jo*. photo - author

Fig. c9 2-4-2 *Siân* in as-built condition on the Fairbourne Railway. photo – N.R. Knight

Fig. c10 *Siân* as now running, largely restored to original external condition except for air-pump and livery. Visiting the Ravenglass and Eskdale Railway in 2001. photo – author

Fig. c11 Ernest Twining's painting, done when
he was 16 and the earliest he retained. (1891) Twining family

Fig c12 Highly
detailed drawing of a
Passion Flower from
1893.
Twining family

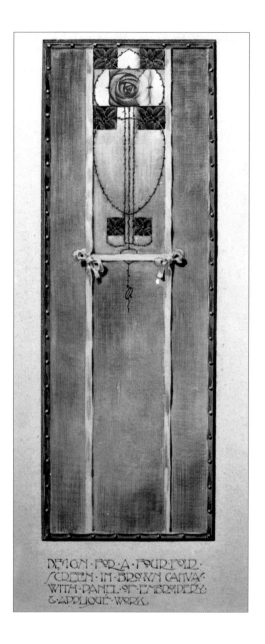

DESIGN·FOR·A·FOUR·FOLD·
SCREEN·IN·BROWN·CANVAS·
WITH·PANEL·OF·EMBROIDERY·
&·APPLIQUE·WORK.

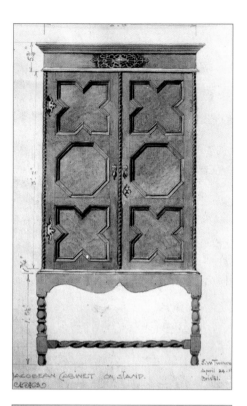

JACOBEAN CABINET ON STAND.
CADOGAD

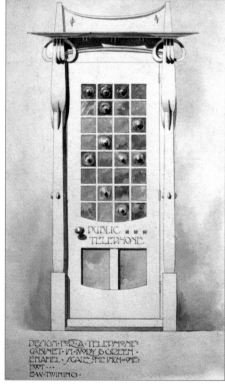

PUBLIC
TELEPHONE

DESIGN·FOR·A·TELEPHONE·
CABINET·IN·IVORY·&·GREEN·
ENAMEL·SCALE·ONE·INCH·ONE·
FOOT···
E·W·TWINING·

Above: Fig. c13 Art deco fire-screen.
Twining family

Top right: Fig. c14 An example of his
carved furniture designs. Twining family

Bottom right: Fig. c15 Twining's exciting
telephone box design. Twining family

Fig. c16 Twining Aeroplane Co. catalogue cover of October 1909. Twining family

Fig. c17 A selection of Ernest Twining's covers for Bassett-Lowke's Model Railway catalogues. from *Art in Advertising*

Fig. c18 a/b Twining Models Ltd catalogues/
brochures. Twining family/Tony Woolrich

Fig. c19 Poster design for the LMS celebration of the Liverpool and Manchester Railway centenary. From *Art in Advertising*

Fig. c20 One of Twining's pictures for his proposed book on arms and armour. Twining family

Fig. c21 Another illustration for the proposed book. Twining family

Fig. c.22 One of Ernest Twining's many landscapes. Twining family

Fig. c.23 GWR *Cobham* class No 157. Michael Gilkes

Fig. c24 Mounted knight in armour, one of several oil paintings of period figures. Twining family

Fig. c25 Christ with crown of thorns. Twining family

Fig c26   C.Hamilton Ellis' favourite amongst the historic locomotive pictures Twining painted for Rosling Bennett's book of 1906, a London Brighton and South Coast Railway *Jenny Lind* type 2-2-2.

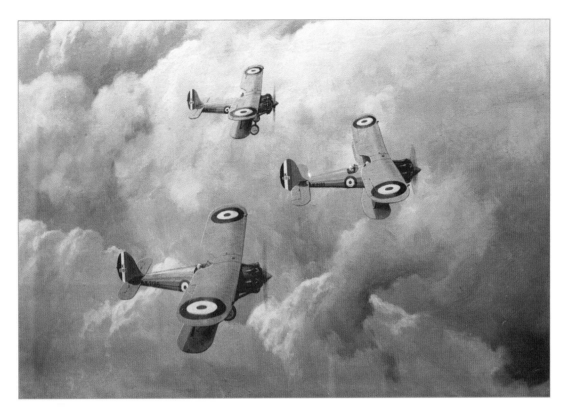

Above: Fig. c27 A flight of Bristol Bulldogs from the Sywell picture depicting the 1930s scene. photo – author

Left: Fig. c28 Details of the Caledonian Railway (ex Highland Railway River Class) 4-6-0 model made by Hawthorn Leslie. photo - author, courtesy NRM

Fig. c29 Model of Metropolitan Railway Bo-Bo electric locomotive No 2.
photo – author, courtesy NRM

Fig. c30 Details of
the Metropolitan
Railway model.
photo - author,
courtesy NRM

Fig. c31 1in to 1ft scale Bengal Nagpur Railway wagon, made for the Midland Railway Carriage and Wagon Company. photo – author, courtesy Acock's Green library

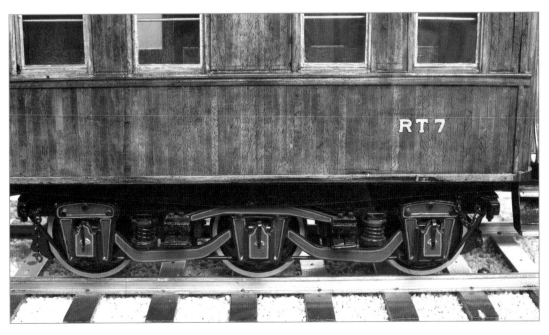

Fig. c32 Detail from the Central of Brazil Railway Dining Car made for Metropolitan Railway Carriage and Wagon Company. photo – author, courtesy Acock's Green library

Fig. c33 Twining Models' Hypothetical Factory model, perhaps used for sales or display purposes. photo – author, courtesy Northampton Museum

Fig. c34 Another view of the Hypothetical Factory. photo – author, courtesy Northampton Museum

Twining's coloured drawings for the 1938 Euston centenary model – Fig c35 Edward Bury locomotive. Twining family

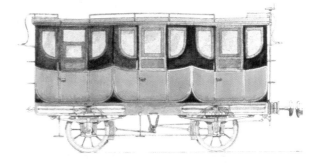

Fig. c36 Passenger carriages.

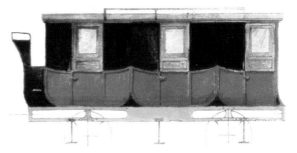

Fig. c37 Carriage truck with Brougham.

Fig. c38 *Sir Galahad's Visione*, Twining's stained glass panel designed and made for his book to illustrate the various stages in the process of making a stained glass panel.
photo – author, courtesy Northampton Museum

Fig. c39 Sketch for *The Angel of the Holy Grail*. photo – author, courtesy Northampton Museum

Left: Fig. c40 Northampton Museum's other Twining panel *The Angel of the Holy Grail*.
photo – author, courtesy Northampton Museum

Right: Fig. c41 Part of Twining's original oil-on-tinfoil painting on which *The Angel of the Holy Grail* panel was based. photo – author, courtesy Northampton Museum

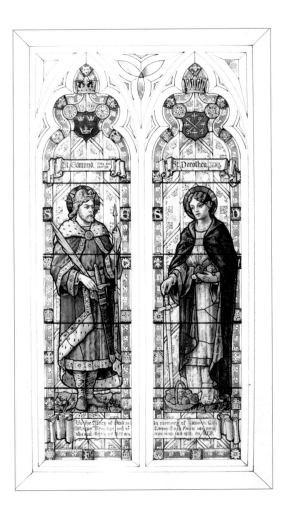

Left: Fig. c42 Original sketch for Hardingstone Church's two light window
St Edmund and St Dorothea. Twining family

Right: Fig. c43 The Hardingstone Window in 2003. photo – author

Left: Fig. c44 Close-up of *St Edmund's* head.
photo – author

Below: Fig. c45 Close-up of *St Dorothea's*
feet. photo – author

Fig. c46 The *St Cecilia and St Catherine* window now in Holy Trinity church hall, Northampton, but originally in St Paul's, Semilong. photo – author

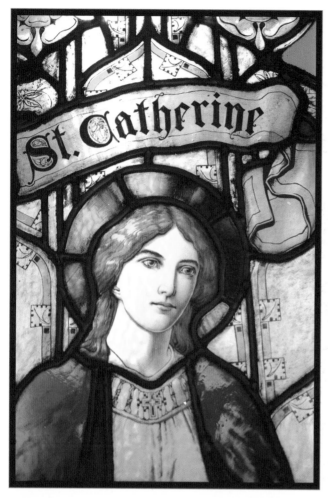

Left: Fig. c47 Close-up of *St Catherine's* head. photo – author

Below: Fig. c48 *St Cecilia's* belt, showing some of the musical instruments.
photo – author

Fig. c49 *Sir Galahad and the Angel of the Holy Grail.* photo – author

Fig. c50 Part of one of the windows of St Mary's church, Fawsley, restored by Ernest Twining. photo – author

Fig. c51 Twining's WWII memorial windows in St Francis de Sales Church, Wolverton.
This pair are *St George* and *Christ our King*. photo – Marina Buck

Fig. c52 The second pair of windows at Wolverton, *Queen of Peace (Mary)* in one
panel and *St Francis with St Bernard* in the other. photo – Marina Buck